In *Psyche and Eros,* Gisela Labouvie-Vief describes historical and current concepts of mind and development, drawing from disciplines as diverse as philosophy, mythology, religion, literature, and psychology. She then presents a powerful theory of the maturing of mind, which brings together her empirical work and her exploration into mythology. The classical Greek myth of the gods Psyche and Eros serves as an evocative illustration of the author's theory.

In most developmental theories, the mind is seen as rational, opposed to imagination and emotion. The author claims that we are taught to develop our rational capabilities to the exclusion of imagination, but that in later life affect and imagination are brought back to the fore. This is often seen as decline and a regression to childhood, but the author views it as a natural developmental stage, in which mythos (imagination and feeling) and logos (rationality) are integrated.

Psyche and Eros asserts that the core experience of development differs along gender lines. Rationality is regarded as masculine, whereas imagination is viewed as feminine. Competition between so-called masculine and feminine parts of the mind has limited our ability to describe the mind and its development over the life course. The author suggests that we overcome the dualistic way of thinking about mind and see how rationality and imagination can complement each other.

Psyche and Eros

Psyche and Eros

Mind and gender in the life course

GISELA LABOUVIE-VIEF

Wayne State University

CAMBRIDGE
UNIVERSITY PRESS

Published by the Press Syndicate of the University of Cambridge
The Pitt Building, Trumpington Street, Cambridge CB2 1RP
40 West 20th Street, New York, NY 10011-4211, USA
10 Stamford Road, Oakleigh, Melbourne 3166, Australia

First published 1994

Printed in the United States of America

Library of Congress Cataloging-in-Publication Data
Labouvie-Vief, Gisela.
Psyche and Eros : mind and gender in the life course / Gisela
Labouvie-Vief.
p.   cm.
Includes bibliographical references and indexes.
ISBN 0-521-43340-1 (hc). – ISBN 0-521-46824-8 (pbk.)
1. Intellect – Sex differences. 2. Psychosexual development.
3. Reasoning (Psychology). 4. Imagination. 5. Androgyny
(Psychology). 6. Mythology, Greek – Psychological aspects.
I. Title.
BF433.S48L33   1994
153.4'2 – dc20   93-21292
                                                      CIP

A catalog record for this book is available from the British Library.

ISBN 0-521-43340-1 hardback
ISBN 0-521-46824-8 paperback

For Alois, Elisabeth, and Irmgard

Contents

Contents

Acknowledgments

This book has been born out of a woman's experience with descent and darkness. Those who have forced me to look at the dark side of development ultimately have strengthened the integration toward which it strives. But what at first seemed merely a personal quest would not have been brought to public light had it not been for the trust and encouragement of many individuals.

Klaus Riegel's and Larry Kohlberg's "You can do it!" has sustained me for many years beyond their untimely deaths. Once I embarked on this book, several colleagues and friends helped me stay with my vision. Bernice Neugarten has provided encouragement and support through the years. I thank Allan Chinen for his enthusiasm and insight into the role of mythos in development, K. Helmut Reich for the vastness of his knowledge and his willingness to share it, the late Norma Haan for the depth of her understanding, and Leonard Pearlin for his friendship. I am also grateful for the continuous financial support that has been provided to me by the National Institute of Aging through a Research Career Development Award as well as major research grants.

The enthusiasm and excitement of my collaborators, students, and friends has been a source of immeasurable comfort and hope over the years; I feel especially indebted to Cynthia Adams, Janet Calle, Lisa Chiodo, Nancy Dougherty, Fredda Blanchard-Fields, Diana Veselka, Lori Goguen, Marlene DeVoe, Julie Hakim-Larson, Gail Mally Mack, Bernadette Meier, Lucinda Orwoll, and Lois Robbins. All of them helped nurture the development of my voice throughout the process of writing.

The final draft of the book was realized while I was on sabbatical leave from Wayne State University and taught at the Committee of Human Development at the University of Chicago. Many lively discussions with Mihaly Csikszentmihalyi, Bertram Cohler, Gil Herdt, Stanley Kurtz, and the graduate class on adult development have made their way into the final conception of this book. Margaret Huyck was a generous source of intellectual and emotional support during my stay at Chicago. Comments on the final draft by Ravenna Helson, Abigail Stewart, and the reading circle at the Institute for Personality Assessment and Research at the University of California, Berkeley, also helped improve the final version of the book.

I was fortunate to have had Julia Hough of Cambridge University Press as an editor. Thanks to Sage Publications, Inc. for permission to reprint parts of Chapters 4 and 6, which originally appeared in my article, "Women's Creativity and Images of Gender" in *Women Growing Older*, edited by Barbara F. Turner and Lillian E. Troll (Newbury Park, CA: Sage, 1994). And I thank Alexandra Brady, Olabisi Davis-Goetz, Diane Hamilton, Catherine Krueger, Susan Schreiber, and Christine Tedjopranoto for their help in putting order into an ocean of notes and references. To all of these individuals, I express my heartfelt thanks; but, of course, I am solely responsible for any errors of fact or interpretation that may have slipped into this book.

Chapter 1

Prelude

THE PARADOX OF MATURITY

Western intellectual tradition has brought us a separation of two aspects of mind and self. On one hand, there is the realm of *logos* – the realm of logic and objectivity, of all that can be stated in terms of rational truths, of our hope that life can be reduced to laws that are mechanical and precise.[1] On the other hand, there is the realm of *mythos* – the realm of all that is felt and organic, of that which is private and imaginative, of all that appeals to the inner world of emotions, of our tendency to leap out of the constraints of analytical precision and to seize the novel.

Recognizing that basic duality, thinkers throughout the ages asked which one of these two ways of being was better. Which one is more worthy of our trust? Through which one do we gain access to true knowledge? Which one can lead us on the path to wisdom and enlightenment? Which one ought to describe the mature adult – indeed, human nature at its best?

The answer we inherited from the past is logos.[2] And in accordance with that answer, it has been usual to think of human nature and its development over the course of life in terms of one single theme. For the Greek philosophers and many of their descendants, the knife that would clear the forest of ignorance and expose the path to knowledge and enlightenment was sharpened through training in logic and mathematics. Mature adults were to leave behind the world of change and flux and to orient themselves to those universal

1

forms of thought in which our organic existence is eclipsed. Development, as a consequence, has been construed as a progressive movement; an onward rush; a heroic and energetic striving for ideals and for perfection; a triumph of conscious, abstract forms of thinking; a victory of a conscious ego over the unconscious and undesirable impulses of the id.

Development as ascent, aging as decent

The view of development as the ascent and onward rush of logos has been a useful and even powerful one when describing changes from birth to young adulthood. But when applied to the total of the human life course, it has created a paradox.[3] When examined from the perspective of logos, later adulthood seems to be a dark period indeed. Yet perhaps it only appears so from a logos-oriented perspective. How are we to reconcile the disappointments of adulthood, the painful reminders of our organic limitations, with the view of an onward rush? How can we account for the second half of life by theories that celebrate the accomplishments of youth? Compared with the unfettered vigor and idealism of youth, adulthood often has been depicted as a problematic period. Indeed, it appeared to be no more than youth's negative: Rather than examining the gains and strengths unique to adulthood, adulthood often is merely examined from the perspective of the loss of youthful accomplishments. As a consequence, scientific descriptions of adulthood abound with accounts of the erosion of biological and intellectual capacities.

The origins of this book lie in my musings about the tendency to see only the failings of later life, not its fruits as well. I started to reflect on this problem some twenty years ago when I embarked on the study of adulthood and aging – that stepchild of the sciences, which may well reveal the deepest wisdom about human nature yet. In the still recent history of the study of developmental processes after adolescence, it has been usual to think of adulthood and aging as a period of loss and regression in biological adaptability and cognitive abilities.[4] And indeed many features of the performance of older

2

adults appeared to point to the conclusion that later adulthood is precarious, at best, as far as the maintenance of intellectual and biological self-regulation is concerned. In contrast to childhood, adulthood is seen as a period of deficiency and regression; indeed, the notion is prevalent that the aging of cognitive functioning reflects a reversal or mirror image of the process of development. Ribot's law of the aging of cognitive functioning states this principle of regression as follows:

> Regression first affects more complex organizations. In mnemonic organization, the "new" dies prior to the "old," the complex before the simple. . . . Volitional control is lost first, the control of automatic action later. In this way cognitive organization follows the reverse order of its development through sequential stages.[5]

Aging and wisdom

Yet in my research with adult and aged participants, I soon found myself engaged in dialogues about our respective concepts of intelligence, memory, and so forth. On the one hand, it was true that many of these adults in their performance on cognitive tasks sometimes showed a concrete orientation often associated with the behavior of children. But on the other, they also showed features not so readily captured by the notion of a "return to the concrete." They often insisted that it was of no use to engage in tasks that had so little tie to the pragmatic constraints of their everyday lives; or, as appeared to happen more often, they simply refused to participate without volunteering any criticism.

This remarkable refusal to sever cognition from its application also displayed features, I felt, that were entirely different from the concrete thinking of the young child. Not only did it reflect a conception of the role of the participant vis-à-vis the experimenter that is entirely more dialogic and autonomous than that found in children and even college students; but it also showed a much more conscious, reflective awareness that the goal of cognition must be that of structuring self-chosen goals and the actions that lead to them. "Have you ever considered," one elderly woman (I shall call her Eliza) once asked me, "that there is no point in remembering just *anything*? That we have to make choices about what is *worth* remembering?"

Eliza was born and raised in what then was the mecca of music and logical positivism, Vienna. The daughter of a gifted woman pianist, she still loves classical music, but she has made a clean break from logical positivism. Once, when reading a paper in which I had quoted the early Wittgenstein as saying that there are no surprises in logic,[6] Eliza imperially disagreed with the implication that logic and subjectivity belonged to different realms of experience. "Logic is completely subjective!" she asserted, tossing aside centuries of intellectual history with such certainty as only springs from ignorance or wisdom.

Like many thinkers of this century, Eliza asserted that at the root of any theory of thought and its development must be a conception of the subjective self, a realization that, ultimately, the impersonal laws of logic must be grounded in what is felt to be true and relevant subjectively. Not all older adults, of course, thus dare raise themselves into the ranks of our most celebrated thinkers. Still, numerous dialogues with research participants throughout the years gradually matured my conviction that something important indeed was contained in what these adults had to say. However disturbing it was for a neophyte scientist embarking on her career, it also had a timely ring. The message was, quite simply, that our scientific concepts of the nature of reason and emotion, the objective and subjective, of thinking and acting were slanted, and we had better spend some time setting them aright.

What makes these elders speak with such authority? Were it not for the fact that philosophy and psychology alike have started to reevaluate the relationship between the realms of "objective" reason and "subjective" feelings, we might explain such opinionated self-assurance as nothing more than the arrogance born of rigidity – the onset, even, of senility. And indeed, this is still one of the favored interpretations of the course of later life.

And yet, I was persistently haunted by a question. Could

these adults' advanced age not have put them at an advantage of wisdom over most of us – scientists or not – who are younger and ponder these very same issues? When they insisted that my notions of the rational cannot be divorced from richly felt experience, could they be expressing some deep philosophical wisdom? Thus an intriguing hypothesis was born. Had we, in our own denial of aging and yearning for eternal youth, perhaps scaled our models of human adaptation uniquely toward the *young* adult? Could it be that the powers of logical thought and cognitive analysis typical of adolescents and youth were supplanted, in mature adulthood at its best, by a new language – one that was not deficient at all, but in effect more integrated, broader, more abstract? Yet even though that language seemed more abstract, it was a kind of abstractness gracefully free of the tension between the theoretical and the applied so typical of youthful thinking. Perhaps this was a way of thinking that achieved what Piaget has claimed truly marks the achievement of wisdom and maturity – the reuniting of "intelligence and affectivity,"[7] the marriage of logos and mythos.

THE LOST DIMENSIONS OF DEVELOPMENT

My dialogues with Eliza and others suggested a view of mature and later adulthood that could not be accommodated very well by most available models of development over the life span. As pointed out elsewhere,[8] these models are usually framed in terms of growth and gain, of "ascending" and "becoming better." Yet it is a popular adage that in order to gain consciousness, we not only experience gain but also give up a sense of innocence and wholeness. My early experience with adult research participants underscored that adage: In order to adjust to the tasks of adulthood, these individuals felt that they had sacrificed a connectedness to the concrete and organic. Mature adulthood for them became an occasion to reclaim that wholeness. Thus, rather than experiencing their advancing age in terms of decline, many of these individuals appeared to experience a rebirth of a sense of organic and connected self that they earlier had surrendered to the demands of growing up.

Maturing into later life, then, often was experienced as the healing of a split, the resumption of an abandoned dialogue. But if adulthood thus revealed its lighter side, earlier development also showed its darker side. Growing up brought not only progression and ascent but also was experienced as the disruption of a sense of unity, a surrendering of organic wholeness, and a resulting feeling of fragmentation. Gradually, my conviction matured that a theory dealing with adult life needed to concern itself with the ups and downs of that dialogue over the life course, rather than merely celebrating a single way of being. Rather than describing development as the ascent and victory of logos, it was necessary to describe development as a tandem progression between logos and mythos. In that dual progression, the two modes might have somewhat different ascendancies, indeed often an antagonistic relationship.

The loss of mythos

In attempting to trace that tandem progression, I soon found myself led back to some of the "grand" theories of development, especially those of Piaget and Freud. Indeed, an analysis of features of those two theories forms a part of my argument throughout this book, but especially in Chapter 3. My extensive discussion of these two theories requires some explanation. Some readers may feel that by focusing on these men, I have erected straw men in order to support my argument; certainly, the work of both theorists has been extensively critiqued and updated. In choosing to discuss the work of Freud and Piaget, however, I am not alone. Several authors also have found it necessary to reevaluate part of these theorists' work.[9] I believe there are cogent reasons for such a reevaluation, since the theories of both of these giants have created a kind of prototypical supratheoretical framework many individuals are attempting to transcend. But, in that attempt to transcend a broad framework, it is often useful to distill clearly those features one is attempting to correct and transform.

What is notable about the theories of Freud and Piaget is that both assert that development is, in fact, based on a dialectic between two modes of knowing. For Freud, for example, development is based on the tension between two modes of being and of defining reality. One is primary process, a mode in which an inner world of desires and wishes prevails. The other is secondary process, a mode no longer directed by the inner reality of wish fulfillment and fantasy. Rather, this mode strives to find out what is objectively true, what holds in the outer world. And it is the developing individual's task to strike a relatively harmonious balance between these two forms of relating to the world.

Piaget, too, proposes that the reality to which we adapt is not merely an external given, an objective world "out there." What we come to understand as "reality" is based on the organismic ground of our biological and psychological being. Hence to develop successfully, individuals must not merely internalize the conditions of outer reality, they also must find outward expression for their inner biological needs and desires and creative tendencies. Piaget explicitly proposes, in fact, that successful development requires that these two movements – inward and outward – form a balance or dialogue: If one pole predominates, adaptation remains disturbed.

By emphasizing such a balance, both theorists were instrumental in transforming the pervasive rationalist bias of classical philosophies of the mind and human nature. That bias dealt with the individual primarily in terms of logos, whereas the processes related to mythos were seen mainly in pejorative terms. As the philosopher Susanne Langer states, mythos, according to rationalist theories, is inferior, not adaptive in its own right. Thus "everything that falls outside of the domain of analytical, propositional, and formal thought is merely classed as emotive, irrational, and animalian. . . . All other things our minds do are dismissed as irrelevant to intellectual progress;

they are residues, emotional disturbances, or throwbacks to animal estate" and indicate "regression to a pre-logical state."[10] Thus, mythos is often defined in terms that imply that it is a merely infantile or pathological way of functioning.

Freud and Piaget begin their work with a radical rejection of that rationalist bias. Both authors maintained that the study of human adaptation must be based, first and foremost, in acknowledging the organismic reality of persons. Paradoxically, however, neither carries that notion to its logical conclusion. Freud's theory, for example, is less aimed at a harmonious balance between inner and outer reality, but more at a fairly complete victory of the secondary-process over the primary-process principle. Indeed, the former is called "reality principle," whereas the latter is termed "pleasure principle." Thus, Freud defines education "as an incitement to the conquest of the pleasure principle, and to its replacement by the reality-principle."[11] Similarly, the ideal of the adapted individual is the scientist who "comes nearest to this conquest."[12] Piaget's theory, too, maintains that rationalist bias. Piaget's writings show that he tends to equate development with a loss of organismic and imaginative relatedness, emphasizing instead the rise of objective, abstract structures of relating to the world.

Thus both theories continued to be faithful to a profound rationalist legacy in which development was equated with the ascent of the rational principle of logos. In contrast, the nonrational principle of mythos continued to occupy a highly problematic status and, indeed, became successively displaced and degraded. This rationalist degradation and fragmentation of mythos has been widely deplored. By classing mythos as an immature form of thought, we deny that mythos, too, can have an important function in development, and one that is not at all characteristic of the primitive and the childlike only, but continues well into adulthood. Since the romantic movement,[13] many thinkers – foremost among them perhaps Rousseau and Nietzsche – have lamented how logos deals mythos a blow of death, and argued for an emancipation of mythos as a worthwhile adult mode. As Thomas Mann claimed in his famed lecture on "Freud and the Future,"[14] most of the lasting mythos products of culture are uniquely *adult* accomplishments, and the emancipation of mythos may be a unique triumph of *mature adulthood* rather than a mere remnant of immature childish ways of being. Thus, mythos provides a separate language, one that is not necessarily inferior, though it is qualitatively different. It is a language in which knowledge is presented in personified images and narratives rather than in analytical and propositional form.

Mythos and development

At this juncture, I became intrigued with what seemed uncanny parallels between the more logos-oriented accounts of development such as those of Freud and Piaget and a more mythos-based one such as has been offered by the theory of Carl Jung.[15] Although I shared with many of my colleagues from academia a deep reservation toward the mystical excesses of Jung's work, I found in his theory the most significant attempt thus far to deal with development not as the single progression of one mode of knowing, but rather as an interweaving of two modes. Specifically concerned with the split between the two modes that had been instituted in Western philosophy and that pervaded the theory of Freud, Jung felt that it was one of the special challenges of an adult's later life to heal that split. Thus, Jung saw the period after about the middle of life as an opportunity to bridge the multiple dualisms between the subjective and the objective, between mind and body, between reason and instinct, between masculine and feminine.

Jung[16] proposed (though that proposal was not systematically explicated by him) that development can not only be seen in terms of the rational structures that theoreticians such as Freud and Piaget had proposed, but that the development of those structures is paralleled by a developmental line of mythos, in which developmental progressions are expressed in terms of symbolic and narrative themes. Unlike the development of logos structures, however, that of mythos structures reveals not a single theme, but rather two separate though complementary ones. One of those themes follows the structure of the hero myth;[17] development is depicted as heroic ascent, the courageous victory of reason over the unruly life of instincts. But in the account of the second type of theme or narrative, a darker, less glorious image of the process of development emerges. Those accounts take, as it were, the perspective of the subdued life of the instincts, showing the resulting degradation and devaluation of mythos. In the concrete imagery of mythos, the metaphors are shocking indeed: Violence, rape, death, and dismemberment are symbols that over and over again speak of the destruction of mythos.

One well-known myth, for example, is that of the marriage between Isis and Osiris. Twin children of Nut, the goddess of heaven, they are engaged in loving embrace in their mother's womb. As adults, they work together in harmony and bring writing, agriculture, and other gifts of culture to their people. But their brother Set is overcome with envy and hate at Osiris' fame and virtue and devises a ruse to destroy him. He has a magnificent wooden coffin made according to the measurements of Osiris' body. He then arranges a feast and announces that the person who can fit into the coffin may keep it as a present. When Osiris steps into the coffin, Set shuts it, takes off with it, and has Osiris' body torn to pieces and scattered over the land. Isis then embarks on a long journey to piece Osiris' body together, and eventually, Osiris is reborn each year as nature abounding with new life and vegetation.

In this myth, early development is depicted as a fall from wholeness, a loss of unity. That very loss, however, sets up a tension that ultimately turns into a positive force. The longing to recollect the lost parts of our selves – if we can only sustain that longing – eventually leads to a rebirth and a new sense of life and vitality. It is that mature vitality that many myths celebrate as the pinnacle of mature being – a vitality that, like that of Osiris, emerges from the surrender to suffering.

The importance of the duality and tension between different aspects or parts of ourselves is also dealt with in Plato's widely quoted story of the origins and healing of fragmentation. In the *Symposium*, Plato relates a mythic account of the origin of love as a symbol of this process. In the beginning, he says, there were complete human beings, some male, some female, some hermaphroditic. These beings were round, with four arms and legs and two faces. So much power and vitality did these beings possess that Zeus grew fearful they might overturn his reign. Thus, he gave the order to

> cut them all in half as you or I might chop up sorb apples for pickling, or slice an egg with a hair. . . . Now, when the bisection was complete it left each half with a desperate yearning for the other, and they ran together and flung their arms around each other's necks, and asked for nothing better than to be rolled into one. . . . And so, gentlemen, we are all like pieces of coins that children break in half for keepsakes – making two out of one, like the flatfish – and each of us is forever seeking the half that will tally with himself.[18]

These and other myths talk about issues of development in astonishing themes. Jealousy and hate, creation and destruction, envy and competition, violence and dismemberment and rebirth are the metaphors describing part of the life course. And in turn, later life in those accounts is not described as regression and loss but rather as a chance for rebirth and balance.

MIND AND GENDER

Examining the language of mythos and its images of development was not only an intriguing enterprise but also proved to introduce a dimension of vast complexity to the questions I am posing in this book. As a mode that speaks of symbolic realities in personified forms, mythos is not only a mode that is personified; but being personified, it is also of necessity based on an imagery of gender. In this way it offers a rather direct and inescapable indication that superimposed on the more abstract themes of modes of knowing is another, much more concrete one: that of gender relations. Just as the myths of Isis and Osiris or of Plato's split beings speak of development in terms of the vicissitudes of desires, so desire is depicted as a transaction between gendered personages. Freud had understood, of course, that this theme is perhaps the most universal, and the most emotionally significant theme of the life course. Hence, that issues of developmental milestones often are depicted as the relationship between masculine and feminine figures appeared to be at the core of understanding changing theories of the mind. And, since those theories affect how we think of development, they have immediate consequences for how we look at development over the life course.

For some while, I had pondered the fact that, historically, the two modes had become identified with gender, logos being associated with the masculine, mythos with the feminine. And just as mythos was a devalued mode, so it had been attributed to the devalued "feminine" pole of human functioning. This association has resulted in several positions regarding the minds and natures of men and women.

The traditional position, and one still widely influential, has been to take this association between mythos and the feminine as proof that women's intellectual status is inferior to that of men. As women's participation in the intellectual and educational life of modern culture has become more apparent, however, the notion of basic and hierarchical differences in the mental capacities of men and women has been almost completely discredited. Instead, a second position has been proposed by several recent writers.[19] Here, the suggestion is that mythos, though a feminine mode of thinking, is an important one in its own right and by no means inferior to logos. This position actually was prefigured by Jung, whose insistence that the "feminine" be reevaluated and upgraded had been one of the reasons for his famous break with Freud.

However, this position also is problematic. Even though the aim of positing a "feminine" mode of knowing was to point to the pervasive devaluation of the "feminine" in our culture, it maintained the traditional split and thus also entailed some grave conceptual flaws. Of those, perhaps the most significant is that it continues to reify aspects of the mind as "masculine" and "feminine."[20] But there is little evidence to support the notion that there are basic qualitative differences between the minds of men and women. In study after study[21] we are finding that differences that once were claimed to be gender-related are disappearing, and thus the ancient mythology of the gendered mind is gradually changing.

Yet study after study suggests that complex feelings about the nature of "masculine" and "feminine" aspects of mind persist.[22] In this book I join a third position – that it is in those feelings, rather than in an objective, perhaps biologically willed reality, that we may find an explanation of the nature of gender differences in mental functioning.[23] The evolving concept of "mind" always had symbolic meanings, meanings related to the use and regulation of social power. How this symbolic meaning enters into social relationships, and particularly into male–female relationships, therefore, seemed to me to be the key that might unlock some important secrets of the continuing puzzle about the nature of the mature mind.

I have come to believe that one major difficulty in formulating more adult-appropriate theories of mind and self was a hidden language and imagery of gender that underlies our theories of development throughout the course of life. It is the same set of images already encountered: images relating to envy of power and to competition for control; images of hierarchy, domination, and subjugation. If these images are basic to our notions of development, I believe it is important to make them explicit. And to decode that hidden language and to show how it has infiltrated our concepts of development and aging seems to me an important step if we want to formulate more integrated theories of mind and self and their development over the life course.

The task of decoding that gender imagery underlying our conceptions of mind and development is not only academic. It also becomes a major personal issue as individuals progress through the life course. I have come to believe that the mythology of the gendered mind profoundly structures core identity issues over the life course. If, for example, Freud's theory depicts the Oedipal resolution as an ascendancy of the masculine over the feminine, he not only expresses an ancient mythic theme but also points to a significant personal reality: the fact that the boy comes to identify his core sense of "I" with the exalted "masculine" principle, whereas the girl needs to define herself along the devalued "feminine" one.

Whereas Freud believed that this core identification could form the basis for adaptive functioning in adulthood, however, much modern thinking and research suggests that adulthood in a modern culture exposes this identification as problematic. Far from securing flexibility and adaptive competence in adulthood, the polarities established in early development can become a major source of fragmentation and disorder. And thus, many modern adults speak of their development in themes that parallel those of the philosopher or the psychologic theoretician. Not maintaining but bridging the splits between masculine and feminine, between logos and mythos becomes a major theme, and an important aspect of mature functioning. The concept of an integration of logos and mythos, often personified by the image of the marriage of the masculine and the feminine, thus offers an important new metaphor for the mind and its development.

STRUCTURE OF THE BOOK

Because the language of mythos thus seemed to complement my more academic quest, I eventually resolved to use a tandem structure for this book. I chose not only to rely on evidence from historical and psychological researches – thus following the rules of logos – but to supplement that language with the language of mythos. I decided to blend my familiarity with fairly rigorous scientific research with other evidence, especially evidence taken from literature, art, and myth, as well as the evolution of public trends that, though they form the backdrop of scientific inquiry, are not necessarily its focus. In addition, I decided to present my argument in terms of a dual structure, using a blend of both narrative and discursive genres. Thus I resolved to supplement the latter with the integrative power of one particular myth.

14

Prelude

I present my argument using the story of Psyche and Eros as a frame story, amplified by a lengthier discussion of historical and psychological evidence. For the purposes of presentation, the myth has been divided into five major sections (as well as a sixth, concluding one). Each section serves to introduce the theme of a chapter, and that narrative introduction is then followed by a more academic amplification.

The reader might well ask, Why yet another interpretation of the myth of Psyche and Eros? Indeed, many excellent discussions are available. Foremost among them is that of the Jungian scholar Erich Neumann who has set the stage for frequent interpretations of the tale as one of prototypical feminine development.[24] Neumann's interpretation has been very influential in my own thinking, and I rely heavily on it throughout this book. Nevertheless, I also believe that his interpretation does not make a distinction that is important in my argument: When can we say that what we call "feminine" development is something inherent in the nature of women, and when, in contrast, should we believe that our notion of "femininity" is a social construction inherent in a system that devalues women?

This differentiation between "femininity" as a characteristic of women versus "femininity" as a prevalent social construction is made more clearly in the work of Maria von Franz, a Jungian scholar who has claimed that the Psyche and Eros myth does not reflect female development but rather the development of the man's projection of the feminine.[25] On that view, the story is not necessarily about women, but about that part of their own selves that men are likely to find problematic and, in the process of disowning it and splitting it off, to call feminine.

My own approach is to argue that either approach reveals a kernel of the truth, but that neither is sufficient in itself. Rather, I suggest that the reaities of masculine and feminine development are not given independently and a priori. Rather, they are realities that are constituted in interaction and in relation among men and women. Moreover, I also suggest – along with Neumann – that these realities ultimately define our images of mind and its development. This approach, I feel, can provide a powerful tool for integrating much psychological evidence about similarities and differences in the life-course development of men and women.

Of course, quite apart from issues of how to interpret a story, mythos has an inherent power of integration and an inherent self-validating function. That function, as suggested in Chapter 2, is to involve the author and the reader alike, to provide a common context for discussion, and – true to the main tenet of this book – to integrate not only academic argument but genres of presentation as well.

The specific integration is developed in the next five chapters, Chapters 2 through 6. These chapters are grouped into two parts. Part I, "The Mind Divided," consists of three chapters. Chapter 2 offers both an introduction to the myth, and a historical introduction to the classical model of mind and human nature that it symbolizes. The chapter begins with an introduction of the main protagonists of the myth: Psyche, Aphrodite, and her son Eros. It suggests that these figures can be seen to stand for an evolving way of thinking about human nature in terms of a hierarchically ordered polarity, and this evolution is traced by discussing the classical Greek concept of the mind. The chapter enlarges on logos and mythos as two modes of knowing, and traces the evolution of the Western way of thinking of them as related in a hierarchical, vertical manner. This evolution has resulted in a divided image of the mind, and it is mythically expressed in the conflicts between the main protagonists of the Psyche and Eros myth.

Chapter 3 suggests that these conflicts form the core of a "classical" view of development, one that – even as it is in the process of being overturned and reinterpreted – still exerts a major influence. Mythically, that view is expressed by the union of Psyche and Eros, a union that is based on subordination and superordination rather than on a cooperative exchange – a union Neumann has labeled with the perhaps ominous term of "marriage of death."

Just as in myth, development is represented as the birth of light and the heroic ascent of the hero-god who represents light and the sun, so in traditional developmental theories growth from birth to young adulthood is described as the victory of reason over the irrational. But here, the myth shows that the image of the hero also implies its dialectical opposite, the image of the slain. To recover what has been "slain" or "sacrificed" to the heroic view of the mind is the topic of many recent reformulations of a model of development. Gain in rationality, according to these more recent views, may often go along with a repression and splitting off, or sacrifice, of nonrational ways of knowing.

Chapter 4 further carries this duality of victory and defeat, of logos and mythos, into the domain of gender. Here, the myth continues to elaborate the diverging pathways for Psyche and Eros, suggesting that male and female development are represented by quite different narrative patterns. These narrative patterns are related to the prevailing classical model of mind. Since logos is culturally associated with the masculine and mythos with the feminine, men and women experience early development in ways that are profoundly different. Men are more likely to experience their early lives in terms of themes of ascent and mastery. For women, however, these themes become increasingly problematic, resulting in themes of renunciation and loss as mastery and competence are split off and projected onto men.

Part II of the book, entitled "The Mind Restored," argues that the potential of later life development is a healing and bridging of the split introduced in early development. This issue is dealt with in Chapters 5 and 6, which continue the more cognitive and the more gender-related themes of Chapters 3 and 4 respectively.

Chapter 5 continues the myth by presenting the envious sisters of Psyche as a reemergence of negative feelings that result from the repression of mythos and the feminine. This reemergence is related to an emerging model of the mind, one in which the previously abandoned and devalued dimensions are reevaluated. I examine that reevaluation both as a general cultural trend and as a task of individual development. This movement of individual development is shown by a review of a number of recent studies that suggest that adults become concerned with forging an integration between the dimensions that become split early in development. I suggest that such movements result from a series of stagelike changes that are akin to those observed in early development, and that result in a model of the mind in which individuals more and more reflect on their own inner structure and motivations, eventually resulting in a reevaluation and upgrading of previously devalued mythos. The result is a new form of thinking in terms of hermeneutical principles.

Chapter 6 relates the notion of hermeneutical thinking to the gender theme of Chapter 4. The myth now continues with a series of trials Psyche must undergo, trials that require her to give up her notion of masculinity and femininity as hierarchically ordered realities and come to understand them as cooperatively engaged and mutually enriching and constitutive parts of the self and social reality. This theme is applied to a discussion of later life development. Just as early development is experienced in terms of different primary paths for boys and girls, so later development is experienced differently for men and women. The primary issues of identity and development for men revolve around a sense of loss and disempowerment as they upgrade modes of knowing and ways of being that they previously experienced as "feminine." In contrast, the main focus for women's development is a deidealization of the "masculine" as they struggle with issues of personal empowerment.

In Chapter 7, the concluding chapter, I relate how Psyche's trials are rewarded as she is raised to a deity and joins her divine husband Eros on Mount Olympus. I expand on this mythic notion of a divine marriage between mature forms of masculinity and femininity, logos and mythos, as a model for mature development. That mature model adopts as its core metaphor one that radically differs from metaphors underlying early notions of development: Rather than using guiding images based on competition and aggression, the core metaphor now is one of a playful dialogue between different forms of knowing and ways of being.

Such a model of "ludic hermeneutics" restores the dimensions of the mind that have been split in classical models. Thus, reason and emotion, self and other, reality and play, and male and female form polarities that retain their vitality as somewhat independent principles, yet are engaged in a cooperative and dialogic relationship in which they mutually define and change each other. Nevertheless, this notion of a cooperative model refrains from reifying idealism, but also introduces a tragic dimension to our models of mind. To the concern with idealized pathways of development, this idea adds a new question to theoretical analysis and empirical research: Why is it that play and reciprocity of self and other are developmental achievements of such rarity and extraordinary difficulty?

Part I

The mind divided

Chapter 2

The rage of Aphrodite:
The vertical mind

A king and a queen had three fair daughters. But by far the most beautiful was Psyche, the youngest. So extraordinary was her loveliness that words could not describe it. Soon people began to worship her as a goddess, and rumors spread around the country that she was no other than a new incarnation of the foam-born Aphrodite, created when "heaven had rained fresh procreative dew, and earth, not sea, had brought forth as a flower a second Aphrodite in all the glory of her maidenhood."[1]

When Aphrodite heard of those rumors, fury and rage engulfed her, and thus she said to herself: "Behold, I the first parent of created things, the primal source of all the elements; behold, I the kindly mother of all the world, must share my majesty and honor with a mortal maid, and my name that dwells in the heavens is dragged through the earthly muck. Shall I endure the doubt cast by this vicarious adoration, this worship of my godhead that is shared with her? . . . this girl, whoever she be, that has usurped my honors shall have no joy thereof. I will make her repent of her beauty, even her unlawful loveliness."[2]

And so she summoned Eros, her son, and cried: "I implore you to avenge and punish this maiden. Strike her heart with your arrow, and cause her to be consumed with passion for the vilest, most horrid of men. She shall have no fortune, no honor, and her misery shall have no peer in all the world." Thus she spoke, and then returned to the shore and plunged down to the deep ocean floor.

23

THE NEW INDIVIDUAL

The tale of Psyche and Eros begins with a conflict. The goddess Aphrodite is enraged, because rumor has reached her of the birth of Psyche, a mortal girl of extraordinary beauty. So exquisite is Psyche's beauty that it is said to rival that of the goddess of love and beauty herself. Even worse, according to rumor, humans are no longer paying Aphrodite the respect due her as a goddess of extraordinary prominence, but are treating Psyche as a goddess, praying to her while the temples of Aphrodite are turning to ruin. Indeed, Psyche is said to be no other than a new version of Aphrodite herself. But unlike "the goddess, who sprang from the blue deep of the sea and was born from the spray of the foaming waves,"[3] Psyche is said to have been born from the union of heaven and earth. So deep is Aphrodite's rage at these events that she calls her son Eros and asks him to help her bring Psyche to ruin.

What is the reason for such deep rage? What does it signify? In the language of logos, such stories may appear to be merely idiosyncratic at best, perhaps a quaint and picturesque way of evading a more direct message. But in the language of mythos, they are believed to speak of something much more coherent, perhaps of something no less compelling and even universal than the "truths" of logos. They speak, however, in a different medium, or use a different genre. Rather than saying what they say in logical and discursive form, they say it in the form of symbols, using images and stories rather than propositions to drive a point home.

Of those theoreticians who have emphasized the importance of mythos as a coherent language of broad aspects of human experience, Sigmund Freud and Carl Jung are probably the most famous and significant.[4] Although their emphasis on mythic symbols has long appeared to give their theories an "unscientific" cast, the social sciences more recently have been swept with a deep interest in the symbolic and narrative construction of our sense of history, self, and reality, asserting that, however "subjective" such constructions are, they nevertheless are at the core of our sense of coherence as individuals or collectives.[5] Thus many of the claims of Freud and Jung appear to have been rather prophetic.

My own approach to myth has been strongly influenced by Jungian and neo-Jungian writings. Such theorists have long maintained that the core experiences of life tend to be codified in terms of symbols and story patterns that are repeated again and again across different cultures and historical times.[6] I was especially struck by a similarity between my emerging reflections on historical changes in conceptualizations of human nature[7] and the work by Jungian scholar Erich Neumann,[8] who had proposed a sweeping account of how such changes are reflected in the imagery and stories of myths around the world.

Following Neumann, I suggest that Aphrodite's rage refers to a complex symbolic event. Aphrodite, as well as the figures of Psyche and Eros, tells a story of certain prototypical issues encountered in the evolution of selfhood. Moreover, this may be true not only if considered from the perspective on individual development but also in a broader historical context.[9]

Background of the myth

In order to fix the symbolic meaning of the story more precisely, it is important to know about the story's origin. The story forms part of the novel, *The Golden Ass,* written by the Roman poet Apuleius in the second century C.E. Thus its date is the close of antiquity, and it derives its texture from the forces that defined views of human nature at that time.

The millennium preceding Apuleius' story had seen many dramatic transformations of ancient beliefs about human and divine natures and their relative order in the cosmos. For the individual at the dawn of antiquity, these two realms were not clearly differentiated, as we will discuss at length later in this chapter. Individuals did not, apparently, feel themselves to be separate entities the way modern Western individuals do. Instead, they felt themselves to be part of, and firmly embedded in, a cosmic order. A sense of reality prevailed in which self and other, mythic and divine, all were closely fused in a common mythic sense of reality. Indeed, the modern concept of the individual as a fairly individuated and responsible center of thought and action did not exist. However, by Apuleius' time a new sense of the nature of individual selves had formed, and the new concept of the individual was firmly in place.

The figures of Aphrodite, Psyche, and Eros, then, can be seen to signify those changes. Aphrodite represents an older order of reality, whereas Psyche and Eros represent a newer, more recent one. These different stages of evolution can be seen both in a historical context and in that of the individual life cycle. Indeed, it is an adage, oversimplified though nevertheless containing a kernel of wisdom, that stages of the life cycle in certain respects mirror historical stages of the development of the individual.[10] In his discussion of the myth, entitled *Amor and Psyche*, Neumann[11] suggests that we can glean the nature of those changes if we pay attention to certain features of the key symbols of the story.

One of those key symbols is the medium from which the two women are said to have arisen. Aphrodite's birth is described in Hesiod's *Theogeny*,[12] a major poem probably written in the 8th century B.C.E. It lays out the elements of Greek mythology concerning the origin of the universe, the gods and goddesses, and humanity. Hesiod gives the famous description of Aphrodite's birth from the ocean: She emerged from the foam that arose in the ocean when Chronos castrated his father Uranos, the primordial Greek sky father. Uranos' genitals fell into the ocean, and from this mating of sky and sea was born Aphrodite.

Aphrodite's birth thus is both divine and miraculous, and related to water, the element of the ocean. In contrast, Psyche's birth is mortal and of the earth; her parents, even though noble, are mere mortals. Even the rumor of her birth makes the earth rather than water the principal element. Because in the language of myth, ocean and earth stand for different stages of evolution in cultural and individual development, Aphrodite and Psyche thus refer to different developmental stages.

Psyche's earthborn nature is a symbolic characterization of a more recent and thus modern consciousness. It is in contrast to

Aphrodite's birth from the sea, which signifies a more archaic consciousness. The ocean in biological evolution was the site of the earliest and most primitive forms of life. Similarly in the language of myth, water and the ocean usually refer to more archaic, instinctual, and unconscious forms of thinking, behaving, and being. The earth, in contrast, signifies those that are more advanced and conscious. Having been born of the earth, then, Psyche does indeed represent a more modern stage of consciousness than is true of the sea-born Aphrodite.

The fact that Psyche is the daughter of mere mortals rather than born of divine parents also is significant, because it helps us gain a more precise idea of what this more advanced form of consciousness consists. It suggests that we are dealing with a transformation that redefines the ordinary reality of mortal men and women relative to the realm of the divine. More and more, individuals came to view themselves as different from the old divine order, as agents who had separate identities and wills.

That the two women represent different stages of evolution also corresponds to historical data.[13] Aphrodite is a much more ancient goddess than Psyche. In fact, her history is much more ancient than Hesiod's account, as she predates the Hellenic period by several millennia. Long before she was enthroned as a goddess on Olympus, she was one of the very oldest goddesses in the countries of Mesopotamia. In Palestine, for example, her forerunner was the goddess Asthoreth, whose name in Syria was Astarte, Ishtar in Akkadia,[14] and Innanna in Sumer. In all of those countries, she was a goddess of extraordinary power, queen of heaven and earth who united in her a multitude of resources. Not only a goddess of love and sexuality, as she was to be in classical Greece, she combined in one figure the aspects of fertility and love with those of wisdom, authority, and warfare. Over the course of time, however, as this goddess became more "civilized," her awesome power also became degraded. By Hellenic times, she had been made into a love goddess who was but one of the women of the patriarchal Greek pantheon – and a somewhat flighty and seductive one, at that!

Psyche and Eros

Psyche, in contrast, is a much more recent goddess. In fact, Apuleius' story deals with her eventual deification, and indeed she appears to have been raised from a human to the status of a goddess relatively late in history. This raising from the human to the divine level is also a deeply symbolic event. Psyche's becoming divine here stands as a symbol for self-realization and for the process of individuation in the modern development of the "feminine." As many writers have noted, however, on that journey toward the realization of the self, the individual must learn to balance precariously the pressures of socialization that would impress on him or her the stamp of cultural conformity. In that process of civilization, many of the more archaic elements of "feminine" power must be repressed.

The feminine dimension

A brief commentary is necessary here on the use of the term *feminine*. As will become clearer in the chapters to come, the term is used in this book to refer to more than the natural inclinations, capacities, and resources of women. Certainly, it is not used to suggest a set of biologically determined characteristics. Indeed over time the term has undergone a complex evolution of meaning. In that evolution society has come to term many characteristics of men as feminine – often in a pejorative sense. In fact, it is often completely unclear just when, by referring to something as feminine, one means a positive set of feminine characteristics inherent in the nature of women or whether one means to label a set of undesirable qualities in a man. Indeed, I will argue in this book that this ambiguity has plagued, and continues to plague, accounts of development in which dangerous repressed powers often have been called feminine and have been attributed to women.[15]

By using the term feminine throughout this book, then, I mean to refer to the fact that our notions of masculinity and femininity are, in large part, socially constructed and not fixed biological constructs.[16] In fact, a major concern throughout

28

this book is how the meanings of masculinity and femininity have been created and have evolved, sometimes amplifying and distorting realities that may be more basic. Nevertheless, these meanings are extremely powerful: They not only *reflect* certain inner self-identifications and outer social realities, but they also come to *create* those very inner and outer realities. Thus, the resulting language of gender attributions becomes a framework within which developing selves define them-selves, attempting to validate their "appropriateness" as men and women in a culture.

Bearing with the resulting ambiguity for the moment, I sug-gest that the repression of a more archaic mode of life, and specifically a mode that came to be called feminine, is the source of the conflict between Aphrodite and Psyche. That conflict indicates, then, that the more modern, civilized con-sciousness often brings with it a profound repression of those attributes that are part of our ancient heritage. However re-pressed, they nevertheless continue to exert a more hidden, underground influence, creating a warlike state between mod-ern consciousness and more ancient and unconscious at-tributes. This, then, is the meaning of Aphrodite's rage: It reminds us that a vital dimension of life is not properly re-spected, and that it exerts its influence, as a consequence, in a negative and destructive form. How to resolve the resulting conflict, and how eventually to carve out a more peaceful and cooperative coexistence between more modern and more ar-chaic layers of the self is, indeed, a major theme of the myth. And since it is the theme of this book as well, the myth seems to be particularly well suited to offer a narrative backdrop for our discussions.

The god Eros

The theme of integration of different layers of the self has a parallel, as well, in the god Eros, although the masculine com-ponent of the story is not as finely developed and differenti-ated as the feminine one. We will return to the meaning of this lack of development in later chapters. Here, it is significant to note that by Apuleius' time, Eros was well established as the god of romantic love, piercing lovers with his arrows and sweeping them away in a torrent of passion. By that historical time, he was said to be the son of Aphrodite. His origins, like those of Aphrodite, are much more ancient, however. According to some accounts, he is one of the very oldest gods. Stories of his origin state that he predates the Olympic gods and goddesses. According to one story,[17] his mother was Night, who produced a silver egg that was fertilized by Wind. From that egg Eros emerged with golden wings, bringing light to the world that had lain in darkness. Graves reports his creation:

> Eros, whom some call Phanes, was hatched from this egg and set the Universe in motion. Eros was double-sexed and golden-winged and, having four heads, sometimes roared like a bull or a lion, sometimes hissed like a serpent or bleated like a ram. . . . Phanes created earth, sky, sun, moon.[18]

In Hesiod's *Theogeny*, too, Eros is one of the very oldest gods. He is created from Chaos along with Gaia, the ancient mother goddess who predates all of the Olympic gods and goddesses. But in Hesiod, Eros no longer is a two-sexed power integrating the feminine symbols of snake and moon. Now, he is clearly masculine, and after Aphrodite is born, he becomes her companion.

By Apuleius' time, this powerful god also had become degraded; he is merely Amor, the insipid boy-god. This degradation, then, offers a masculine parallel to that of Aphrodite. Thus, Eros could be seen as a masculine complement to, and equivalent of, Aphrodite. If Aphrodite represents a powerful, primordial female vitality, Eros represents her masculine equivalent.

This interpretation of Eros is perhaps most similar to Freud's. For Freud, Eros represents the primordial fountain of instincts, desires, and passions that compel the individual to relate to the outer world of objects and individuals – a force identified with sexuality and termed libido. As in Hesiod, libido for Freud is primarily understood in masculine terms and

indicates an earthy, powerful masculine principle of relatedness that, in the interest of civilization, also became tamed and
powerless. But this striving toward love and relatedness (retained in the Freudian notion of cathexis) has resulted in confusion, since relatedness stereotypically is termed a feminine
attribute.

The resulting confusion is most clearly visible in Jung's theory, for whom Eros has become a feminine principle of relatedness, in contrast to the principle to logos, which he believed
was a masculine principle. This same differentiation is also
mirrored in many contemporary discussions of sex differences
that argue that relatedness is a uniquely feminine principle.[19]
Along with Whitmont,[20] I suggest that this is not a constructive interpretation. As Whitmont suggests, because Eros is a
phallic god, he should be seen as a masculine principle of
desire striving toward union. Indeed, I believe that the failure
to separate masculine and feminine sources of connectedness
remains a pervasive problem in providing an unbiased account of development.

In this book, therefore, I suggest that Psyche and Eros both
represent forms of libido and connection, but ones we experience in unique masculine and feminine forms. We will be concerned with defining those forms throughout the chapters to
follow. To anticipate, however, Eros is a principle in which
desire connects through heroic conquering and gaining control over, through piercing and penetrating, through phallic
intrusion. In contrast, Psyche is one in which desire and connection are achieved through opening oneself, through being
receptive, through "giving up" control and surrendering. Similarly, I also reject the classical identification of logos with the
masculine, arguing instead that logos forms a gender-neutral
principle – even though one that, in the course of history,
became gendered and associated with the masculine.

The fact that historically Eros became associated with desire
is interesting in itself, since it indicates that neither the Greeks
nor most of subsequent Western intellectual tradition acknowledged feminine passion and desire as a positive principle. Being overwhelmed and in the grip of passion (as opposed

to being the one who deals the arrows) was one correlate of the principle of Eros that took on rather frightening aspects for the emerging new consciousness, which emphasized rational control. Such control was personified in the god Apollo. As this god grew to major stature, the principle of Eros also became tamed and powerless. One form of disempowerment is, in fact, the effeminate, mother-dominated figure of Amor in the present story.

Although the story does not speak of this, the more ancient figure of Eros also continued to persist in many forms reminiscent of the original, primordial one. We will encounter one of those forms, a terrible dragon, in the next chapter. Other forms continued to retain features of the primordial monster Eros, such as horns, hoofs, lion-headed creatures, and so forth. But these features, too, were more and more driven into the domain of the repressed. In myth, this disempowerment became represented as the death of the god Pan, eulogized in Byron's famous poem:

> The Gods of old are silent on their shore
> Since the great Pan expired, and through the roar
> Of the Ionian waters broke a dread
> Voice which proclaimed "the mighty Pan is dead."
> How much died with him! false or true – the dream
> was beautiful which peopled every stream
> With more than finny tenants, and adorned
> The woods and waters with coy nymphs that scorned
> Pursuing Deities, or in the embrace
> of gods brought forth the high heroic race
> Whose names are on the hills and o'er the seas.[21]

I attempt to show in this book that the metaphor of Pan's death, or of Aphrodite's and Eros' degradation has parallels in historical and individual development. Both require that powerful desires be civilized and tamed. In that process, they are degraded and represented as dangerous. We will explore the specific results of these degradations for individual development in later chapters. In the current context, we will follow this process of degradation, showing that it did not only occur in mythic themes and stories, but that these mythic stories form a powerful undergirding of philosophies of the mind and the individual – philosophies that developed parallel to the historical changes we are discussing, and that came to form the basis of later concepts of mind, self, and human nature.

ORDERS OF REALITY

The belief that human consciousness has evolved through a series of different stages has been widespread since ancient Greece. Although in the story of Psyche and Eros it is expressed in the forms of images and personified symbols, in much of the intellectual history of the West it has been described as forms of thinking, as ways of speaking, or as aspects of the mind and consciousness. And just as is true of the relationship between divinities in the story, so in philosophical theories these aspects of the mind came to be represented as a confrontation of older and newer forms of thinking and speaking. I have already referred to those forms as logos and mythos in Chapter 1. In this and the following section, I will further explain those terms and how their meaning changed during the course of history.

A new language

Plato, living from about 428 to 348 B.C.E., discussed these changes when speculating about the effects of writing and literacy on thinking.[22] Writing implied an altogether new language form than the previous oral language of nonliterate cultures. More recently, such writers as Havelock, Goody and Watt, McLuhan, Olson, Postman, and, most recently, Donald[23] have expanded Plato's analyses and suggested that these forms or modes were based on different ways of thinking and speaking. In fact, writing per se appears to be only *one* possible factor in the evolution of that new form of thinking, as will be suggested later in this chapter. Nevertheless, the differentiation between the two modes remains important, and it is useful to introduce it with the help of these thoughts on the importance of written language. In the following, I base my analysis on these authors as well as the work of Scribner and Cole.[24]

Prior to written language, according to Plato, all knowledge was tied to oral information transmission. Think of the recitation of an epic like the *Iliad*. Such a recitation took place in a setting that was inherently interpersonal. Knowledge was based on a sense of participation and immersion, of emotional directness, of a close identification between the orator and the listener. Plato calls this mode *mimetic* and in the *Republic* he says of the reciter of Homeric poetry:

> I think you know that the very best of us, when we hear Homer or some other of the makers of tragedy imitating one of the heroes who is in grief, and is delivering a long tirade in his lamentations of chanting and beating his breast, feel pleasure, and abandon ourselves and accompany the representation with sympathy and eagerness, and we praise as an excellent poet the one who most strongly affects us in this way.[25]

Plato, to be sure, remained quite aware that this way of relating to reality was a mixed blessing and brought not only advantages but also some drawbacks. Thus he also suggests that it might require cognitive activities, such as sharp and vivid memorization, that were lost with more modern times. Nevertheless, on the whole his work is concerned with showing the flaws of that mimetic mode of thinking, one I will refer to as mythos. This mythos mode is an organic one. We are not distanced but immersed in a flow of events. We participate in an event; our attitude is performative. We are embedded in an interaction: It would be impossible, indeed, to tell where the event and the information passed on with it is located between speaker and listener. There is a merging, thus, between the experiencing subject and the object experienced. A skilled orator indeed draws on this very lack of differentiation so as to optimize the experience of mimesis in the listeners.

At its most effective, the mythos mode implies a surrender. We are being moved; we emote. And we process information in an intuitive, feeling fashion that involves us in the most direct way. The philosopher Martin Buber[26] wrote extensively on this mode, suggesting that it involves a particular relationship of the self to another person or an object. That attitude could be described as an "I–thou" relationship, to be constrasted with the "I–it" attitude we take on in the logos mode. When we are in that "I–thou" mode, the person or object beheld is not experienced as an entity outside of ourselves. Rather, experience is holistic and based on a bond of close identification between the self and the object of thought. Thought and thinker, knower and known, are one single, indivisible unit, and it is from this bond that derives the meaning of an experience. To judge what is true requires no criteria external to an experience; rather each experience carries the conditions of its own validity within it, in the very quality of the communion between subject and object. The object's qualities are not out there, distanced from the self; rather they are located within a deep core of the self. Cassirer has eloquently characterized that feature of mythos thought in his essay, *Language and Myth*:

> Mythical thinking . . . does not dispose freely over the data of intuition, in order to relate and compare them to each other, but is captivated and enthralled by the intuition which suddenly confronts it. It comes to rest in the immediate experience; the sensible present is so great that everything else dwindles before it. For a person whose apprehension is under the spell of this . . . attitude, it is as though the whole world were simply annihilated; the immediate content, whatever it be, commands his . . . interest so completely that nothing else can exist beside and apart from it. The ego is spending all its energy in this single object, lives in it, loses itself in it.[27]

This is a mode, then, identified with myth, with the performative, the concrete, the emotional, and with passivity. It is also often related to archetypal differences in gender: The intuitive, emoting, and surrendering aspects of the mimetic are often called feminine.

But it would be wrong to associate the mimetic with the more tender, gentle, feminine feelings *only*. Many writers, to be sure, have tended to romanticize the mythic mode as one that exhibits our natural unspoiled nature, that compels us toward a paradisiacal sense of unity with others and with nature, that leads us toward a sense of universal respect and community. This, I believe, is a grave error, since it does not take account of the fact that mythos has its dark side, too. Destructiveness, aggression, and the so-called masculine emotions are no less prevalent states of feeling typical of mythos. Thus, the lack of differentiation can be experienced not only in surrender and desire for union, but also in attack and the desire to destroy the other to which we are relating.[28] Depending upon the emotional system concerned, the mythic mode can aim at underdifferentiation – or its aim can be overdifferentiation and denial of similarities between self and other.[29] This important issue will concern us repeatedly in this book.

We already pointed out that since Plato, many writers have associated this way of relating to reality with preliteracy. In contrast, he suggested, and many writers of this century elaborated, that written language allowed another mode of knowing. Writing was based on permanent visual symbols, and that feature permitted an altogether different attitude toward the text. Readers could disconnect the message from its carrier and its original setting and take it to other settings, there to be read and reread at times of their own choosing. The undifferentiation between the knowing subject and the object of knowledge hence gave rise to a separation. Reader and listener no longer were united by some mimetic bond. The sense of awe, of mimetic immersion an orator might have fostered, was no longer effective. Instead, one could distance one's self emotionally and examine the text from a new perspective.

Written communication hence also implied a different kind of interpersonal relationship. It was less participatory and more distanced and afforded the reader a greater measure of independence. The distancing brought about by written discourse was not only interpersonal and emotional, however, but tied to dimensions of space and time as well. Messages could be uncoupled from the communicative process in which statements flow unidirectionally in time. Instead, the reader could break up that organicity and sequentiality, select individual statements for inspection, disconnect and transpose them in time or space, systematically compare and critique statements.

Thus the text had become the object of intellectual operations of a new kind. These operations were no longer organic and mimetic but mental and analytic. No longer dependent on others or on the context, they, too, afforded the reader a measure of independence and self-centered control. And all of these new functions, then, supported the evolution of a more analytical and logical mode in which information was represented.

Greek culture, then, brought into being a new mode of thought. Plato called this new mode *reason*, and he thought that reason was a more advanced and more mature mode of knowing. He thought that mimesis, through its appeal to the emotions, undermined the "higher" faculty of reason. And since reason played a more significant role in written modes of discourse, he thought that the faculty of reason was fostered by written language.

According to Havelock,[30] Plato's differentiation between the two modes of thought and knowing was based on the contention – surprisingly modern in many respects – that each mode affords not only different opportunities of thinking, but was actually based on a quite different language structure. Epics were memorized and recited in front of an audience, and thus had to rely on linguistic tools that would support the memory of both speakers and listeners. Rhythm, vivid imagery, and narrative style were important, as was the personality of the speaker. Both the language and the setting in which poems were recited fostered emotional identification. The listener was unlikely to adopt a reflective and distancing attitude.

The mimetic function of language, then, employs specific structural features. Language is situated in the particular, the here and now, and it is this language a poet or bard might use to evoke specific meanings in the listener. Aiming at reproducing as vivid as possible a sense of the concrete and felt texture of an experience, this language is emotive, associative, and sensuous. Words are chosen so as to convey immediate and obvious relationships to the events and objects they signify. The language thus relies on figurative and analogical elements. Like a map that is to represent territory, the aim is to give an almost pictorial impression of events. This aim is accomplished with the use of imagery, metaphor, rhythm, and punctuation.

The introduction of literacy, however, brought the evolution of a language of quite a different character. That "rational" language was at odds with the language of oral discourse. Havelock has commented on this antagonistic relationship between the two languages:

> Oral information is likely to be unfriendly to such statements as "The angles of a triangle are equal to two right angles." If, however, you said, "The triangle stood firm in battle, astride and posed on its equal legs, fighting resolutely to protect its two right angles against the attack of the enemy," you would be casting Euclid backwards into Homeric dress, you would give him preliterate form. . . . Oral storage is hostile to the expression of laws and rules which are stated in such terms which are connected by the timeless present. It is unfriendly to statements which place cause and effect in analytic relationship.[31]

Plato's differentiation between mimesis and reason, then, has profoundly shaped Western thinking about the nature of rationality. However, we no longer believe that it is necessarily the *setting* of language that forms the critical distinguishing feature. The languages that underlie mimesis and reason are not inevitably tied to the oral versus written settings. For example, a poem, though written, could rely primarily on features of the oral mode; or a scientific lecture, though presented in an oral and interpersonal setting, could predominantly draw on those of the written mode. What is at issue, therefore, is not just the context in which language is used; rather we are concerned with the fact that Plato's lifetime is widely associated with the differentiation between two modes, or types, of language and thought.

Logos and mythos

Throughout this book we will encounter many similar distinctions between two different forms of language and different modes of knowing and ways of experiencing. I shall use Plato's analysis of the process of reading as a model for these two modes of knowing, and I shall refer to their more intellectual aspects by the Greek words of mythos and logos. I have already introduced these terms in Chapter 1. However, since I will use them in a rather specific technical sense throughout this book, a more detailed definition is in order at this juncture.

Both of these terms have carried broad and diverse meanings through the centuries. Yet these meanings derive from rather precise roots. Indeed, both are terms for *word*, although in two different senses.[32] Mythos can be translated as speech, narrative, plot, or dialogue. It refers to word in the sense of spoken language and mimesis, to those aspects of language and its meaning which, though intuitively gripping, are not readily argued, demonstrated, or formalized. Yet despite that elusive quality there is a distinct meaning that is connotative rather than denotative: It is organically felt rather than logically derived, pregnant with emotive significance rather than "objective" evidence. Mythos refers to the language of poetry, myth, and dreams – a language that imparts psychological rather than logical knowledge. We can sense or feel the meaning of mythos, but it may remain entirely opaque to our attempts to justify or define it.

Logos also means word, but the term refers to the more conceptual aspects of words and, more generally, of states of the world. Logos was originally used to mean gathering, or reading, and came to connote counting, reckoning, explanation, rule, or principle and, finally, reason. In contrast to mythos, it refers to that part of knowledge that is arguable and can be demonstrated. It is more tangible than mythos to the extent that it can be defined with precision and agreement. But it is less tangible in another sense, since logos refers to the immaterial and disembodied aspect of concepts. Thus, by using the term logos, we do not mean the psychological effect produced by the word, but rather its representative, denotative function. Words are disembedded from a reality of flux and change and related to stable systems of categorization. The complexity of mythos is reduced, multisensory images are canalized into single modalities, and multivalence is contained in fixed meanings. Thus the logos function imparts on the word a dimension of stability and abstractness that is in contrast to the mythos function.

These two modes can be said to reflect the human capacity to construct and communicate meanings in two separate languages.[33] One of those is an *analogic* language. Here the sign usually has some immediate and obvious – often iconic – relationship to the thing it signifies. It is a language of imagery, metaphor, and symbols. It is the stuff of dreams, fantasies, myths, and inner world experiences. It is a language that delights in and thrives on the unexpected, on idiosyncrasy, on the juxtaposition of illogical relationships. But rather than creating chaos or illogicality, analogic language uses that feature creatively and exploits it in jokes, word games, innuendos, and condensations. It is a language without which artistic creation would be unthinkable. But scientific creation, too, is highly dependent on such language to the extent that it is permeated with holistic images that form laws into sometimes unexpected patterns.[34]

The other language, in contrast, is one that tradition has come to associate with the concept of reason. It is an objective, definitional, and analytic language. It is poor at discerning holistic patterns; but it can examine the components of such patterns for logical cohesiveness and noncontradiction. It dissects relational networks into their constituents and examines those for their logical adequacy. It follows a grammar and syntax that are intersubjective or objective rather than intrinsically motivated and idiosyncratic. This language is context-free rather than context-sensitive. When it does refer to context, it is *digital* rather than analogic. Thus, it relies on a relationship between sign and signifier, which is conventional and arbitrary rather than iconic and organic. And, to make this arbitrary assignment of sign and signifier work, it is necessary that the assignment be accepted by all users of the language within a specified community of thinkers.

These two languages partake in a relationship that is often antagonistic and paradoxical.[35] What is appropriate and well formed by the criteria of one can be inappropriate by those of the other. Consider, for example, metaphor. If we say of woman, "she is a lioness," we draw on a network of connotations that renders the statement meaningful and informative to competent speakers. Presumably, a combination of fierceness and protectiveness is evoked. Yet though appropriate in a connotative sense, the statement is false in a literal and denotative sense; it violates logical and lexical categories and creates a biological monstrosity!

The notion that two modes of thought underlie our processing of language has a long and distinguished history. It is a differentiation so broad as to cut across virtually all of Western thought, and it suggests that there are two distinct ways in which we experience reality. Indeed, there are different meanings of what constitutes reality altogether. According to one of those, a mature definition of what is real could be described as a reign of logos over mythos; according to the other, the ultimate reality is that of mythos, and logos is but a sterile and impoverished mode of being.

In philosophy, the debate about which mode is more desirable is often cast as a question about the origins of knowledge. Depending on theoretical tastes, that question has been metaphorically answered by proposing two different images of the knowing process. One of those images represents knowing as a mirror that objectively reflects to us the goings on in the world out there, and the other image, as a lamp that illumines our understanding from within.

The metaphor of knowledge as a lamp is a romantic one. In answer to the question, How is it possible that we perceive reality not as an aggregate of disconnected facts, but rather as a coherent unity? it suggests that such unity cannot originate from without but rather must be located within. Thus at the origins of our perception and experience of reality is a creative leap, a spontaneity of the mind, a synthesis that is purely imaginative. Rather than grasping reality discursively, we experience it as an immediate and intuitive unity of opposites, apprehended through an act of faith rather than reason.[36]

On the other hand, the image of knowledge as a mirror[37] holds the mind to a more disciplined attitude. To the romantics, adherents of the mirror view reply, How can objective knowledge be built on a spontaneous synthesis of faith? To accept that at the root of knowledge lies faith, that knowing is an imaginative integration rather than an objective account, amounts to claiming that knowledge is fictional rather than factual, that it is invented and constructed rather than based on some record of what is objectively out there. Thus, a second major current of our intellectual history has been the rationalist assertion that knowledge is, in essence, based on a receptivity rather than spontaneity of mind. For empiricists, this receptivity is a relatively peripheral one as reflected in Locke's image of the mind as a blank slate, to receive its imprints by what we perceive through the senses; for idealists, the problem is a more central one and framed in terms of those categories of the mind that permit a universal and veridical view of reality.

Religious systems, too, divide along such a duality. On the one hand, there are those from Western thought that tend toward hierarchic structure, tight ethical principles, and closely guarded dogma. These systems are usually based on the primacy of a single masculine deity – the foremost symbol of logos.[38] On the other hand, there are those systems that favor more mystic openness and individual insight. In those systems, polytheistic and inhabited with goddesses as well as gods, a mystic sense of at-one-ness between knower and known is the ultimate aim of spiritual illumination.

Many psychological theories, too, are based on a duality between two modes of knowing. Freud's distinction between primary and secondary process is a good example of that duality. When thinking in the primary-process mode, the reality of inner life – of dreams, wishes, and a sense of unity of knower and known – prevails. By contrast, the secondary-process mode is one in which the demands of an outer, objective reality prevail.[39]

Freud's distinction has recurred in many other major theories. Piaget,[40] for example, has distinguished between assimilation, a mode in which reality is defined in the imaginative, ludic approach defined by our inner life, and accommodation, a mode in which we adjust to the dictates of the outer world. More recently, Bruner[41] similarly has proposed a differentiation between a narrative mode, based on the inner reality of imagination, intention, and psychological causality, and a paradigmatic one, based on the objective reality of agreed-upon frameworks of classification and procedures of verification. Indeed, many thinkers believe that the distinction between two modes of knowing may be based on the organization of a duality of neuroanatomical and neurophysiological control structures.[42]

Vertical and lateral models of the mind

We noted that the two modes of knowing and ways of being often partake in a paradoxical relationship. One of the first philosophers to point out the paradox that arises from the different modes of experiencing reality was the sophist Zeno of Elea. On the one hand, Zeno pointed out, we can experience reality dynamically, in terms of movement, process, change, and becoming; on the other hand, statically in terms of equilibrium, structure, rest, and being. Zeno showed by force of logical argument that the two modes were related in a paradoxical fashion.

Consider, for example, Zeno's paradox of the runner running for the finish line. What is the initial distance he will run? Zeno argued that there is no such distance, and that the runner hence will not be able to take off. This is because to reach the finish line, he must first reach the halfway mark. Before reaching the halfway mark, however, he first must reach the point halfway between the halfway mark and the starting line. But again, before he reaches *that* point, he must reach the one-eighthway mark, the one-sixteenth mark, and so on, ad infinitum. Therefore, the initial distance vanishes into something infinitely small, and there is no initial distance the runner can run; he can never take off, and never will reach his destination!

Zeno's paradox derives from asking the question, Which of the two is right: that reality is something dynamic, continuous, and changing or that it consists of a series of stable images, of stops and discontinuities? With the wisdom of hindsight we can answer, of course, that both are in their own way true. Runners *do* run, and arrows *do* fly, though we can *represent* their movement as a series of images, much as a camera lens decomposes movement as a series of discontinuities. Nevertheless, as Hofstadter[43] has shown so well, the paradox often can entangle the thought processes of some of our most powerful thinkers. Indeed, it has been the source of much controversy throughout our intellectual history, and many thinkers have taken one side or the other on the issue of which is the "true" view of reality.

One answer to the question of which reality is true was that of Heraclitus who held that the only reality was that of change and dynamic tension – the reality of mythos. The person who would take logos as the true reality, who would look for the real in frozen, stable images, pursues an illusion. The only thing real, Heraclitus proclaimed, was an ever changing flux of time. We might try to fix that flux, arrest it, hold it constant, but even as we thus abstracted an image from the flow of reality, that flow moved forward and reality no longer was the same.

Unity and harmony, according to Heraclitus, are to be found only in change; truth and beauty are not to be found in sameness but in diversity and the juxtaposition of opposites. New forms of being emerge out of dynamic opposition: "What is at variance agrees with itself. It is an attunement of opposite tensions, like that of the bow and the lyre."[44] Or again: "Sickness makes health pleasant and good; hunger, satiety; weariness, rest."[45]

Heraclitus' reality serves as a model for one mode of relating to experience. He himself did not provide an elaborated theory of that mode, but rather wrote a series of aphorisms about what is the source of order, harmony, and stability in our experience of reality. For Heraclitus, order derives from rhythm and process. As in organic life, opposites and complementarities form interrelated processes: They combine, separate, and recombine. The resulting view of reality is one emphasizing constant transformation: becoming rather than being, evolving rather than arriving at end points, change rather than stability.[46]

Heraclitus' attitude is based on a form of logic that appears paradoxical. It asserts that the conflict between opposites is the basis of unity and order. This paradoxical mode of thought also was predominant in Chinese and Indian thinking. Its basic premise has been expressed by Lao-tse for Taoist philosophy: "Words that are strictly true seem to be paradoxical. . . . Gravity is the root of lightness; stillness is the ruler of movement."[47] This view holds that logos thinking – the process of categorizing and naming – is merely a device of thought we use to contain the dynamism of mythos. It is necessary, of course, for the individual to rely on conceptual tools by which a stable network can be mapped onto a reality of change. Yet that act of classifying and categorizing is merely a temporary gesture, and once it has been performed we must not hold on to it but return to the reality of mythos. Hence, what is real is not what we can articulate or name: "The Tao that can be trodden is not the enduring and unchanging Tao. The name that can be named is not the enduring and unchanging name. . . . He who knows [the Tao] does not speak [about it]."[48]

Heraclitus thus equates order with rhythm, process, and dynamic tension. The view that order is to be equated with process and tension rather than stability and rest has often been associated with some philosophic, religious, and mystic traditions, especially those of the East. It has also recurred in more modern Western thought, as will be discussed in Chapter 4. It is not an attitude, however, rooted in the urgent dictates of societal life, and it proved ill suited to the active, heroic sense basic to expanding Western thought. That expansion could only happen with the stability provided by logos. Heraclitus' teachings, though they eventually recurred in more modern forms of dialectical theories such as those of Hegel and Whitehead, were not very influential in the early development of Western thought. His emphasis of change and process contrasts with that of Parmenides who anticipated the Western preference for structure and stability – the reality of mythos. Parmenides taught that only that which does *not* change is real:

> When you think, you think *of* something; when you use a name, it must be the name *of* something. Therefore, both thought and language require objects outside themselves. And since you can think of a thing or speak of it at one time as well as another, whatever can be thought of or spoken of must exist at all times. Consequently there can be no change, since change consists in things coming into being and ceasing in time.[49]

Parmenides anticipated a particular model of how we are to understand the relationship between the two modes of knowing. According to that view, the two modes are to be arranged vertically and hierarchically. Thus we view the mature mind almost exclusively in terms of the logos mode of thought. The mythos mode, in turn, was considered less advanced. Here, we have a model in which logos is seen to dominate or control mythos. Reason is seen within a model of competition and conflict, and the attempt is to resolve that conflict by making logos the ruler of mythos. This is a view that is vertical and *rationalist*.

Of course, the rationalist ideal of severe control easily leads to the opposite excess. Just as in the myth, Aphrodite's wrath suggests that the rationalist model has not achieved a peaceful coexistence between new and old forms of being, so throughout our intellectual history thinkers have attempted to invert the image of logos dominating mythos. Martin Luther, for example, criticized the rationalist model, calling logos a whore who would prostitute herself to tradition and dogma.[50] Rousseau, too, believed that the domination of logos, far from assuring the highest reaches of human rationality, corrupts an inborn innocence and organic harmony inherent in mythos. But in these romantic visions of the mind, the vertical image with its connotations of competition and conflict is not, in essence, changed. In fact, it merely stands the rationalist model on its head, but it does so without changing the basic metaphors on which that model rests – those of control, of hierarchic organization, and of the "rage" of part of the mind against another.

Both models are limited. Rather than holding the tension and paradox that results from the dual nature of the mind, each offers a one-sided view at best, and a view that is distorted and fragmented, at worst. Thus many contemporary writers are suggesting that we adopt an alternative model – one that, in lieu of the conflictual image of control and domination, substitutes that of a mutually enriching exchange.

Within such a lateral view of the mind, logos and mythos could be described as participating in a dialogue. One mode provides precision, and the other, richness. One performs analysis, while the other gives direction and significance. Without one, the dialogue would be without rule and form; without the other, it would not matter to anybody – it would not stir our fancy, capture our interest, incite our feelings. It is not the dominance of one mode, but rather their cooperation that makes for a mature individual; indeed, that is a prerequisite for successful adaptation. The two modes share in a bond of cooperation that is not to be broken. Because if we do break the bond, different parts of the mind and self engage in war and struggle for domination.

This, indeed, is the wisdom revealed in the language of myth by the figure of the raging, vengeful Aphrodite. Aphrodite here represents that part of human nature that, in the ascent of logos, has become devalued and is being delegated to an underground existence. But, the myth suggests, being thus delegated to a peripheral position she is not disempowered. Rather, her range of action has been banned from the arena of public ideals and thus continues in a less direct and more

47

distorted way. How to transform that distorted energy and turn it into a cooperative exchange of the various divinities of the story is indeed the object of the myth.

The idea that the mind is best described by such a lateral and cooperative model has been an exception rather than a rule, however. As I argue in a later chapter, it requires that the individual be able to hold the tension between seemingly opposite visions of reality. Most of the models proposed in the course of history have not been able to integrate that tension. Beginning with Plato, who – as discussed earlier – thought that reason was a better mode of thinking than mimesis, our culture has equated the mind primarily with logos processes. Indeed, Plato's lifetime was a major historical milestone in that emergence of a vertical model of the mind. We will turn to a discussion of the beginning of this model next.

THE RISE OF LOGOS

We have already noted that the vertical model of the mind found a first formulation in the work of Plato, and in this section, we will examine in more detail how a vertical and dualistic model began to emerge with Plato's theory. To be sure, Plato's model of the mind was merely a precursor of more modern forms of dualism. Indeed, in his dialogues the dualisms are merely set up as tensions; they are not nearly as sharply drawn as they would be about a millennium later. In fact, there still is in Plato's work an infusion of mythos. Separations are set up tentatively, but not always systematically, and still one feels in his work the breathing of an animated, alive cosmos. Often, when more formal knowledge fails him, Plato resorts to myth to amplify his points. Indeed, to many interpreters Plato's work has suggested a theory that embodies a mystical union of the mind's polarities.[51]

There certainly is no consensus, then, about whether to call Plato a dualist or a mystic. Why, then, offer a somewhat detailed discussion of the dualisms in his theory of mind? I believe that Plato's work is particularly interesting because here we can observe the *setting up of dualisms* – mind and body, outer and inner, abstract and concrete, universal and particular, and so forth – that have animated theoretical debate ever since, and that have become the focus of much recent reevaluation. Of course, in setting up these dualities Plato was merely the spokesperson of a much broader historical trend or zeitgeist.

The birth of reason

I have already noted that Plato himself related that trend to the emergence of literacy. Recent research, however, suggests that the existence of a written language, per se, is not enough to account for so profound a reorganization in the nature of language and thought.[52] Rather, these reorganizations were part of a much more sweeping transformation of the social fabric and intellectual life in ancient Greece,[53] which began several millennia B.C.E. and reached its culmination around 400 B.C.E., during Plato's lifetime. That span of time brought the worldwide transformation of social life from nomadic gathering and hunting communities to ones characterized by complex and stable social hierarchies.

The rise of complex social organizations brought with it the necessity for profoundly different forms of life. In his study of the civilizing process, Elias[54] has commented on the way in which the emergence of more complex social networks affect these forms of life and the individual's conduct within them. In simpler societies of the past, Elias claims, life was regulated by a form of control rooted in the predominance of instinctual forms of expression, without the mediation of complex explicit rule systems. Such unmediated control contrasts profoundly with the way modern individuals regulate their conduct. Modern life is organized less by a dimension of concrete physicality and the immediacy of more or less automatic and instinctual programs, than by individuals guiding their behavior with reference to a complex web of social expectations and cognitive controls that are standardized and socially shared. Thus, logos acquired more and more significance – not merely as a novel linguistic form but, indeed, as an extraordinarily broad new way in which self, mind, and reality were understood.

This new way of speaking and thinking about self and reality has been studied by contrasting the way philosophers and poets talked about reality. One important source of evidence, for example, relies on analyses of the Homeric poems, probably written in the 8th century B.C.E., and of the writings of Plato and his contemporaries. Another is based on a comparison, stretching over about the same time period, of how philosophers talked about the nature of reality. Over this relatively short time span a dramatic reorganization occurred in how the actions and capacities of adults and their reality are described.[55]

Many philosophers before Plato already asked such questions as What is the nature of reality?, or What is our nature, and what is our place in the order of things? To the pre-Platonic philosophers, answers to these questions were permeated with mythic and organic concepts. Reality still presented itself as an organismic happening integrated with the world of nature. Like nature, reality was animated with life and subject to growth and decay.[56] Mythological and poetic accounts of the universe were beginning to be mixed with systematic and abstract thought.

To the question of what was the nature of reality, Greek philosophers, however, came to evolve a characteristic answer. Conceptions of reality gradually were bared of their concrete and mythic elements. Instead, they were reframed in terms of the more abstract, immaterial laws of logos.

This process of demythification or disenchantment[57] of the human view of the order of things was one of extraordinary breadth. It was animated by a broad worldview that provided a pervasive and coherent sense of how reality was structured. At its center stood no less than a profound revolution of the conception of the nature of human beings, their faculties, their responsibilities, and their destinies. All of those provided a comprehensive view of the kinds of skills and concerns the mature adult ought to demonstrate. Thus, the new model of reality as logos came to lay the foundation for more modern views of the nature of persons and their faculties.

That new model of the person has been widely studied by comparing descriptions of the individual in the Homeric poems to those in Plato's writings. In the Homeric poems, there is little evidence that individuals were equipped with the attributes we associate with the modern mind – abstract thought, control of impulses, a sense of individual uniqueness. The Homeric heroes do not engage in thought and reflection but are embedded in action and impulse. Theirs is a concrete, sensory existence. It shows little evidence of the mental types of regulation mastered by the modern adult: impulse delay and monitoring and self-ownership of action and feeling.[58] There is no language of a self different from its concrete actions and assets – a self as a permanent, persistent agent who authors its actions but is not identical with them. Indeed, there is no word at all, no specific designating concept, for the self, since "no one in Homer thinks by himself, but rather engages in an interaction or dialogue, be it with another person, with a god, or with a part of himself."[59]

Thus, the language of the self is one of concrete action and of participation with other figures, whether human or divine. Nor is there a specific differentiation between mental and physical, bodily processes. Mental activities such as wishing, thinking, and planning are often described as the automatic occurrence of bodily processes and physical actions. There is no concept of an individual reflective mind. Rather, mind and self are inherently interactive, dialogic, and participatory. The boundaries between inner processes and states and outer events are fluid, and inner states are often attributed to outer events. For example, dreams are seen not as emanating from within, but as originating from without. Thus, when Zeus in the *Iliad* ponders how best to avenge Achilles, he sends "evil Dream" to go to Agamemnon to send him a message. Dream is not an inner process (as it will be for Plato), but an outer event, a personified agent. Disguised as Nestor, Dream stands at Agamemnon's bedside and repeats Zeus' message to him.[60]

The same tendency to externalize one's inner process is also evident in the language of emotions, wishes, and desires. In the time of the *Iliad*, there was no concept of inner motives; rather individuals saw themselves moved by divine forces. Personal feelings and intentions were perceived as injunctions from the outside. Thus, when Achilles is about to slay Agamemnon, he interrupts himself because "Athena comes down, pulls him by his hair, and says, 'Cease.'"[61] The self expressed in such language is a self, then, undifferentiated from inner organismic states and functions on one hand, and fused with its physical and psychological environment on the other.

By Plato's lifetime, a dramatic change in the language of the mind has occurred, and Plato's writings represent the culmination of a new way of speaking about the mature adult. For Plato, the adult is no longer embedded in a concrete, organic, and participatory reality. Rather, the new reality is one defined by a new function, psyche, variously translated as soul, mind, or spirit. Most of Plato's writing is concerned with delineating the new faculty that allows us to live in that new reality, and with differentiating it from a reality of concrete sensory textures.

For Plato, mental functioning is no longer identified with the organic and the mythic – with the senses, with actions, with poeticized accounts of reality. Rather, it resides in our ability to step back from the purely sensory. Plato addresses this issue in the dialogue *Thaetetus*, where Socrates challenges Thaetetus' belief that knowledge is a form of perception. Neither knowledge, suggests Socrates, nor the faculty from which it springs – the mind – is to be identified with sensory functions. The senses, he argues, are merely the *instruments* of knowledge and the mind, but they are not *identical* with them. The senses merely point to the workings of a more abstract agency, the psyche or mind. Mind draws on the activity of the senses, yet it is something that goes beyond them, an inner abstract agency that does not merely act but that coordinates activity and operates on it.

With that inward movement, the mind has become an autonomous agency. This autonomy is evident in its changing social nature as well. As it turns inward, as it claims ownership and conscious control of bodily impulse and sensory activity, the mind also becomes less tightly embedded in the network of regulations provided by those that surround the self. The new mind thus is more individuated and self-authored. It becomes distanced from a concrete reality of interpersonal exchanges and located inside the individual, instead. It is no longer communal but becomes the purely internal discourse of a solitary agent, the self, with itself. Thus, in his dialogue with Thaetetus, Socrates maintains that thinking is

> a discourse that the mind carries on with itself about any subject it is considering. . . . So I should describe thinking as discourse, and judgment as a statement pronounced, not aloud to somebody else, but silently to oneself.[62]

The demythified mind

The writings of Plato and his contemporaries are witness to the emergence of a concept of mind that is marked by a sense of individuality and responsibility and a concept of self as a cognitive and moral author and decision maker. The evolution of this new set of cognitive capacities was of momentous significance in the process of civilization. It made possible a way of life necessary in a complex social organization in which systems of abstract concepts and symbols played an increasingly significant role in the individual's conduct.

Plato's theory of mind delineated the mental functions that would accomplish a new way of life. The person who would think and behave according to the new theory is a person of virtue and wisdom. However, this theory of wisdom also contained its negative side, as it formulated the new functions in a dualistic way. It delineated previously undefined differentiations – mind and body, inner and outer, flux and change, being and becoming, knowledge and opinion, universal and particular – as dualities around which the new concepts of mind and self are structured.

Such differentiations were an essential accomplishment of abstraction essential in the progress of cultural evolution. Still, the classical Greek model of reality anticipated a view of the mind and self that provided no effective synthesis of these dual terms. Thus, the preferred, more valid mode of knowledge was logos, while mythos was considered an inferior, a more primitive one – a lesser or degraded version of logos. Hence the project of building a new concept of mind was equivalent to one of demythification or, as Max Weber would put it, "disenchantment."[63] That reconceptualization and demythification encompassed a number of dimensions of mind and reality – both ones that are more collective and outer, and ones that were more private and inner.

The disenchantment of the natural world. A first example of this "disenchantment" was the emerging concept of nature. Greek culture, as the philosopher Cassirer points out, was involved in a sweeping process of denaturalizing nature, of divesting it of organic and concrete texture. Instead, nature came to acquire meanings that were purely theoretical and mental. This demythification and denaturing of nature is well demonstrated by Cassirer's[64] discussion of this process of inversion as it occurred in the change in meaning of the concepts of time and space. Originally, time encompassed meanings that were primarily qualitative and concrete. It indicated experiential and cyclical phenomena. It was biological time, conditioned by the emotional color of the seasons, of the succession of cosmic events, of stages of life. The new concept of time, however, was gradually emptied of these concrete associations. Time came to be a purely neutral and abstract frame of reference; none of its elements was charged with a particular value or significance, but each was understood as merely quantitative and abstract.[65]

Similarly, the concept of space also underwent a devaluation of its mythic and concrete connotations. The individual of the *Iliad* had moved in a space that was sensuous and concrete. His was a space that could be walked in; it had a concrete, sensual texture; it was defined and differentiated by the range of the specific feelings, actions, and experiences it afforded. The elements of which it was composed were concrete elements, as well. This was not a space composed of ideas and axioms, but of the forces and textures of nature, and of experiences within it.

Greek science, however, transformed this notion of a concrete and sensuous action space. The new space was no longer concrete, physical, and experiential. It was, instead, a mental or conceptual space and was captured, ideally, by the space of mathematics. It, too, had moved inside entirely. It no longer afforded pragmatic potentialities but was a space to be contemplated, a theoretical or scientific space. No longer constructed of concrete organic substances, it was composed of elements merely created in inner mind space, not the outer space of material things. It was a space in which the mind could free itself from the fetters that tied it to the life of the physical world, a space constructed out of purely axiomatic, Euclidian "elements," and the functional relations that could be constructed out of these mental building blocks:

In . . . [geometrical space] . . . all the concrete differences of our immediate sense experience are wiped out. We no longer have a visual, a tactile, an acoustic, or olfactory space. Geometrical space abstracts from all the variety and heterogeneity imposed upon us by the disparate nature of our senses. Here we have a homogenous, a universal space.[66]

Indeed, the Greek interest in geometry was excited by the hope that such knowledge could help create a new kind of reality. Unlike their predecessors from Babylonia and Egypt, the Greek thinkers did not value geometrical knowledge primarily because of its pragmatic utility – predicting the cycle of the seasons or the coming and going of droughts and floods. For them, geometry came to stand as a promise for a new reality, one in which you no longer needed to move physically but in which only the mind could move, free to roam in an ideal reality that can negate the constraints of organic life. Geometry thus became the symbol par excellence for how the rational man should conduct his life. Plato is reported to have inscribed on the door of the academy "Let no one ignorant of Geometry enter my door"[67] and to have believed that god continually "geometrizes." Virtue and wisdom were seen to derive from the study of geometry in a way that was impossible by living a more sensuous life. Thus, in Plato's *Gorgias*, Socrates admonishes Callicles:

> Wise men, Callicles, say that the heavens and earth, gods and men, are bound together by fellowship and friendship, and order and temperance and justice, and for this reason they call the sum of the things the "ordered" universe, my friend, not the world of disorder or riot. But it seems to me that you pay no attention to these things in spite of your wisdom, but you are unaware that geometric equality is of great importance among gods and men alike, and you think we should practice over-reaching others, for you neglect geometry.[68]

Frankfort and Frankfort[69] also have discussed this process by which reality was more and more dissociated from the concrete textures of nature. These authors note that early Greek philosophers typically proposed cosmogonies inter-mixed with mythic elements and imaged mythopoetically rather than scientifically. But gradually, natural phenomena come to be described in terms of discursive processes, qualities that can be analyzed, discussed, and judged intellectually. The relationship between self and nature changes from "thou" to "it." A good example is Thales' theory in which water is no longer a god but a thing. Similarly, for Anaxamines air is no longer the god of air or storms but a sustaining principle characterized by quantitative functional relationships:

> When it is dilated so as to be rarer it becomes fire; while winds, on the other hand, are condensed air. Cloud is formed from air by felting; and this, still further condensed, becomes water. Water, condensed still more turns to earth; and when condensed as much as it can be, to stones.[70]

Here, personified representations are abandoned with passionate consistency, and reality is more and more understood as a purely axiomatic realm. In that realm, man is revealed at his best.

The demythification of human nature. Another major consequence of reducing mythos to logos was the changing concept of *human* nature: of the mind and self that lived in the natural world. More and more, the belief emerged that the mature mind could be described without reference to an intersubjective, collective reality. Instead, thinking was to be described exclusively by propositional forms, universal ideas, and stable principles that transcended the dynamics of social order and interpersonal exchanges. These new laws of thinking were to replace the forms of decision making of the past, forms that had relied primarily on the authority of myth, tradition, and social power.[71] Instead, the Greeks envisioned a new form of decision making that was located purely in the realm of the abstract and the universal. In that realm, everybody could examine statements and be led to the same conclusion. The individuality of the thinker, then, no longer entered into the process of thinking, except in the sense that one might make an error of logic.[72] The qualitative individuality of participants in dialogue was completely transcended, however, by universal laws. There were no unique selves, therefore, to be accounted in a theory of thinking. Rather, each self was a mere replica of other, similarly universal selves, and the self entered into thought merely quantitatively.

The attempt to come up with universal decision forms resulted in the formulation of laws of logic, which were assumed to transcend subjective personal and interpersonal forms of decision making. Truth claims and the laws of thinking on which they were based were taken out of the communal and interpersonal and referenced only with respect to universal forms that were not dependent on the characteristics of individual thinkers.

Again, this program had at its core a message of liberation: If one were to judge by one's own mind, no longer dependent on the power of social coercion, one could come up with truths that were a matter of a new kind of power, one rooted merely in intellect rather than social control. The exciting connotations of that message are hardly to be understated, leading as they do to visions of an emancipated society.

Yet once again, Greek philosphy overstated the power of such rule systems. As DeLong[73] notes, this overstatement was evident in the contempt many philosophers held toward the Sophists, a philosophical school that held that logic and subjectivity were intricately related. To be truthful, the Sophists claimed, a thinker must be able not only to follow the logical structure of arguments but also to evaluate how reasonably truth values have been assigned to premises. Hence, truth cannot be dissociated from, or even displace, a general discussion of wisdom.

Plato, however, would have no theory of truth or thought that opened the door for the discussion of such subjective processes. In the *Protagoras*, he has Socrates oppose truth based on logic alone to rhetoric, which aims at argumentation and persuasion. Socrates compares Protagoras, the Sophist, with a mere peddler who, by using the tools of narrative, seduces people, "charming them with his voice like Orpheus, and they follow spellbound."[74] Thus he tries to lead the soul away from its necessary aliment, truth:

> We must see that the Sophist in commending his wares does not deceive us, like the wholesaler and the retailer who deal in food for the body. These people do not know themselves which of the wares they offer is good or bad for the body, but in selling them praise all alike, and those who buy from them don't know either.[75]

Plato thus thinks sophism a shameful practice, based as it is on the folly of the body. Following his lead, for centuries to come theories of truth and logic focused on rational structures only, while the mythic and narrative forms of artists and poets were not considered to be as advanced.

One correlate of the devaluation of communal and narrative aspects of knowing was a similar degradation of the individual's inner world, of the material and organic aspects of knowledge. Plato's theory, accordingly, defined the new way of life in direct opposition to the sensual, bodily, organic, and interpersonal. The ideal man's thinking (and thinking, we shall see, is very much a masculine activity) was no longer supported by the concrete texture of sensory impressions and interpersonal exchanges. Rather these were defined as perils, as dangers that constantly threaten to pull the new self back into its former, more primitive mode of existence. In Plato's *Phaedo,* the mind or psyche, says Socrates to Simmias,

> can best reflect when it is free of all distractions such as hearing or sight or pain or pleasure of any kind – that is, when it ignores the body and becomes as far as possible independent, avoiding all physical contacts and associations as much as it can, in its search for reality.[76]

Thus, it is necessary that the philosopher aims at "despising the body and avoiding it, and endeavoring to become independent."[77] There is a constant disparagement of everything associated with the body and the senses:

> As long as we possess the body, and our soul is contaminated by such an evil, we'll surely never adequately gain what we desire – and that, we say, is truth. Because the body affords us countless distractions . . . it fills us up with lusts and desires, with fears and fantasies of every kind, and with any amount of trash, so that really and truly we are . . . never able to think of anything at all because of it . . . for all these reasons it leaves us no leisure for philosophy. And the worst of it all is that if we do get any leisure from it, and turn to some inquiry, once again it intrudes everywhere in our researches, setting up a clamour and disturbance, and striking terror, so that the truth can't be discerned because of it.[78]

Here we see the emergence of dualistic reason. On one hand, such values as truth and morality are erected as ideals to live by. While this in itself can be considered an advance, it is also problematic because these ideals become dissociated from the organic reality of living things and beings. Indeed, the attributes of "real" and "natural" became more and more decoupled from the organic, mythic processes of life, and more and more associated with the nonliving world!

Just as the mind must maintain discipline over the body and its impulses as Plato claims in the *Republic,* so it must cultivate a deep suspicion over everything concerned with the imagination. For Plato, the inner life of feelings and the imagination lurks with dangers. As a consequence, his project of denaturalizing and demythifying mind and self is carried to such imaginative products as dreams, myth, and art. For example, in the *Republic* Plato says of dreaming that desires

> are awakened in sleep when the rest of the soul, the rational, gentle and dominant part, slumbers, but the beastly and savage part, replete with food and wine, gambols and, repelling sleep, endeavors to sally forth and satisfy its own instincts. You are aware that in such case there is nothing it will not venture to undertake as being released from all sense of shame and all reason. It does not shrink from attempting to lie with a mother in fancy or with anyone else, man, god, or brute. It is ready for any foul deed of blood; it abstains from no food, and, in a word, falls short of no extreme of folly and shamelessness.[79]

In a similar vein, Plato wants to ban other imaginative activities from the *Republic.* The artistic, the poetic, and the mythic, he claims, deal not with the truthful eternal nature of things, but rather with their phenomenal appearance. Pictorial representations, for example, are lies and apparitions only, superficial and illusory. "That kind of art . . . ," says Plato, "seems to be a corruption of the mind of all listeners who do not possess as an antidote a knowledge of its real nature."[80] The activities of poets are no less dangerous since

> the poet himself, knowing nothing but to imitate, lays on with words and phrases the colors of several art in such fashion that others equally ignorant, who see things only through words, will deem his words most excellent, whether he speak in rhythm, meter, and harmony about cobbling or generalship or anything whatever. So mighty is the spell that these adornments naturally exercise, though when they are stripped bare of their musical coloring and taken by themselves, I think you

know what sort of a showing these sayings of the poets make. . . . The creator of the phantom, the imitator, knows nothing of the reality but only the appearance.[81]

Plato thus believes that just as the rational life requires that the self steer away from the seduction of the senses and matter, so the philosopher must be careful not to succumb to the deceptions of art. In actuality, this contempt of imaginative activity is quite undeserved, because the arts, no less than philosophy, were part of the very transformation discussed in this chapter. Simon[82] has demonstrated, for example, that as the rational, discursive language of the philosopher became transformed, so did the language of the poets. In the great plays of Aeschylus, Sophocles, and Euripides, for example, mental processes are clearly located in an individual mind. Thus in *the Oresteia* by Aeschylus, Orestes is told by the chorus of Clytemnestra's dream: She had given birth to a snake. When she held it, swathed for sleep like a baby, to nurse it, it drew blood from her nipple. Orestes, saying, "No void dream this. It is the vision of a man,"[83] indicates that the dream refers to him who will turn into a snake and kill Clytemnestra. Thus artistic productions, too, reveal evidence of a new self who claims responsibility for an inner life.

CONCLUSION: BEYOND THE VERTICAL MIND

In this chapter, we have examined how modern notions of rationality and maturity emerged some two and one-half millennia ago. I have suggested that these notions elaborated one component of mental functioning and one that forms the major part of modern conceptions of the mind and human nature. Thus historically, theories of the mind and its development were associated with the evolution of abstract, theoretical modes of functioning, what I have called logos in this chapter. Those abstract modes themselves evolved from earlier modes of functioning that appear to have been based on mimesis and myth.

The elaboration of this pole of the mind was an enormous accomplishment in cultural history. It is rightly considered to form a foundation of much of Western civilization, and it has determined not only our scientific orientation, but also our democratic and humanistic traditions. Nevertheless, the one-sided evolution of logos-oriented theories also has had major drawbacks, and these drawbacks have become the focus of much recent discussion of theories of mind (see especially Chapter 5). Since the logos mode of functioning was defined as a tension against mythos, mythos tended to be devalued and considered an inferior mode, rather than one that also can partake in development.

As these two modes became differentiated and refined, they also became related vertically and hierarchically. I detailed that vertical model by examining features of Plato's theory of the mind. Plato's analysis of the mind has profoundly influenced our Western conception of the individual and his or her capacities. Thus more modern rationalist conceptions of the mind – those theories often referred to as modernist[84] – have taken the dualities Plato elaborated and arranged them in a hierarchy in which the more mature and desirable logos reigned over the more primitive and less desirable mythos.

Again, it is important here to point out that Plato's theory is not nearly as dualistic as its more modernist decendants. Nevertheless, it set up those tensions by describing the faculties of the adult as one end of a polarity. On the one end, that duality is defined by forms of knowing that are tied to an intimate interpersonal context; imitation, intuition, the analogical and figurative, the organic and the instinctual, change and conflict, all define that pole of his theory of knowledge. The second pole, in contrast, is defined by forms of knowing less dependent on the immediate context: Abstract understanding, rational analysis, the intellectual and analytical, the mental and voluntary, stability and harmony all refer to what Plato thought were the better parts of the human being.

The nonrational functions, accordingly, were believed to be a lesser, reduced version of the rational. They made us similar to animals and children; they were associated with illusion, darkness, and ignorance. In turn, reason's function was to control those lower functions. Thus Plato's theory also outlined a theory of development, and one that is still exerting its influence on modern views. As we will see, the ability to dissociate and hierarchize mind and body, self and collective, reason and imagination – inner and outer – are widely held to be the hallmarks of mature development. In turn, how the abstract is to be grounded in mythos, in lived, felt experience, continues to be a problem for our accounts of development. We will turn to this problem in the next two chapters.

Chapter 3

The marriage of death:
Ascent and loss in development

Psyche, meanwhile, felt no joy in her beauty. Men marveled at her as at a lovely statue finely wrought, but none came to ask for her hand. Her sisters had long been married happily to kings who came to claim them, but Psyche grew increasingly broken in spirit. And so it came that her father the king, suspecting that something divine had gone awry, consulted the oracle of Apollo. To his horror, he was given this advice:

> *on some high crag, o king, set forth the maid,*
> *in all the pomp of funeral robes arrayed.*
> *Hope for no bridegroom born of mortal seed,*
> *But fierce and wild and of the dragon breed.*

But though they mourned and wept, the oracle must be followed. In her ghastly bridal dress of funeral robes, and with the mournful wailing of the procession that led her, Psyche walked to her doom.

THE SURRENDER OF THE FEMININE

Here, the story takes a precipitous turn. Aphrodite's warning that Psyche is to be united with a vile and monstrous being turns into reality as Apollo's oracle ordains that she is to be married in a funeral ceremony to a terrible dragon. But even before this terrifying oracle, we learn that Psyche's extraordinary fame and beauty are not entirely positive gifts. Not only have they enraged Aphrodite, they also have alienated her from other humans. So beyond the reach of mortals is her loveliness that she cannot find the ordinary creature comforts of life – home, husband, and family – that come naturally to her less beautiful sisters.

Psyche's beauty with its disastrous consequences here calls our attention to what Jung calls the "shadow" – the fact that ideals of necessity have their negative, or "dark," side.[1] On the one hand, Psyche reflects the ideal of a new way of being. She is a person who lives in a mental and spiritual realm rather than one that is dictated by lusts and desires, by immediate organic needs. On the other hand, by having distanced herself from the organic texture of life, she is forced to lead a one-sided existence. So close is her fit with the new ideal that she is almost completely abstracted and spiritualized. Much as Plato suggests that the mature individual is raised beyond the world of matter, imagination, and attachment, Psyche also represents these refined spiritual qualities. Having relinquished her organic wholeness, she has become an idealized figure standing above earthly desires, divorced from love and lust. No longer a whole woman, she no longer is home in the realm of the mythic, organic, and divine. She is an ideal created by her culture. Thus Psyche sits at home, broken-spirited and lonely.

Development and renunciation

In Chapter 2, I discussed the price we paid for the development of consciousness as history defined new models of the individual. Psyche's lot addresses a similar price the individual pays in his or her development. Her unhappy fate reminds us that in individual development, too, gains in consciousness are often associated with losses. These losses are dealt with in this section of the myth in a two-tiered fashion. When she is still a girl, these losses are the result of a purely "inner" victory in which Psyche's organic self is alienated from her idealized, mental aspect. But as she grows into adulthood, they are represented by the more dramatic and terrifying image of her sacrifice to a monstrous dragon.

The language of myth here suggests that, as is true of cultural development, individual development brings not only growth and gains but also decline and loss. Let us discuss the gains first. As the growing individual is born into the reality defined by a culture, he or she must learn to define self and reality along certain conventions. In the process of mastering the rules of our culture, we learn to be good sons and daughters of our culture, to idealize ourselves along the guidelines provided by that culture. The advantage we gain from this process of self-idealization is that we are able to participate fully in the riches our culture has to offer: protection, security, knowledge, and so on. It would be difficult indeed to underestimate how vastly we extend the potential for our development by participating in a rich culture, rather than being left to our own devices. Thus the rewards for seeing ourselves in the light of our culture's ideals are enormous, as well.

But we also pay a price for these cultural gifts. To become a good member of the collective, the individual must renounce more spontaneous and instinctual forms of behavior. The selfish demand for our own pleasure must be sacrificed to the well-being of the collective, and thus, the individual not only gains but also loses potentialities by participating in culture. Neumann, in his book *The Origins and History of Consciousness*,[2] has elaborated on the losses encountered as the child thus attempts to adjust to the "reality principle."

> Characteristic of the process of differentiation in childhood is the loss and renunciation of all the elements of perfection and wholeness, which are inherent in the psychology of the child. . . . The very things which the child has in common with the man of genius, the creative artist, and the primitive, and which constitute the magic charm of his existence, must be sacrificed. . . . The drying up of the imagination and creative ability, which the child naturally possesses in high degree, is one of the typical symptoms of impoverishment that growing up entails. A steady loss of the vitality of feeling and of spontaneous interests of "sensibleness" and "good behavior" is the operative factor in the conduct now demanded of the child in relation to the collective. Increase in efficiency at the cost of depth and intensity is the hallmark of this process.

The marriage of death

Neumann here suggests that in the interest of cultural adaptation, the individual surrenders part of the self. This surrender enables the development of a sense of "I," of a bounded self that is the center of action and experience. Yet this accomplishment is achieved at a cost: The individual is required to split off the yearning for the mythic, organic, and interpersonal connectedness referred to as mythos knowing in Chapter 2.

Formation of the ego

Instead of experiencing the self in terms of those dimensions of connectedness, the growing self needs to be defined more and more in terms of logos processes. Mythos, in contrast, is no longer experienced as part of the self. Instead, it becomes objectified and experienced as something outside the self, an "it" rather than a "me." Part of the self's vitality is killed off, moved outside where it can be looked at objectively.

This process of splitting the self into an "it" and a "me" is well reflected in the common terms for these aspects of the self: *id* and *ego*, respectively. It is interesting here to reflect on their historical origin. Freud, of course, introduced these terms to refer to two aspects of mental functioning – one dominated by the "pleasure principle" and the world of instincts and desires, and one determined by the faculties of rational judgment. What is less well known, however, is that Freud's actual choice of concepts had connotations that were lost when his work was translated from the original German into English.

Bettelheim[3] has pointed out that Freud's translators chose the abstract, scientifically sounding Latin words *id* and *ego*, rather than the simple, common-language words *it* and *I*, for the German *es* and *ich* used by Freud. The word *I*, of course, indicates an immediate, direct personal identification with part of ourselves. And it is interesting that for Freud, that direct place of self-identification is that structure that mediates decision making, planning, and conscious thought. Thus, the self is, in effect, equated with logos functioning. This is where we are assumed to feel ourselves most "at home," where our sense of reality is most secure. The word *it*, in contrast, connotes a distanced, rejecting, and critical attitude toward that other part of ourselves – mythos.

The division of a formerly unitary self and the "expulsion" of part of that self outward as consciousness develops parallels, then, the process of the historical formation of mind we discussed in Chapter 2. The same process also is a pervasive mythological theme. Indeed, Neumann[4] has suggested that myth provides a general account of the formation of conscious thought both in individual and historical development.

Consciousness in creation myths

Creation myths are especially revealing in that regard, since they depict the polarization and the growing inner division of different aspects of the self. The original forces of creation, mythically understood, usually are primordial and chaotic ones; they combine all creative powers, both those that are benign and constructive and those that are terrible and destructive. In creation myths, this often is expressed in the figure of a single godhead who embodies all the powers of creation and destruction. Such myths of creation, Whitmont[5] suggests, were prevalent at a magicomythical level of cultural development. Only gradually do these forces become divided and sorted, with the result that the original integrated godhead eventually is split into two classes, one representing the "light," benign, and rational side of the divine and the other, its "dark" and destructive side.[6]

The Greek creation myth as reported by Hesiod[7] is an example of such progressive differentiation. In the beginning, Hesiod tells us, there was the void, and Gaia, the earth mother goddess, emerged out of this void. Gaia gave birth to the mountains and the sea, and to her husband, Uranus, the sky. Uranus mated with Gaia, and from the union emerged the Titans – primordial powers of nature who were the predecessors of the Olympian gods.

Hesiod's account suggests that even at this early time, the god's mature powers were based on an expulsion of infantile, more primitive aspects. Uranus, according to Hesiod, grew so envious of Gaia's procreative powers that he attempted to prevent her from giving birth by pushing the children back into Gaia's womb. In terrible pain, Gaia called the Titans for help, and her son Cronus responded to her cry. Taking a sickle that Gaia gave him, he waited for Uranus to come and mate with his mother. When the couple lay together, Cronus approached the couple and castrated his father. He then married his sister Rhea, and from their union was born the first generation of Olympian gods and goddesses – Hestia, Demeter, Hera, Hades, Poseidon, and Zeus.

But like his father, Cronus grew envious of his wife and jealous of his children. Forewarned that one of his own sons would some day overcome him, he swallowed each child immediately after its birth. But Rhea invented a ruse: When her last child, Zeus, was born, she hid him and wrapped a stone in swaddling clothes. Cronus swallowed the stone, not realizing that he had been tricked.

Zeus eventually did overthrow his father and became the supreme god of the Olympus. But in this generation of gods, the dark and light powers became separated when Zeus and his two brothers, Hades and Poseidon, divided the universe among them. They drew lots, and Poseidon won the sea, and Hades, the underworld, but Zeus won the sky – the realm of light and of exuberant, procreative mental powers.

Zeus, then, represents a more "civilized," tamer power than his forefathers; abusers of their own children, Uranus and Cronus embody both the positive and the abusive effects of magnificent powers. In Zeus and his brothers, we also see a division among the gods of light and of darkness. Still, this division is only emerging, and Zeus still is a rather primitive god, throwing thunderbolts in fits of rage and pursuing and violating women in indomitable lust. But in Zeus' sons, these powers are further separated. No longer united in one single individual, they instead become divided into different figures.

One of those is Apollo, who, like the girl Psyche in the story, represents the new ideals of consciousness. He is a god of harmonious balance, the epitome of heroism, a wise and just

69

god, associated with rational thought and with sun and light. In contrast to Apollo is his brother Dionysus, who represents unpredictability, ecstatic excess, and orgiastic irrationality, and who is associated with wine, death, and darkness.

Even among these two gods, the division grows sharper over time. Early in Greek history, they were closely associated. Whitmont, indeed, refers to them as "twin bothers," and originally Dionysus was admitted to Apollo's precincts at Delphi for part of the year.[8] Over the course of time, however, they were seen in more and more of an oppositional relationship. It was Apollo only who was admitted publicly; his cult had enormous influence and in many ways he became the quintessential Greek god. In contrast, the Dionysian element went underground. First, it descended into the mystery rites, cults whose initiates were sworn to secrecy. But eventually, the Dionysian element was outlawed altogether. Indeed, his goat image was turned into the face of the devil, and followers of Dionysus from the Middle Ages on "were branded as demon- and devil-worshippers."[9]

Neumann[10] shows that this process of splitting of divine figures is a very general one in the history of myth, involving male as well as female figures.[11] Many original godheads represent a unity, but a unity of the paradoxical coexistence of dreadful and magnificent aspects; they are benign and malevolent, both givers and devourers of life. Emerging consciousness experiences this union of opposites as overwhelming, and reorders it so that it can be assimilated with less dread. Thus, from the primal *coincidentia oppositorum*, an ideal and positive side is split off. That positive side is recognized by consciousness. It is symbolized by light, gold, and the sun, and is established in the conscious world as a value that one confesses to and celebrates. The other part, however, is largely repressed and excluded from the conscious world.

The process by which the ideal self overcomes the split-off instinctual part in myth is often described as the heroic confrontation of the god of lightness with the powers of darkness: serpents and dragons. This heroic slaying of the dark side of the self by its light, ideal side is, in fact, already visible in the pair of Gaia and Uranus: Gaia representing the dark, fruit-bearing earth, and Uranus the light-bringing sky. This separation of the powers of light and darkness – associated with the masculine and the feminine from the beginning – and the beginning antagonism between them continues from this point on. It is also a part of the myths surrounding Apollo. One story, for example, tells how Apollo, when still a little boy, though precocious on a diet of ambrosia and already holding bow and arrow in his hands, slew the primordial she-dragon Delphyne.[12] At Delphi, they encountered the monster, a huge serpent, and Apollo shot arrow after arrow until the dragoness was defeated.

The feminine as victim

It is significant, now, to observe that in the myth of Psyche and Eros these processes are not only personified but also gendered: The feminine principle is sacrificed to the masculine one. And indeed both in myth and in our popular assumption the values represented by Dionysus are most often associated with the feminine: Dionysus was a god who loved women and who was loved by them, and as a god of fertility, his followers were mostly women.[13] In contrast, the values embodied by Apollo are usually called masculine. Hence the coexistence of different parts of the selves mythologically often is represented as a marriage – a marriage, however, in which part of the self, and specifically, the feminine part is killed, torn apart, subjugated, or raped.

The images of subjugation and rape, to be sure, are coarse and terrifying ones. But such is the language of mythos that it distills desires that offend our more conscious sensibilities into stark, personified processes. The sacrifice of primordial feminine powers is such an image, often referred to as the "marriage of death."[14] This death marriage, then, is the dramatic image of this killing off of part of the self so as to adapt to the new order. Because Apollo himself is a representative of that new order, it is not without significance that the prescription that Psyche be sacrificed to the dragon comes from this god of light.

To be sure, from the perspective of the hero and his growing consciousness, the primordial power is often represented as a feminine being. But here it is interesting that the story does not adopt this heroic perspective, from which the killing of the primordial monster strikes us as a rather glorious act of sublime courage. Rather, it adopts that of the slain, and thus the source of beastly deadliness is shifted. Neumann[15] argues that in many myths from the perspective of the masculine hero, danger and aggression are projected onto a feminine serpent figure. From the feminine perspective, however, the process is experienced as one of victimization, and danger appears to come from the masculine source. Hence we find that from the perspective of Psyche, the danger and darkness of organismic life, of the split-off "animal" self, are seen to come from the figure of Eros – for no other than the god of love, we are soon to learn, is to appear as a fierce and wild dragon.

Because the Psyche and Eros myth thus involves a change in perspective from the masculine to the feminine viewpoint, Neumann argues that the "marriage of death" theme in the Psyche and Eros myth makes it, in essence, a tale of feminine development. But it would be just as correct to say that it is a tale of masculine development, looked at from the perspective of those aspects of a man's self he has split off as feminine. In either case, however, the myth has very direct and obvious implications for the development of men and women and their interactions. This point will occupy us at length in the following chapters.

In the context of the present chapter, however, we will interpret the myth less literally and look at this death marriage as a purely *inner* union of opposite tendencies. That union may occur not only in males, but also in female figures, whether they be mythological or actual people. Thus, in the god Apollo as well as in many adult men, the slaying of instinctual powers shows as a problematic attitude to one's instinctual, feminine side. Not surprisingly, therefore, we also find that Apollo's relationship to love is problematic. Most of his loves, and the most famous ones, end tragically as the god accidentally kills his would-be lover and/or transmutes the lover into a more primordial form of life, such as a plant.

But even though it lacks wholeness, this "Apollonian" structure can make for successful adaptation in young men for whom it can bring a great deal of status and success. It also can characterize female adaptation. Before she is called to surrender to the death marriage, Psyche in our story represents such a form of adaptation, which consists of the refusal to surrender to the feminine destiny and a desire to participate in the masculine world. In that regard, Psyche is reminiscent in many ways of the goddess Athena. Like young Psyche, the Hellenic Athena was a highly spiritualized goddess. But her relationship to femininity – her own or that of other women – was problematic. Born from her father's head rather than the womb of a woman, already clad in armor, her primary allegiance remained to the masculine principles of the new order.

But on the question whether a masculine adaptation is possible for Psyche, the myth is without ambiguity. The heroic form of adaptation is not to be tolerated for Psyche. To marry and to grow into maturity, Psyche must not resist the surrender of the feminine but must actively embrace it. And embrace her fate she does: In the end, Psyche accepts the oracle's words and leads the funereal wedding procession herself.

The mythic theme of the marriage of death, then, presents development as the tandem evolution of two inner tendencies. One is the heroic tendency, symbolized by the slaying of the primordial monster. In this heroic act, the instinctual power of the body and the fusion of self and world are overcome. From that activity emerges the hero – an "acting, willing, discriminating ego which . . . performs new and extraordinary deeds, and battles its way to victory."[16] The other, however, is the attitude of the victimized feminine, which is forced to submit to a death marriage.

In the remainder of this chapter, I suggest that this dual

mythic perspective on development has significant implications for more scientific discussions of the process of development. This is because it suggests that if we focus only on the evolution of reason, we inevitably paint a partial, and partially distorted, picture of the individual's journey to adulthood. Thus, if we ask what room is left for further development, we are apt to find that in choosing too logos-oriented an account, no room or dynamic tension is left for further change.

DEVELOPMENT AS RISE: PIAGET'S THEORY

The feeling that an important dynamic of development has been excluded from our traditional accounts of development has been widely voiced in the community of developmental psychologists.[17] Many recent writers have noted that our grand theories of development have remained embedded in the assumptions of classical rationalism, with its devaluation of mythos processes. Thus they have exclusively focused on the positive side of that process of devaluation: efficient acculturation and the standardization of communal life. But the negative side, the suppression of individual creativity and its damaging consequences, has been less apparent.

I suggest that in reconceptualizing the process of development, it is extremely important that we reevaluate the balance of gains and losses that may come with such a rationalistic and heroic image of development. To focus the discussion of the interweaving of these two movements, I propose an analysis of one of the giant theories of development, that of Jean Piaget. As was the case with my discussion of Plato in Chapter 2, the reason for choosing one particular thinker is not to "blame" any one individual for faults. Rather, it is because Piaget in many ways was a particularly articulate and erudite spokesperson of a zeitgeist. Hence, to discuss assumptions of his work ultimately offers an avenue for clarifying our own thoughts and for proposing our own recommendations for future theory development.

The marriage of death

The vision of Piaget's program

It is useful to begin this discussion with a question: Why has Piaget's theory, despite all the criticism it has evoked, continued to fascinate theoreticians and researchers? The answer, I believe, is that the theory is linked with a major intellectual movement of this century and one that, to an extent, is concerned with reversing the trend we saw rising in the work of Plato and his contemporaries. That trend, I suggested, eventually led to a particular ideal of human nature – one in which criteria of mature conduct were severed and dissociated from organic forms. In contrast, Piaget asserts a view of the human organism and its mental equipment as part and parcel of the organismic and biological world.

Piaget's theory, not unlike that of Freud, thus represents a first step toward bridging the dualisms that had been set up by classical philosophies of the mind. The attempt was to integrate the polarities of the mind that had been dissociated. Against the classical dualism, Piaget's theory squarely proposes a more integrated view of the human organism and its capacities.

The attempt to integrate the two poles of knowing is apparent in several propositions basic to the Piagetian program. First and foremost, Piaget proposes that the organic realm is the very ground out of which more abstract mental capacities evolve. The continuity between the organic and the mental is assured, according to Piaget, because every adapted act is based on a balance of assimilation and accommodation. Assimilation tends to preserve the existing inner form, while accommodation tends to modify actions according to the demands of the outer world.

Even though the bulk of Piaget's work has traced the development of formal and scientific forms of thought, at the core of his program was the belief that these forms of thinking reflect pervasive reorganizations in the way in which the individual structures reality, generally. Thus, much of Piaget's work has carefully charted how, early in infancy, intelligence is closely identified with this organic ground. Instincts and he-

75

reditary reflexes form organic adaptations from which later, more complex forms of intelligence evolve. These organic forms soon become extended cognitively, empowering behavior with a greater degree of foresight and planning. Ultimately, however, for Piaget the roots of conceptual activity were organic.

Piaget[18] also asserts that mental operations are continuous with the emotional and imaginative realms. Thus, Piaget rejects a reductionism that would claim that emotions are the cause of cognitions or, alternatively, that cognitions are the cause of emotions. Instead, Piaget thinks of the two rather as two sides of the same coin: Cognition provides the structure, while emotions provide the dynamics and energy. As the individual develops, the cognition and emotions codevelop in essential interdependence.

In this way, affective experience develops along with cognitive development, creating feelings that become more differentiated and more internalized. First, affect is dictated by inborn affective reactions, which, however, soon become modified with increasing mastery over the world. The toddler's mastery of language and symbol adds increasing stability and internality to feelings. Emotions related to norms, morality, and one's evolving will are soon added. Finally, in adolescence, "feelings for other people are overlaid by feelings for collective ideals. Parallel to this is the elaboration of personality where the individual assigns himself a role and goals in social life."[19]

Piaget[20] also proposes that it is impossible to separate levels of intellectual understanding from ways of relating. The child's cognitive immaturity and the adult's sophistication create an imbalance that is not only cognitive but social as well. Because of that imbalance, relations between children and adults are asymmetrical and reflect the power differential between the two age groups. In the child's eyes, parents are all powerful; their rules are seen as unalterable and as representing something akin to universal order. Piaget calls that asymmetrical relationship a "unilateral relation of constraint." He states that reason proper cannot develop in such a relationship. This is because reason implies a reciprocal relationship:

one where individuals are equal in power and exchange their views without social coercion. This ideal is not possible, however, in the relationship between children and adults. Instead, in the interaction between children and adults, understanding "is imposed from without [and] it leads to a calculation of [individual] interests or remains subordinated to ideas of authority and external rules."[21] Piaget, following Kant, calls this orientation to rules and knowing "heteronomous."

In adolescence, Piaget claims, these unilateral relationships of constraint give way to ones of reciprocal exchanges and cooperation. A good example of such exchanges is that of a peer group. In such a relationship, rules are no longer understood as coming from some outside authority. Rather, they are created from within the group. Ideally, Piaget says, they are being coconstructed cooperatively among a group of individuals equal in power. In such a setting, there is "continuous comparison, . . . opposition . . . , discussion, and mutual control,"[22] placing on each individual a system of checks and balances that modulates subjectivity and caprice of any one member of the group. The new orientation to knowing is "autonomous," based on the recognition both of one's own individuality and that of other members in the group.

Thus, for Piaget, increasing levels of cognitive development involve also a restructuring of power relations. Indeed, cognitive development implies that processes of decision making are decoupled from conventional structures of authority and, instead, subordinated under processes accessible to every individual. In this way, a more lasting equilibrium of rationally motivated laws is substituted for the coercive quasi-equilibrium of social power and convention.

Here Piaget[23] proposes, in effect, a view of cognitive development that is no less integrative than that encountered in Plato. What was so exciting to the Greek philosophers was the realization that a move to the new world of thought also required a new way of relating. It is no accident that classical Greece was the birthplace not only of formal laws of logic but of democracy as well. For Plato and his contemporaries the formation of democratic rule was made possible by a decline in the dependence on the concrete here and now, an ability to control bodily sensations, a censoring of the imaginative, and a lessening of the awesome power of the sacred. Similarly, for Piaget increasing levels of cognitive development imply the very same movements. By differentiating an inner imaginative, animistic reality imbued with the sacred and an outer objective one and by projecting beyond the immediate demands of one's organic reality and expanding experience across space and time, more powerful and coherent structures of mind and self were formed. In addition, Piaget proposed, this process also involved a restructuring of power relations. Indeed, cognitive development implies that processes of decision making are decoupled from structures of authority and convention. Instead, they become dependent on laws that are purely based on intellectual power and that are, therefore, accessible to every individual. In this way, a more mature balance based on the laws of reason and equality is substituted for an imbalance of individuals differing in social power.

Thus, Piaget's theory is one of extraordinary sweep, and one that places itself within Western ideals of democracy and humanism. Nevertheless, there are also telling ways in which Piaget has fallen short of describing that ideal of social life dictated by a concerned and principled exchange among individuals. Before exposing those limits, let us first review some of the major milestones of development as proposed by Piaget.

Piagetian stages of development

As I have noted, Piaget's theory of cognitive development is one that explicitly focuses on the role of organismic factors in development.[24] Like many other theories of development, it, too, suggests that the individual slowly comes to distinguish between a world centered around one's own body and self, and a world that is out there and objective. With increasing age, the child eventually begins to understand that more is involved in "reality" than the momentary appearance of objects. Specifically, Piaget believes that this transcending of a body-based and action-dependent reality moves through several cycles or stages.[25]

Sensorimotor period. According to Piaget's theory, the infant's thought is completely based on a reality focused on the body and the actions it is able to do. He calls the infant's intellectual functioning sensorimotor, since at first the world does not appear to have an existence independent of what the child can feel and do. For example, Piaget has shown that the infant's early grasping is merely a reflex action. Different objects are grasped in the same undifferentiated way, with no regard to the object's unique and differentiated properties. It is as if each object were merely an extension of the same primordial grasping pattern.

For instance, in one set of observations Piaget traced the baby's reaction as an object, say a rattle, is removed from vision. When the baby is about 5 months, "out of sight" is literally "out of mind"; the child does not search for the object or otherwise indicate that it has not simply vanished. At about 8 to 12 months, in contrast, the infant will engage in deliberate search, thereby indicating that the object indeed continues to have an existence even if it cannot be seen.

Thus, from rather modest beginnings eventually emerge much more complex skills. The infant gradually learns that different objects require very different kinds of grasping and reaching. After a few months, an infant's actions become finely differentiated and adjusted to the unique properties of different objects. Soon, out of these more differentiated actions the child can create higher order, composite actions; for example, once the child masters the action of throwing a ball and creating a certain bounce, that action can be made part of a game between the child and an adult.

Representational period. When they are about 2 years old, Piaget believes that children have a firm understanding of a world somewhat independent from their own actions, perceptions, and feelings – a world that is populated with objects whose properties are less dependent on a child's own experience. Now, children are capable of representing reality rather than merely acting in it. However, this advance is relative only, and Piaget distinguishes between a preoperational and a concrete-operational stage of this general period.

During the preoperational stage, from about 2 to 5 years of age, a new set of confusions between inner and outer becomes evident in the toddler. Now, however, that confusion becomes more psychological and results in the child's attribution of the self's feelings and intentions to an inanimate world. Thus, unlike the adult, the child has no sense of uniform, impersonal, scientific laws that dictate part of nature. Rather, there is a thorough confusion between physical and psychological mechanisms. Piaget calls that aspect of the child's thought "animism" and comments:

> When children between 5 and 8 are asked whether the sun could go away if it wanted to, they always answer that it could: if it does not go away it is because it "has to shine a little longer," or because "it has to lighten us during the day." Clouds cannot go because they show us the way, etc. In short, if there are natural laws at work, it is not because the bodies in question are physically determined; they could perfectly well evade the law if they wished to. It is simply that they are obedient.[26]

This animistic attitude by which the child imbues the world with her or his own intention also is related to a high level of concreteness. The child's mind at this level of development is still tied to the here and now, immediate appearance of objects and events. One method by which Piaget studied this concreteness is the famous "beaker" problem. The child is shown two beakers filled with a colored liquid to an equal height, and the child affirms that both contain "the same amount to drink." Next, liquid from one of the beakers is poured into a third beaker. This third beaker is of the same volume as the other two, but of very different shape; it may be either wider and lower or higher and narrower than the first two beakers. Piaget found that preoperational children are convinced that by having changed its shape, the water has changed in amount as well. Thus, because of their very extreme concreteness, the children are misled by the changing appearance of the liquid's volume.

Piaget designed many similar tasks attesting to the concrete nature of this period of thinking. For example, preoperational children think that a quantity of chips changes if it is bunched out or pushed together, or that a clay "sausage" changes in amount if it is flattened into a "pancake." However, a few years later, children are able to understand that quantities do not change despite their visual form; presumably, children can now coordinate the various dimensions (e.g., height, width) in such a way that increases in one can compensate for decreases in the other. Thus, the notion of "amount" actually becomes a more abstract thing that requires the coordination of several dimensions.

More generally, Piaget was also interested in showing that concrete operations brought a move of experience onto a more complex, abstract plane in which such systems as numbers and physical quantities can be mapped. However, he believed that this accomplishment was not only important for the child's beginning ability to understand scientific concepts, but that it also has profound consequences for how children think about their social world. He studied how individuals under-stand simple rules, such as those that direct marble games or jumping hopscotch.[27] Here, too, young children display a view of reality that is exceedingly concrete, and in which judg-ments are based on direct, literal evidence. For instance, chil-dren under about the age of 6 years judge a transgression by the amount of physical damage that results, rather than by such psychological criteria as intention. Similarly, young chil-dren are not aware of the difference between a lie and a state-ment that is simply untrue; only at a later stage does the child understand the difference between a lie and a purposive deception.

Piaget argues that this move from a confusion between inner and outer reality to a more psychological worldview is paral-leled by another move: The young child has a rather magical understanding of the origin of rules. When asked where the rules of games come from, young children indicated that they considered rules as sacred and unalterable. They seemed to come from divinelike superiors, authorities, and all-powerful agencies such as parents, god, or public officials. Here, once more, we observe a parallel to the historical processes discussed in Chapter 2: Just as for the early individual, the world was the seat of divine and unalterable powers that reside outside of the self, so for the child rules appear to have a similar sacred quality. Thus Piaget suggests, "The young child believes in a Great World Order, wherein everything 'meshes' according to a grand plan of cause and effect, right and wrong, and everything equalizes in the long run."[28]

Abstract period. During the concrete-operational period, the child – not unlike the historical process I discussed in the previous chapter – begins to operate from a worldview that is more and more "disenchanted," based on an understanding of physical causes and scientific laws. But even so, experience remains rather tied to the concrete. That concreteness is overcome in the next and final stage, *formal operations.* The degree to which the growing mind leaps beyond this personal "here-and-nowness" is dramatically shown in the following study reported in Piaget's book *Experiments in Contradiction.*[29] Children ranging in age from about 5 years to early adolescence, about 12 years, are asked to assess a rectangular board with seven sockets. In each of those sockets is fitted a disk. The disks are all of the same thickness, but although their diameters *look* the same, they actually increase progressively in steps of .2 millimeters (about 1/125th of an inch). The disks, A through G, are arranged in a zigzag pattern. Each disk is held in place by a fine chain in such a way that it can be moved to be compared directly with its immediate neighbor. However, disk G is completely unattached and can be moved about freely, so that it can be compared freely with all others.

The trick in this study is, of course, that the disks increase in steps so small that they are imperceptible. Yet when the disks at the extreme end, disks A and G, are compared, those imperceptible differences add up to a small though perceptible and measurable difference of about 1/20th of an inch. How is the young child going to reconcile that even though one does not *see* a difference between adjacent disks, there nevertheless *is* a small difference that eventually adds up to something that can be perceived?

Piaget's answer is that very young children cannot understand what is happening here. They begin by comparing all adjacent disks and ascertain that they are all the same size. But now, when asked to compare disks A and G and finding their beliefs inaccurate, they are not bothered by the contradiction at all. However, by about 8 years of age, children are puzzled and try to figure out what happened. One girl, for example, concludes that, since disk A equals B, B equals C, and so forth, it follows that A equals G. Surprised, she goes back and checks to see if she has committed an error. Perhaps, she thinks, A, B, C, D, and E all are equal, while F and G are larger. But comparing F and G, she finds that this hunch is not true. She then goes on to redefine the boundaries of the "big" class and the "little" class from trial to trial, contradicting herself at every trial.

A boy about 2 1/2 years older than she, however, soon comes upon the notion that can resolve the contradiction. After first stating that A is equal to G, he immediately notes that this prediction is not true: Noting that G is larger than A, he immediately exclaims, "They're not all equal. Yes, they are all different."[30] But even though this child has an idea of what is happening, he remains hampered by what he sees: Adjacent disks always look the same size. He says that maybe the differences are too small to see, and that perhaps they can be felt by touch and goes on to carefully feel the disks. Thus, children like him try to set out to "prove" that perhaps invisible differences are involved here. Some children even hit on the ingenious notion that one could get a microscope and in this way show increases in size that, though invisible to the naked eye, can be seen with magnification. But lacking a concrete proof of their ideas, these children give up the correct hypothesis, ending up feeling quite confused.

A critical step is reached when children a few years older say they "know" what is correct, even though it cannot be proved with sensory evidence. For example, one boy, aged 13 years, when seeing that G is a little larger than A checks to see if he measured properly. Then he immediately says that it is "just a little bigger. Not much. You can't see it. . . . They get bigger and bigger all the way along, and the last one is bigger than the first (meaning visibly bigger)."[31]

Here, something extraordinary has happened. Adolescents no longer think that proof is dependent on concrete sensory data. Instead, it has become merely a matter of making a logical derivation: It *must* be so, since the only logical explanation for what is happening is that all contradictions are removed in this way. This movement from a concrete reality of being dependent on a sensory reality of here and now, to one that has to do with thoughts, ideas, and ideals, according to Piaget, is the most extraordinary step the individual makes when growing from childhood to adulthood.

For Piaget, the ability to step out of what is concretely perceivable and into what is abstract and imaginable constitutes perhaps the most important ingredient of adolescent thinking. "Reality" no longer is dependent on the visible and felt here and now, but rather is shaped by ideals, thoughts, and notions of what is possible. By this reversal "between what is real and what is possible," a person is able "to escape the concrete present toward the realm of the abstract and the possible."[32] This leap of thought forms the basis of a variety of intellectual feats that were not possible in childhood.

One of those is the ability to orient one's thought systematically toward the future – to ponder about one's role in life, to make plans toward the future, to begin building, in a relatively conscious way, an identity. Related to this capacity is the one for reflective thinking, to take the products of one's thought as an object and examine them, to think, in other words, about thought. This revolution of thinking has enormous consequences for the adolescent's social and affective life as well. Now, feelings relative to ideals are added, and the individual has complex affects related to social roles and scales of values that are societal in nature:

We are struck by the fact that feelings about ideals are prac-
tically nonexistent in the child. A study of the concept of na-
tionality and the associated social attitudes has shown us that
the child is sensitive to his family, to his place of residence, to
his native language, to certain customs, etc., but that he preserves both an astonishing degree of ignorance and a striking
insensitivity . . . toward his own country as a collective reality. . . . [in contrast] The notions of humanity, social justice . . .
freedom of conscience, are ideals which profoundly influence
the adolescents's affective life; but with the child's mentality,
except for certain individual glimpses, they can neither be understood nor felt.[33]

DEVELOPMENT AND THE LOSS OF MYTHOS

Piaget's theory had an enormous influence on the study of
children's intellectual development. Before his work began
making an impact in this country some 30 years ago, there was
no comprehensive theory available that could provide a
coherent and attractive theoretical underpinning for the observation that children's ability to make sense out of their world
varies dramatically with their stage of life. Piaget's attempt to
show that these progressions from stage to stage affect not
only children's ability to grasp abstract conceptual issues but
also major aspects of their everyday lives. This attempt influenced not only the study of the former, but also has spawned
similar explorations into children's understanding of their social world.

On the less positive side, however, the theory has recently
fallen on hard times.[34] Limitations quickly became apparent
when Piaget's concepts and tasks were extended to cultural
groups other than those on which the theory had been
developed – Swiss children. Especially when children from
developing countries were studied, it appeared that the theory
perhaps tapped forms of reasoning more strongly related to

such factors as education and industrialization than development per se. Specifically, it seemed Piaget's theory contained an overall bias toward logical, mathematical, and scientific forms of thinking. Thus, it was not appropriate for cultures less exposed to these forms of thinking.

Somewhat similar criticisms also arose when the theory was extended to age groups older than intended by Piaget.[35] Piaget had constructed his tasks with a brilliant and almost infallible knack for what works with young children. His tasks are extremely interesting, engaging, and compelling for young children. But the same is not true when the tasks are applied to issues of adult and later life. Thus the question arises: Are these populations deficient or does the theory not work for them?

As a result of these and similar criticisms, a number of so-called neo-Piagetian theories have been developed. Although these theories show many similarities, and although all of them owe a profound debt to Piaget's original formulations, they tend to restrict themselves to somewhat more delimited problems and issues. Some deal with cognitive developmental stages in the narrower sense,[36] but others extend to more interpersonal areas such as morality,[37] concepts of self and other,[38] and even emotions.[39]

In these attempts to extend and clarify Piaget's original formulations, many of these efforts have begun to confront an even deeper core problem: It has become evident that, even if cast into a more modern form, a theory like Piaget's retains a profound objectivist bias. Thus, at its core, Piaget's theory remains a vertical model in which the relationship between two modes of knowing is translated into a hierarchical rather than a cooperative relationship. In that way, it adopts as its guiding metaphor that of the "marriage of death" in which maturity is translated into the heroic victory of reason. Is this death marriage a necessary aspect of development, or is it a view that results from a particular theoretical bias? To examine that question, we need to examine in more detail how Piaget's theory – and many more recent accounts that are derived from it – ultimately remains a vertical theory of development.

The marriage of death

Development as dialectical balance

It is paradoxical in many ways that Piaget's theory should have become criticized for its vertical view of mature reason. At the core of the theory is a broad and sweeping vision of human development. It is a vision not unlike that of Plato, who was aware that the new model of the human being implied no less than a vast reorganization of the nature of life – one rooted in our nature as rational, mental beings. But while Plato had planted the seeds for uprooting reason from its organic moorings, Piaget's intention was to heal the resulting schism. Writing his early works only some 60 years after Darwin's theory, Piaget asserted that human reason must be studied first and foremost as a function that originates in our nature as organic, biological beings. That conviction is evident in his discussions of early development of the mind, as outlined in the previous section.

To study the mind as something that is rooted in biology meant for Piaget that human adaptation is more than a matter of adjusting to a cultural milieu. To internalize the rules and norms by which the external environment functions for Piaget merely forms *one* aspect of mental functioning. It merely represents *one* movement, a movement in which we learn that there is an "outer" world independent of our actions and desires. Thus, in some sense, we come to perceive a reality that is objectively "out there," that is quite independent of our inner life, that is populated with persons and with impersonal objects. Piaget calls this movement "accommodation."

But, maintains Piaget, accommodation is only *one* movement required for adaptive mental functioning. Much as we need to learn to orient to a "world out there," to do so *only* would create a mind that is primarily imitative. No innovation and no creativity would be possible. Hence, accommodation needs to be balanced by assimilation. In contrast to accommodation, in assimilation the individual is not concerned with the demands of outer reality. Instead, a playful attitude prevails in which the individual acts and feels according to the demands of an inner reality.

87

A good example of such assimilation is play activity. In play, the child (or even adult) may take any object (a wooden block) and playfully use it as something else (an airplane) by enacting appropriate sound and motor patterns (acting out the takeoff of a plane). In such a case, no concern is given to the objective reality; rather, the object is merely assimilated to an imaginative inner world.

Accommodation and assimilation then, also imply two different notions of what is "real." For Piaget, reality never is merely an external given that the individual aims to reproduce or copy. Rather, the outer reality must be matched to an inner reality; and that inner reality is more than a mere copy of outer reality. As a result, development should be seen as a back-and-forth movement between two tendencies. Such a view yields not a vertical but rather a cooperative and lateral structure of development. On the one hand, the demands of an inner reality require that we externalize our creative and imaginative syntheses; that is, we give it expression in the outer world, even modify that world to fit our desires. But on the other hand, the requirements of an outer reality dictate a more receptive attitude – an attitude that permits us to reproduce and internalize what is objectively given "out there."

Now Piaget is adamant in asserting that adapted forms of mental activity involve a balance of these two movements. On the one hand, an individual's needs and desires, organic existence, and imagination give to mental activity organic significance and creative flexibility; on the other hand, negotiating these inner products with the demands of outer, objective reality ensures that the individual does not merely stay stuck in a private world of impulsivity and perpetual play, but, instead, transforms these inner tendencies so that they can find useful and constructive expression in the outer, objective world.

Piaget's position here is similar to that of another major developmental psychologist, Heinz Werner. Werner and his colleagues[40] propose an organismic theory of development that also suggests two modes of perception. One of these Werner calls "physiognomic," the other, "formal-technical" or "geometric-technical." In the physiognomic mode, reality appears to us dynamically. The object of thought is not articulated separately from the motivational and organismic states of the thinker; rather the thinker's whole organism participates in the articulation of the object and animates it with its own motives and intentions. As in Piaget's playful and creative assimilation, there is no concern, then, with what the object means in a formal, "outer world" sense.

Like Piaget, Werner believes that this mode does not lend itself, however, to many meanings that are shared by a social collective. Social functioning requires that many symbols be standardized or so defined that individual feelings, intentions, and other organismic states do not affect them. Thus, the individual must adopt a more informal, technical mode, the one here identified with logos. In this mode, the object is differentiated from its organismic ground and related to stable, abstract, and collective categories. Nevertheless, Werner asserts that the resulting process of disembedding can only be relative, never absolute: The two modes form an essential interaction and must not be dissociated. If the organismic tie between them is broken, symbolization will fragment and lose meaning.

Piaget would agree with this statement. Paradoxically, however, that agreement remains abstract in his theory. In more concrete discussions, Piaget often shows a bias toward equating development with the development of logos only. In creating this break, Piaget is not unique, however, but was following a trend of the times. Freud, too, fails to establish a true discourse between the two processes. On the one hand, Freud introduces primary process as the repository of our "animal" nature. On the other, he asserts that this mode must be superseded by the ego principle, which is aimed at dealing with objective reality. Like Piaget and Werner, Freud argues that the ego principle must be well integrated with the primary process mode. Indeed, notes Freud, "the substitution of the reality-principle for the pleasure-principle denotes no dethronement of the pleasure-principle, but only a safeguarding of it. A momentary pleasure, uncertain of its results, is given up, but only in order to gain in the new way an assured pleasure coming later."[41]

Nevertheless, Freud's theory, too, is less aimed at a harmonious balance than at a fairly complete domination of the pleasure principle by the ego. Thus, the process of development essentially involves a gradual "substitution of the reality-principle for the pleasure principle."[42] As a consequence, that which is pleasant comes to be dominated by that which is "real, even if it should be unpleasant."[43] More generally, many mythos processes according to Freud are considered remainders of infantile, primitive tendencies, just as in Plato's theory dreams and other inner symbols (as in Michelangelo's art) are merely the eruption of infantile processes into consciousness. Religion in Freud's theory is devalued as a mere longing toward fusion with the mother's breast. Our strivings toward social connectedness are expressed either in the form of a tyrannical superego or in a tendency to escape from that tyranny by fusing with mass hysteria. The feminine, finally, is only considered to be a devalued and infantile form of the masculine.

I began this chapter by discussing the notion of the death marriage, a symbol that suggests that often in the process of development the feminine theme is sacrificed to the masculine one. Here, we see how pervasively this mythic theme structures the more complex theoretical "stories" we tell about development as well. The creative, playful, mythos mode gradually is abandoned as an "immature" way of functioning, while development is equated with the growth of the logos mode. Thus, in the end, these theories adopt the heroic myth of the hero slaying mythos.

Giving up the imaginative

In Piaget's theory, that "slaying of mythos" specifically can be observed in how playful activities of assimilation are treated. On the whole, his account of development is biased toward processes of accommodation. One example is Piaget's discussion of play.[44] Piaget believes that early in development, play takes on an extremely important function, since it ensures that development does not merely become an imitative concession to the demands of adults:

Obliged to adapt himself constantly to a social world of elders whose interests and rules remain external to him, and a physical world which he understands only slightly, the child does not succeed as we adults do in satisfying the affective and even intellectual needs of his personality through these adaptations. It is indispensable to his affective and intellectual equilibrium, therefore, that he have available to him an area of activity whose motive is not adaptation to reality, but, on the contrary, assimilation of reality to the self, without coercions and sanctions. Such an area is play, which transforms reality by assimilation to the needs of the self, whereas imitation (when it constitutes an end in itself) is accommodation to external models.[45]

However, Piaget does not believe that such playful activity retains its importance throughout later stages of development. With regard to playful activities and symbols, he very much maintains that progress in development brings a decrease in private symbolism as play is transformed and incorporated into objective thought. Thus, it no longer functions to distort reality along with affects and desires but comes to represent the external world. Piaget's adult reality is very much an external, collective, and impersonal one.

A particularly good example of this driving out of the organismic dimension is given in Piaget's book, *The Language and Thought of the Child*.[46] Here, Piaget's differentiation between assimilation and accommodation returns in the form of a differentiation between "inner" and "outer" speech. Piaget notes that the very young child typically engages in what he calls "egocentric" speech: The child is often not so much interested in "objective communication" but in more playful uses, such as deriving pleasure from the mere repetition of sounds and hearing oneself talk. Much of this early speech is a form of monologue in which the child talks as if thinking out loud. For Piaget, this is a form of inner speech that is not at all aimed at objective communication. But as the child grows older, Piaget argues, a child adopts more socialized forms of speech: Now speech serves such aims as to exchange information, to question and answer, to voice criticisms, commands, and requests.

Note that Piaget here equates the development of language with the dropping out of inner speech. Why should this be so? Here, his thinking is revealing. Piaget distinguishes – and follows Freud – between two forms of speaking and thinking. The first he calls "directed or intelligent" thought, and defines it thus:

> Directed thought is conscious, i.e., it pursues an aim which is present to the mind of the thinker; it is intelligent, which means that it is adapted to reality and tries to influence it; it admits of being true or false . . . and it can be communicated by language.[47]

This directed form of thought is contrasted with an "undirected" form, which, says Piaget,

> is subconscious, which means that the aims it pursues and the problems it tries to solve are not present in consciousness; it is not adapted to reality, but creates for itself a dream world of imagination; it tends, not to establish truths, but to satisfy desires, and it remains strictly individual and incommunicable. . . . On the contrary, it works chiefly by images, and in order to express itself, has recourse to indirect methods, evoking by means of symbols and myths the feeling by which it is led.[48]

Now, it is most significant that Piaget pathologizes this latter form. Indeed, he calls it "autistic" and contrasts it to the former, which he calls "intelligent." Noting that undirected, autistic thought "remains individual, is still tied to imagery, to organic activity, and even to organic movement,"[49] he further distinguishes the two forms by giving the example of a concept such as water:

> To intelligence, water is a natural substance whose origin we know, or whose formation we can at least empirically observe; its behavior and motions are subject to certain laws which can be studied, and it has from the dawn of history been the object of technical experiment (for purposes of irrigation, etc.). To the

autistic attitude, on the other hand, water is interesting only in connection with the satisfaction of organic wants. It can be drunk. But as such, as well as simply in virtue of its external appearance, it has come to represent in folk and child fantasies, and in those of adult subconsciousness, themes of a purely organic character. It has in fact been identified with the liquid substances which issue from the human body, and has come, in this way, to symbolize birth itself, as is proved by so many myths (birth of Aphrodite, etc.), rites (baptism, the symbol of a new birth), dreams, and stories told by children. Thus in the one case thought adapts itself to water as part of the external world, in the other, thought uses the idea of water not in order to adapt itself to it, but in order to assimilate it to those more or less conscious images connected with fecundation and the idea of birth.[50]

How extraordinary is this statement! It discounts a whole class of mental activities and completely devalues them as childish and primitive. Bettelheim, in his book *The Uses of Enchantment*, has noted how prevalent this devaluation of mythos is in Piaget's theory. As an example, he discusses Piaget's interaction with a young child who insisted that elephants have wings. Piaget attempted to resolve this issue through a rationalistic approach in which he pointed out to the child that elephants cannot fly. Yet, argues Bettelheim, this rationalism, based as it is on highlighting the parameters of an outer reality, threatens completely to overlook and deaden the subjective experience of the child:

> If Piaget had engaged in conversation about where the elephant needed to fly in such a hurry, or what dangers he was trying to escape from, then the issues which the child was grappling with might have emerged, because Piaget would have shown his willingness to accept her method of exploring the problem. But Piaget was trying to understand how this child's mind worked on the basis of his rational frame of reference, while the girl was trying to understand the world on the basis of her understanding through fantasy elaboration of reality as she saw it.[51]

From an anthropological perspective, Turner[52] also argues that Piaget focuses on an outer rational world that is independent of the inner world of feelings and purposes. What is more, that devaluation of feeling and inner purposes is carried over to a devaluation of the organismic. Thus, in a very general way, Piaget's is a bias toward thinking rather than acting, conception rather than perception, the abstract rather than the concrete. However, argues Turner, how is that abstract world to be integrated with concrete sustenance, with affect and value? Such integration is not achieved by purely objective forms but by the imaginative and the symbolic as well. Thus, ideally, thinking should be described as a dialogue between two modes. These modes, then, are not arranged hierarchically but are complementary and mutually reinforce each other.

The novelist Thomas Mann, in his celebrated essay "Freud and the Future," also maintains that mythos is far from being an immature and childish form of thought. In fact, he claims that it is a uniquely *adult* form of meaning making. Through mythic activity, the adult is able to see and experience his or her life in terms of patterns that are felt to be meaningful, universal, and necessary. In that way, individual experience can be grounded in the broad and typical patterns of life that form the stuff of myth, art, poetry, religion, and, indeed, all mythos forms of experience. Thus, in the slaying of mythos, a profound split is introduced into our accounts of development – a split that becomes especially evident when dealing with adulthood.

Knowing and relationship

Piaget's censorship of the imaginative, animistic, and mythical is matched, though in a subtler way, by how he accounts for the interpersonal dimension of knowledge. Here, too, his account is based on the logos metaphor of "I–it" rather than the relational mythos metaphor of "I–thou." Consider, once again, Piaget's description of the young child's language. That language is purely inner; in fact, Piaget compares it to a monologue rather than a dialogue. Thus in Piaget's view, the child remains locked in an egocentric world, and only advances in cognitive development can save the child from that egocentric predicament.

Many recent authors have sharply disagreed with that account. Careful observations of mother–child dyads have shown, for example, that even in preverbal infants, during the very first few months of life, there emerges something akin to a dialogue.[53] Trevarthen describes such dialogues in terms of "protoconversations" in which mother and infant engage in a nonverbal "dialogue" that has clear audible and visible features. To be sure, such dialogues are not based on a coherent verbal exchange; in fact, the mother often may utter not speech but nonsense sounds. But what is important is that her vocalizations and other expressions display a particular emotional form of what has been called "intuitive motherese," and that this type of vocalization is directly responsive to the infant's equally coherent emotional expressions – in terms of face movements, coos or frets, hand gestures, and body movements.

Trevarthen believes that these forms – he calls them "primary intersubjective engagements" – are universal and unlearned forms of communication. He believes that their primary form is based on a direct emotional contact between the infant and the caretaker: "The eye-contact, smiling and other facial expressions, coos of fretting and crying, and the varied postures and gestures of a young baby constitute a coordinated display of changing feelings that may interact immediately with the affect in a partner's expressions."

Following a host of recent theorists,[54] Trevarthen suggests that this basic emotional linking forms the ground for later stages of development. If such exchanges are successful, the infant gradually forms an inner image of the world (and more specifically, of self-in-relation-to-mother as the main embodiment of the world) as something and somebody reliable and emotionally responsive. Establishing later relationships that are characterized by more complex forms of intersubjectivity will be a natural consequence. But the establishment of such relationships does not await the development of complex thought structures; it is a primary given of human functioning.

Piaget's theory is not based on this primacy of human inter-subjectivity. In fact, he does not primarily focus on the individual's relationships to other selves, but rather to a world of objects. That bias is seen most clearly in Piaget's account of infant knowledge. Here we see infants exploring, and interacting with, inanimate objects. But what is almost completely missing is the presence of others: There is no mother, for example, whose interactions with the child can influence and modulate relationships to the outer world. Indeed, Piaget claims that the infant is, in essence, lost in an egocentric world, with cognitive mechanisms too primitive to relate to other selves.

How, then, does the self come to relate to others? Piaget thinks that relationships to others are possible once the child has reached a certain level of cognitive sophistication. For example, once the sensorimotor child acquires the ability to conceive of the object as something outside and independent of the self, Piaget argues, the child can develop feelings of attachment and dependence. Years later, the individual is able cognitively to construct the logical necessity of a social dimension to knowledge. That realization comes when the child becomes aware that knowledge is not something given by the "gods," but something that is coconstructed cooperatively among a group of individuals equal in power. In such a setting, there is "continuous comparison, . . . opposition . . . , discussion, and mutual control,"[55] placing on each individual a system of checks and balances that modulates subjectivity and the caprice of any one member of the group. The new orientation to knowing is "autonomous," – based, however, on the simultaneous recognition both of one's own individuality and that of other members in the group.

Note that the social dimension of knowledge here is slightly different from what Trevarthen suggests. Piaget's view is based not on the primacy of playful cooperation in development but on the assumption that the group serves to check the natural tendency toward egocentrism. Piaget's account is not unique in that respect, however. It is typical of a problem our intellectual tradition has faced: How, once we begin with a model of knowledge that does not inherently include the other, can we reconstitute the other? Even Freud, whose model of mind and self is much more explicitly based on the self's relationships to others, could not solve that problem. Freud, too, believes that the infant originally is egocentric and narcissistic; his or her primary goals are selfish – the maximization of pleasure and the minimization of pain. In his system, the infant is essentially autistic, narcissistic, and unrelated to another – significantly called an "object" by Freud and his followers. As for Piaget, the child turns toward the mother and toward others only as a result of the development of more complex conceptual functioning.[56]

Trevarthen's view suggests, instead, that playful and cooperative communication is a fact of human life from the very beginning. Such intersubjectivity does not involve a sharp separation between "inner" and "outer," or "self" and "other." Rather, these dimensions are woven into a seamless mutual dance performed with no other aim than that of sharing and delighting in each other's presence. This mutual dance is not motivated out of defensive and selfish aims, but represents a primary, playful expression of an "I–thou" attitude. In terms of the modes of knowing discussed in this book, such intersubjective engagements represent an area where logos is functionally integrated with mythos.

Such a view of the integrated and cooperative relationship between the two modes began to evolve gradually in the wake of Freud's work. Most significant in this respect is the writing of Winnicott,[57] who maintains that the primary intersubjective attitude forms a domain where inner and outer, self and other, are integrated in one single shared reality. For Winnicott the most typical expression of that domain can be found in play. Playing, argues Winnicott, involves creating a bridge between dream and reality, between objective and subjective. But unlike Piaget, who believes that symbolic play is carried over into the adult world only in relatively "unintelligent" activities, Winnicott claims that it forms the very basis of meaningful adult existence:

> It is in playing and only in playing that the child or adult is able to be creative and use the whole personality, and it is only in being creative that the individual discovers the self. . . . Bound up with this is the fact that only in playing is communication possible.[58]

According to Winnicott, being able to function within that playful space allows the individual to translate the experience of early omnipotence into the capacity for creativity. What is important in creativity is that it involves the individual in spontaneous action, in deep experience. Winnicott calls playing an experience, and satisfying experience, playing. Both enable the individual to "engage in significant interchange with the world, a two-way process in which self-enrichment alternates with the discovery of *meaning* in the world of seen things."[59] They permit the individual to reach those intense sensations that belong to the early years, and thus to an awareness of being alive. Such sensations are most profound in such domains as arts, religion, music, and interpersonal experience.

Ultimately, then, the pervasive devaluation of mythos may reflect a problematic attitude toward the interpersonal world. Playful cooperation with others forms the bridge that allows the individual to span the objective reality of logos with the felt one of mythos. On this view, the development of a strong logos orientation at best can form one component of healthy development. Ultimately, that orientation needs to be integrated with mythos knowing, allowing the individual to build a bridge between two modes of knowing.

THE LOSS OF BALANCE IN DEVELOPMENT

How, then, could we picture development not from the perspective of a single mode but from that of a tandem progression of the two modes? I propose a brief sketch of what such a progression might look like.[60] The main feature of the account I am proposing is to suggest that, as individuals pass through different stages of development, integration is only an ideal and a possible outcome. In reality, each stage brings with it not only opportunities for integration but also for fragmentation. The kind of outcome not only depends on the individual's level of conceptual complexity as in Piaget's or other neo-Piagetian theories; it also is a function of the kind of social embedding the individual finds. On the one hand, as the individual advances in development, he or she redefines what is experienced as the primary social world: from parents, to peers, to culture as a complex system of rules and ideals. On the other hand, that embedding may enhance or hinder integration. Does the self find an embedding structure that mirrors, affirms, and enhances? Is there a constructive environment to relate to?

Whether integration can be achieved will depend to a degree on how these questions are answered. Of course, such answers ultimately are not in an either–or form. Both constructive and destructive environments, both affirming and hurtful experiences make up the background of every individual. As Erikson[61] has suggested, the individual's adaptation ultimately is characterized by some balance of positive and negative outcomes. Hence, most individuals are able to achieve a minimum of adaptive integration; yet, they also retain sectors of unintegrated and fragmented forms of experience.

Sensorimotor period

Many recent authors agree that in accounting for development, we need to start from the primary given of self in relation to others. Recent research has widely upheld that given: Rather than an infant that is narcissistic, we see an infant that from the first moments of life is exquisitely equipped to engage in relationships. Even at birth, when cognitive capacities are quite limited, the infant is actively related to another, especially the mother.

Werner[62] has referred to such an original situation as a "primordial sharing situation," a term close to Trevarthen's concept of intersubjective engagements. But as the child develops more complex cognitive capacities, that shared dyadic world begins to include the world of outer objects. Such "shared reference" is evident, for example, when 9-month-old infants follow their mother's pointing gestures, realizing that such gestures involve some communication about the world of objects, or when the infant is aware that the mother's frowning gesture involves a communication about a third event.[63]

The child's attitude toward the world emerges out of a first sense of self that is laid down in such "primordial sharing situations." Stern proposes that this first sense of a core self encompasses several features. First, the infant comes to experience the self as the center of his or her actions. That is, he or she comes to realize that actions originate from the self and that they are met with consequences and fairly coherent responses by others. Second, the infant comes to experience self as an integrated whole characterized by particular core affective qualities. These core affective experiences form a bridge across both time and space. Temporally, that bridge integrates past, present, and future; spatially, it ties together experiences from different spatial and interpersonal contexts. The result is the emergence of a relatively continuous, coherent experience of self and others.

Such a continuous and coherent sense of self and other forms under relatively optimal conditions. In less optimal conditions, the other can become problematic because he or she does not support the development of a bond or of a coherent sense of self and others. In general, this can happen if the caretaker is not properly sensitive to the infant's signals. An example of such insensitivity is given by Stern's descriptions of "affect attunement." Such attunement between self and other happens when the mother responds to her child's actions with a kind of affective "commentary." For example, one mother characteristically may display relatively flattened affect to the child's conversational overtures; another may respond to her baby's fast, joyful up-and-down movements with the arms by a fast, energetic, undulating vocalization. Each of those infants learns to respond with his or her own characteristic response or "affective signature."

Problems may arise in this process if a mother consistently disavows or discounts the infant's affect as indicated by such "affect contours." For example, Stern describes the case of a depressed mother who consistently "underattuned" to her infant's energetic and joyful affect. A mother may also "overattune" by consistently expressing a "cheerful" attitude that is not attuned to the infant's affect. Such differences in attunement may signal to the infant from the beginning that parts of the self are to be enhanced and expressed preferentially, whereas others are to be suppressed.[64]

Stern's account is similar to accounts of object relations theorists such as Winnicott or Kohut[65] who talk about processes of mirroring. Ideally, the parent can mirror the child's self unconditionally, supporting the development of a sense of self that is characterized by the experience of self as a "joyful center of initiative." In the less ideal, and perhaps more usual, case, parents react preferentially to selected aspects of the child's self: For example, they may welcome and affirm his or her independence and precociousness, while responding negatively to other facets of the self. In such cases, the individual develops a "false self": That is, the worth of the self is felt to be dependent on the welcomed facets of the self but threatened by those not welcomed.

Usually, such faulty attunements or failures of optimal mirroring may not have pathological effects. Indeed, Kohut claims that a slight degree of such failure causes the individual to give up narcissistic grandiosity and thus enhances ego development.[66] If severe, however, they can result in disturbances of a sense of continuity of self and other. This is shown in an extreme way in multiple personality, where the self is split into different personalities with separate identities in different contexts. But it may happen in a less severe way in more normal development as well; in fact, psychodynamic theorists have tended to suggest that such disturbances in the continuity of the self may be a normal part of all development.

The evolution of such disturbances in self- and other-representations has been studied most specifically so far with Ainsworth's "strange situation" paradigm. The purpose of that paradigm is to assess the security of the attachment relationship between mother and infant, and that assessment follows a routine procedure:[67] A mother takes her baby into an experimental room, where she sits the infant on the floor next to some toys that have been placed there by the experimenter. Once the mother has the infant playing with the toys, she leaves the room for 2 minutes. During that time, a woman stranger comes into the room and tries to entertain and comfort the infant. At the end of that period, the mother returns, and the infant's behavior in that reunion is observed.

In this situation many children become distressed. However, their behavior upon the mother's return shows characteristic differences. "Securely attached" infants will approach the mother, greet her, and seek comfort from her, and, perhaps after expressing some feelings of anger and distress, calm down and return to exploring and playing with the toys. Mothers of such secure children have been found to provide sensitive caring during feeding, crying, holding, and face-to-face play in previous independent observations.

However, a considerable proportion of the children show "insecure" patterns of attachment. Of those, "avoidant" children typically snub the mother by turning or walking away from her or refusing to interact with her; instead, they may turn to the toys and play with them in an effort to comfort themselves. The mothers of those infants had been found to provide less affectionate holding during the first 3 months, and often rejected the child when he or she expressed a need for close physical contact. Infants called "ambivalent," in turn, will display a desire for proximity with the mother, combined with angry, resistant behavior. If they turn toward play, these children have difficulty calming down.[68] The mothers of the latter group were not overly rejecting of their infants but were inconsistently sensitive and frequently ignored the babies' signals.

Careful study shows that between these classifications,

there are remarkable differences in the ability to maintain continuity of a sense of self and other. Securely attached children can integrate both positive and negative feelings. They can represent the mother as both positive and negative. They can calm down quickly and "use" the mother as a secure base from which to explore and play. Insecure children show disturbance in these two features. This is especially clear in the case of avoidant infants, who ward off the experience of negative affect by turning away from the mother. Instead, they turn toward playing with the toys. As Case[69] notes, in time this may lead to a tendency to turn away from people to the world of objects as a coping strategy to attempt to maintain a sense of continuity in a weakened self and to deal with the distress related to interpersonal interaction.

Representational period

As they acquire the ability for somewhat more abstract representations (though ones that are still relatively concrete; Piaget called them preoperational and concrete-operational), children's ability to represent aspects of the world become more powerful and internalized. Children now are less embedded in the direct here and now of action, but are able to form more internalized representations. This permits toddlers to move from a level of action to more abstract, internalized "working models" or expectations regarding stable aspects of their environment and their interaction with others. Children now can coordinate events into more generalized social scripts. For example, they are able to describe "typical" sequences related to simple roles of parent and child or boy and girl or describe routine social scripts such as going to a birthday party or restaurant or having dinner at home. Also, the child now develops a primitive "theory" of affect and other inner states such as motives and intentions. For example, children are able to identify and label primary affects such as sadness, anger, fear, or happiness and to give typical social situations that elicit these feelings.

The advent of more powerful cognitive mechanisms permits

children a form of intersubjectivity that is more complex, being based on the interchange between individuals that are somewhat more autonomous. Self and other now are no longer so closely tied to immediate action but can be understood within a more complex framework about individuals that fits into a network of generalized roles, expected actions, and typical affective patterns. However, more abstract functioning not only can have positive consequences but also can result in more powerful ways of distorting reality. Stern[70] has recently commented on this when discussing the emerging sense of self in infants and children. The preconceptual self of the very young child, Stern argues, is profoundly altered by the child's beginning mastery of such an important cultural tool as language. While part of that transformation no doubt is an enhancement, part of it is a loss, as well. Thus Stern comments:

> Infants' initial interpersonal knowledge is mainly unshareable, amodal, instance-specific, and attuned to nonverbal behaviors in which no one channel of communication has privileged status with regard to accountability or ownership. Language changes all that. With its emergence, infants become estranged from direct contact with their own personal experience. Language forms a space between interpersonal experience as lived and as represented. And it is exactly across this space that the connections and associations that constitute neurotic behavior may form. . . . With the advent of thinking, children now have the tools to distort and transcend reality.

How do such distortions happen? Elsewhere[71] I have argued that they are a normal part of development. When moving to a higher level of representation, individuals often form overly generalized concepts that actually distort more direct aspects of more concrete, organismic experience. The child can represent experience on a more abstract plane but then cannot relate it back to the more concrete plane. For example, in one study children were asked to recall simple event sequences such as describing dinner last night. Interestingly, in such cases the child may not recall specific actually experienced episodes but rather more generalized expected sequences.[72]

Similarly, in the affective realm, even though children can *experience* a flow of positive and negative feelings, they cannot conceptually integrate positive and negative. In fact, positive and negative are split: Children think, for example, that an individual is all mad or sad or happy, but not that these feelings can occur in sequence or even at the same time. It is only in adolescence that these opposites can be integrated in relatively complex ways.[73]

In the domain of attachment, Bowlby[74] discusses such splits as resulting from problematic relationships between caretaker and infant. Bowlby suggests that the insecure child develops at least two "internal working models" or "representations" that are mutually contradictory. One is more conscious, and highlights the good and caregiving aspects of the parent. The other model represents the hated and disappointing side of the parent; that aspect is defensively excluded from awareness. Correlatively, "good parent"–"bad parent" splits go along with splits in the self as "good" and "bad."

Bowlby focuses on relatively major forms of disconnection that form the precursors of pathology. He believes that such distortions arise when the parent creates contradictions in what he or she tells the child and what the child experiences. However, as Bretherton[75] notes, less blatant contradiction between parental and child experience may have the same result. For example, a caretaker may disavow or discount a child's signals and perceptions, with the result that special topics are eliminated from reciprocal, mutually validating communication.

Similar processes of disconnection are not necessarily characteristic of pathology alone, to be explained as a child–caretaker bond that has gone wrong. Rather, since children now can fit themselves into a more general framework of simple roles and normative expectations, they also may be subject to distorting varied experience in terms of these simple normative frameworks. We already noted that children of this age are apt to "recall" events in terms of expected sequences. Similarly, there may be a tendency to develop a preference for stereotyped roles, such as those related to gender.[76] Thus, splitting and disconnection may occur also in "normal" development.

An example of such disconnections that are rooted in social structures larger than the family per se is offered by Elias,[77] who claims that the very process of civilization is based on that form of disconnection by which whole areas of organismic experience are excluded from verbal discourse and public reference. Elias exemplifies this exclusion by historical changes in how individuals' reference to body-focused practices related to eating, elimination, and hygiene. In all of those domains, socialization implies that large segments of private experience be shrouded in layers of shame; indeed, Elias thinks that the very process of acculturation and civilization is based on making such areas too "delicate" to admit to public discourse.

Note that such a process repeats the processes of splitting discussed in the previous section, although it raises them to a higher level of abstraction. The failure of "mirroring" now is not predominantly at the level of the primary caretaker, but rather of more complex cultural practices. Such cultural practices can be based exactly on removing from discourse the kind of primary intersubjective experiences that so dominate the sensorimotor period of development.

Such exclusion of discourses about normal organismic functioning is possible because more abstract levels of functioning redefine "primordial" intersubjective situations and raise them to a more general level at which socialized discourse becomes possible. As Werner[78] notes, how we represent experience now is more distanced from the directly experienced, and thus discourse can be conducted in terms of patterns of oughts and expectations rather than the actually experienced here and now. As a consequence, aspects of self and reality can become split from each other in ways that are more powerful than was possible previously.

It is just because those more general discourses typically involve specific forms of restriction that psychoanalysts maintain that play and symbolic behavior are important. In them, the individual can create a discourse about otherwise unacknowledged aspects of reality. Indeed, recent research suggests that secure children are able to use play in that way, giving free expression to the whole of positive and negative affects. Insecure children, in contrast, show many signs of inhibition and denial of negative affect, or else of unmitigated aggression and threat.[79]

During the school period, the mechanisms by which children adjust to a prevalent cultural discourse become even more powerful. Now the child begins to develop a clear and explicit differentiation between inner and outer, and that differentiation can become the basis for learning to "hide" parts of the self. Thus, in adjusting to the outer world, the child does indeed acquire an orientation to reality in which aspects of the inner world are downgraded, while reality is primarily defined in terms of outer, consensual criteria. One of the areas in which this "external" attitude becomes apparent is the area of emotional development. Here, we find that children actively adopt culturally sanctioned displays of emotion. Such cultural standardization of display is especially important in the area of sex-role behaviors where shame and guilt for "inappropriate" behaviors may increase.[80]

The result of this "external" attitude is that children learn to "discount" aspects of their inner life that do not fit into "affect contours" favored by family, peer group, or culture. Such downgrading and demythification is apparent in the development of children's imaginative products such as dreams, art, and play. As far as dreams are concerned, once children learn that dreams do not have the same objective existence "out there" as other aspects of reality, they are able to divest such products of the attribute "real."[81] Part of this process is, of course, necessary, since the individual does need to learn that different kinds of events are associated with inner and outer realities. In this way, initial mastery over one's inner life is accomplished, and such mastery is an important task of early development. Indeed, young children's dreams suggest this struggle with mastery in such themes as gaining control over the intrusion of animals or villains.[82] However, on the other hand, the concern with control and mastery eventually may result in an increasing negation of the subjective world, with the result that much inner symbolism is given up in favor of that imposed by the outer world.[83] Research on play and artistic activities also suggests that with increasing age, children are more concerned with reproducing objective aspects of the outer environment.[84] Overall, the spontaneous productions of children decline, and adolescents become more and more critical of their artwork, with the result that many adolescents stop drawing altogether.[85]

Abstract period

Around adolescence, further advances in the individual's ability to represent reality are evident. Now, representational capacities are even further generalized and internalized; the youth begins to be able to relate to even more abstract networks of ideals and norms. Following the work of George Herbert Mead, cognitive-developmental psychologists such as Kohlberg and Selman[86] have demonstrated that whereas for preadolescents such networks still are mediated through concrete dyadic exchanges with close reference figures such as parents or friends, the adolescent is able to relate to more abstract sets of norms such as those of an interpersonal group or even society at large.

We noted earlier in this chapter how widely these new skills influence the adolescent's understanding of self, others, and reality. Nevertheless – and in line with the current argument – there are limitations to these skills, as well. One major limitation is that adolescents' thinking, though it can function at the level of abstract generalizations and theoretical systems, is still relatively "concrete" when compared with that of many mature adults. For example, as will be further discussed in Chapter 5, adolescents, while they can understand the connections in abstract theories, are very limited when it comes to systematically mapping complex systems and developing a deep understanding for the interrelationships among such systems. Thus, when it comes to such complex systems as fact or value, reason or emotion, inner or outer, and nature or nurture, adolescents typically engage in either–or, dualistic thinking. As a result of that characteristic feature, what is "true" or "real" comes to be defined primarily in terms of criteria that are understood to be "objective" or "outer." This emergence of an "objectivist," mythos-devaluing attitude may reach an apex in adolescence, when the youth is able to define what is "real" along dimensions that reflect societal ideals and norms.

This outer orientation is shown, for example, in studies of how individuals solve problems. Many studies[87] suggest that youth often acquire a rule-based orientation in which they come to disregard more concrete, intuitive, and subjective facets of their own experience. Problems are viewed in terms of abstract, "objective" criteria such as rules and culturally appropriate classification systems. Although this represents an advance in thought over childhood abilities, it may not be the apex of development. Rather, it may only be a transition to a more flexible approach to be developed later on (see Chapter 5).

There is a plethora of consequences. The first may be an overly literal approach: As an example, consider a study by Benner[88] in which novice nurses overgeneralized the rules they had learned concerning the caretaking of infants. In their intake routines, novices were likely to adhere to an unvarying sequence of steps. If an emergency arose, for example, and two infants were to be taken in simultaneously, they were unable to set priorities and vary the two sequences. Thus, they took a narrow and literal interpretation of their newly acquired skills. In the absence of rich experience, they stuck to clearly defined, deductive rules. Experienced nurses, however, were unabashedly intuitive in their approach and not as rule-bound as the novices. Thus, to some extent, intuition must be suppressed by the novice individual who is in the process of acquiring complex knowledge. But for the individual who possesses complex knowledge, a more intuitive approach may afford greater flexibility. (This notion is further expanded in Chapter 5.)

Thus for the youth (or even adult) who embraces youthful objectivism to an extent that is too fervent, disconnections can become created that, over time, can rigidify into a structure

that is maintained by complex explicit assumptions and theoretical formulations about self, others, and reality. Such
disconnection was observed, for example, in a study on how
children of advantaged, wealthy families adjust to the perception of inequalities they observe.[89] Before they reach adolescence, these children often are profoundly troubled by the
plight of their less advantaged peers, wondering about the
justification for what they feel to be an inequitable and unjust
distribution of rights and resources. As they move into adolescence, however, these youth sometimes resolve their conflicts
by forming a view of a reality in which such inequalities are
justified by some abstract principle. An example is one child of
prominent social-activist parents who had been disturbed by
the social inequities related to social status and race. When
entering adolescence, however, this boy was able to resolve his
distress by coming to think of such inequities in terms of a
social Darwinist theory.

Similarly, adolescents now can learn to directly discount as
"unreal" aspects of inner experience that are not admitted to a
cultural discourse. An example is dreams, of which Tedlock
notes:

> Individuals in American society who experience vivid dreams
> may allow them a certain reality during sleep, but upon awak-
> ening dispel or try to forget them. . . . However, although most
> Americans publicly profess the cultural belief, or stereotype
> that dreams are meaningless fantasies or confused mental
> imaginings with no true or lasting reality dimensions, a dream
> occasionally carries such a strong emotional impact that it is
> remembered and returns later to consciousness. When this
> happens, cultural belief wavers slightly, causing the dreamer to
> wonder if dreams, or at least this one dream, might mean some-
> thing after all. But if the dreamer tries to tell this dream it may
> prove difficult. The first problems concern the choice of au-
> dience and discourse frame. Since dream telling is not an ordi-
> nary public communication in American society, the potential
> dream sharer faces a difficulty in finding the proper context for
> the speech event. For example, should it be told at the univer-

sity to a group of colleagues over lunch? Or is this too public a discourse frame?[90]

This problem of excluding from self that which is not admitted to public discourse is, as I have noted repeatedly, a ubiquitous one in development, at least during the first part of life. In fact, I have suggested the very process of cultural development depends on the adolescent's ability and willingness to internalize and master the languages and rules of culture. However, the result is that young individuals often see themselves primarily in terms of ideals, while many actual lived parts of the self are not integrated into that ideal view.

The fact that ideal views of ourselves can be rather poorly integrated was demonstrated rather dramatically in a recent study in which individuals' concepts of ideal, actual, and feared parts of the self were compared.[91] College students in that study typically related their usual experience of self to a positive and idealized self. However, the worst parts of the self were not integrated. This was especially true for the males of the sample: 86% of the males (as compared with 46% of the females) had concepts of self in which usual and ideal selves are linked and integrated, while the worst self remains in an unlinked or isolated position. When examining the specific terms that describe aspects of the self, further research[92] showed that the ideal self tends to be described in rather general and abstract terms that convey little actual quality of experience. However, the worst self is described in very concrete and felt terms, suggesting that it is rooted in actual experience. Not suprisingly, too, that little valued but experientially real self predicts adjustment much better than the ideal self so often studied in research.

Other research concurs with these general results. For example, adolescents' descriptions are strongly structured by what they want to be: They see themselves in terms of ideals and norms. In fact, this tendency toward idealization may begin to form a lifelong habit of thought, since study after study has shown that individuals tend to view themselves and reality in a way that is positively biased.[93] On the one hand, such a positivity bias may help buffer individuals from negative feelings and negative self-concepts. But on the other, it does so by discounting dreaded aspects of the self. Since the mechanism by which this works is that real, concrete, negative feelings are blocked while normative and idealized ones are enhanced, the result is that a sense of cheerful coping ability is bought for the price of significant reality distortion.

The most general formulation of such distortions of self and reality still is Jung's conception of the process of early development. Early in life, suggests Jung, the individual develops a *persona*. This concept is taken from Greek theater, where it referred to the masks that actors wore to represent particular protagonists. Thus, for Jung, early self-formation is akin to putting on a mask as individuals come to idealize themselves along cultural-conventional dimensions. And, argues Jung, that mask has a negative side: The ideals' opposite elements are relegated to the nonself and projected outward. These elements then become the despised and frightening embodiment of our own abandoned vulnerabilities. Jung calls these elements "shadow," and suggests that the formation of the shadow is one issue of early development. However, he suggests that the main task of mature adulthood remains to integrate these rejected aspects of self, a process I discuss at length in Chapters 5 and 6.

Jung's notion of shadow formation actually points to mechanisms of splitting, distortion, and fragmentation that are part of normal growth and development. Also, these distortive mechanisms become more powerful as the individual grows older. Thus, in contrast to formulations that trace possible mechanisms of distortion to the original caretaker–child dyad, the formation of the shadow ultimately must be confronted at the level of cultural practice, ideology, and ritual. The very issues of creating dualisms, including those of gendering of human capacities, are examples of such culturally maintained forms of dissociation and fragmentation that form the very basis of "healthy" adjustment in youth. At the same time, however, these processes also create barriers to continued development, barriers we will discuss in detail in the chapters to come.

CONCLUSION: PRIMARY DEVELOPMENT

In this chapter, I draw a parallel between the components of cultural development discussed in Chapter 2 and some prevailing theories of development. As a polarization has evolved in cultural development between the concrete, organic, and feminine on the one hand and the abstract, mental, and masculine on the other hand, so a similar polarization is characteristic of many traditional views of development. I examine this notion with special reference to Piaget's theory, and to a lesser degree, to that of Freud. In both, the individual learns to define criteria of what is "real," "true," or "right" in large part by those criteria that are offered by the conventions of culture. Thus, the individual in growing up adopts an external orientation in which dimensions of reality are validated by outer criteria.

To some extent, this external orientation results from the fact that development is an embedded, interactive, social process: As individuals, we grow up embedded in structures that have already been elaborated by others (parents, institutions, history, and so on), and our task is, to a great degree, to learn to appropriate and to mirror these preexisting structures. To another extent, the external orientation also may result from the way this mirroring and internalization is accomplished. The very process of early development depends on the child's ability and willingness to "internalize" and master the languages and rules of culture, sacrificing a sense of selfhood for cultural community.

Dabrowski[94] calls this aspect "primary development." In this chapter, I show that such primary development is evident both in mythos and in logos languages of the process of development. Mythically, primary development often appears as the slaying of a primordial monster who represents the

113

danger of primitive emotional life. In theoretical and empirical accounts, a similar process is evident. First, in many traditional theories, development often is discussed as a gradual displacement and disowning of organic and mythic forms of functioning. These forms are considered to be more "primitive" and "infantile" than the abstract and mental forms of functioning that become accessible to the adolescent. Second, in the actual process of early development we observe many parallels to this process. Youthful adaptation often elaborates a preliminary view of the world in which self and others are defensively idealized in terms of the ideals of family and culture. In turn, those aspects of self not fitting that language of idealization remain split off and unintegrated. We turn to some implications of this process in the next chapter.

Chapter 4

Night and day: Reason and gender

As Psyche sat trembling and weeping on the crag, a soft breeze suddenly raised her up. Gently Zephyr, the west wind, carried her down the cliff and lay her in a soft grassy place. A deep sleep came over Psyche but when she woke, she beheld a lovely grove, with a fountain of water and a palace behind a glistening stream. So beautiful a dwelling it was, she knew it must be the abode of a god. Entering it, she found treasures and heard wondrous music. The voices of spirits began to tend to her in the most exquisite manner, offering her refreshments and entertainment. Psyche eventually went to her bed, for the hour was late.

But as she lay on her bed in the dark, a visitor entered, lay down next to her, and made Psyche his bride. Then, before the dawn rose in the east, he departed in haste. Psyche shook with fear at first, but soon what seemed strange became a source of delight to her. Every night her husband clasped her to his body, and every day he flew away before the rise of dawn.

But as time passed, Psyche grew restless in her luxurious setting. She longed for her sisters whom she had not seen in a long time. She fell into mourning, refusing food and drink, and implored her husband to yield to her wishes and let her sisters come visit. But Eros pleaded with her not to yield to her curiosity, for he feared that the sisters would incite Psyche to wonder about his identity. He warned Psyche again and again "with words that struck terror in her soul,"[1] never to let her sisters persuade her to find out who he was. "Do you see," said he, "what great peril you are in? . . . Those false she-wolves are weaving some deep plot of sin against you, whose purpose is this: to persuade you to seek to know my face, which, as I have told you, if once you see, you will see no more."[2] *And again and again he told her: "Sweet Psyche, beloved wife, be cautious and beware. Do not go forth from the house, or you will drive me to bitter despair and yourself to utter destruction."*

A UNION IN THE DARK

This chapter expands on the notion of the death marriage and introduces a related theme: that of the union in the dark. More explicitly than the first, this theme of making love in the dark suggests that the marriage of death is not without payoffs. Indeed, it can be a source of rapture and bliss. Thus, rather than being devoured by a wild and terrible monster, Psyche is gently lifted up and deposited in the most lovely, most enchanting dwelling, and in that dwelling, Eros visits her night after night. Their union is one of deep passion and profound emotional fulfillment.

But much as night remains the realm of passion and rapture for the couple, so the union between Eros and Psyche takes on a rather prosaic, conventional air if examined in the light of day. Psyche finds herself in the most paradisiacal setting, with every one of her needs attended to. No effort is required of her, she does not need to display agency or thinking. Her every wish materializes in this magic realm of disembodied spirits. Eros, in turn, seems to lead a rather conventional life, too. He leaves each morning to tend to his day's business in the outside world, piercing humans with his dangerous arrows.

Not surprisingly perhaps, Psyche soon finds out that she must pay a price for this blissful union. In time, her living arrangements become a source of boredom, and her curiosity stirs. It is then, however, that her husband pleads with her, asking her to surrender her curiosity and telling her that she must stifle her desires to find out about him, and about the outside world. She is not to see him, she is to live in darkness and blindness.

Marriage in the dark

The theme of making love in the dark as a symbol of early romantic love is one that often recurs in myth. In "Beauty and the Beast,"[3] for example, a young maiden is given by her father to a Beast who takes her into his palace and cares for her. Beauty does not give in to the Beast's pleas to marry her, but at night she dreams of a beautiful prince who comes to visit her. In time, however, the spell is broken and the Beast turns into none other than the prince of her dreams.

The tale, "East of the Sun, West of the Moon" has a similar structure. In one version of the tale,[4] a young girl is given by her parents to a Bear who lives in an elaborate dwelling with many rooms. During his visits at night, the Bear turns into a beautiful young lover, but he asks his bride never to look at him in the light. When she finally yields to her curiosity and lights a candle, he disappears to a magic troll kingdom, from which he is eventually released by the girl.

The union between the lovers can be seen as the condition of development at earlier parts of the life span. Since early development is based, as shown earlier, on a dualism between conscious and unconscious processes, the self is represented as the somewhat precarious and symbiotic joining of two halves. One of those halves represents striving for consciousness, agency, and control over affect. This is the heroic part of the self that aims to transcend its bodily limitations in order to reach for a transcendent treasure. Since this half is thought to be masculine in our cultural tradition, it is represented by a male figure. Yet the language of myth also provides a cautionary comment. This masculine version retains beastly and undomesticated features, signaling that development is not yet complete.

The other half of the self, in contrast, refers to those elements that are not integrated by the conscious, masculine self: the "lower," passive, organic, and material. These aspects also are associated with the feminine. In contrast to the "higher," active, abstract, and spiritual-mental aspects of the self, these characteristics must be suppressed and controlled. Thus it is that the bridegroom entreats his bride not to disturb this union by giving in to her curiosity and by reaching for conscious knowledge. Indeed, Psyche's curiosity is reviled and split off and represented as her evil sisters! This theme of the marriage in the dark repeats and extends, then, that of the death marriage. Like the death marriage, it suggests that the surrender of the imaginative to the formal – of mythos to logos – may be a necessary stage in development, as I discussed in Chapter 3.

The marriage between Psyche and Eros, here, is symbolic for a dilemma the individual confronts in his or her development. Not only has our tradition divided human functioning into two classes – the "lower," passive, organic, and material as opposed to the "higher," active, abstract, and spiritual-mental – but it has attributed the two also differentially to each sex.

At the same time, the masculine and the feminine have always carried very different cultural valuations. The man can derive a positive sense of self-worth from his identification with agency-mind-spirit. But for the woman, such positive self-identity remains extremely problematic. Indeed, she is pressured to surrender her claim to consciousness and knowledge, a major source of positive self-identification. Thus, her main source of identification remains negative, since she carries the devalued aspects of culture: Passivity, materiality, embodied existence are her supposed elements.

As a result of this duality, the conditions of development – symbolized by the union of masculine and feminine parts of the self – are represented by quite different, opposing though complementary patterns. Heroic ascent, searching for light and gold, and slaying monstrous creatures all are important ways in which the masculine and its development are represented. But the theme that predominates tales of feminine development is one of fall and descent.[5]

A well-known example of this progression is Mozart's opera, *The Magic Flute*. The story on which this opera is based tells of the prince, Tamino, who happens upon the realm of the Queen of the Night. It is an enchanted realm where the bird man, Papageno, lives in the forest, converses with birds and beasts, and is provided with food by the queen. But this realm of childlike bliss has been disturbed. The Queen of the Night shows Tamino a picture of her daughter, Pamina, telling the prince in a dramatic and melancholy aria of the abduction of Pamina by Sarastro, the master of a neighboring realm. The queen implores Tamino to go to the temple of Sarastro and save the girl. On seeing the portrait, Tamino is seized with love, and, in a melting aria, he announces his love and his determination to find Pamina.

Arriving in Sarastro's realm, however, Tamino learns that Sarastro is not at all the evil man that the queen claimed. Rather, his is a realm of wisdom and of reason, of sun and of light, and he has abducted Pamina to save her from the queen's evil magic and witchcraft. And, Tamino learns, the way to save Pamina is not to reunite her with her mother, but to save her from the queen. To save Pamina, he must undergo a series of trials that will initiate him into Sarastro's temple. By resisting such temptations as fear of the dark, greed for food and drink, and his desire to talk to Pamina, Tamino eventually is initiated into the temple, where Pamina joins him as his bride.

Tamino's story is a story of the young man's ascent – from the realm of the earth and mother to the realm of the sky gods. It shows how in that ascent, the old, infantile past is represented as evil and female, as a sorceress and seductress that the young man must learn to beware of and to be contemptuous of. But while the story depicts the masculine as an ascent from instinct to reason, Pamina's development is depicted differently, as an abduction and theft.

What is the meaning of this "theft"? The story suggests that Pamina cannot be initiated into Sarastro's temple in and of herself. It is not her own activity and effort that will allow her to rise to reason and wisdom; rather, she does so by becoming passive, by assuming the role of a victim, and by letting the men in the story act. Thus, for her, development is represented not as active ascent, but rather passively as loss and descent.

Psyche and Eros

Male and female pathways of development

In his book *Sex and Fantasy*, May[6] has discussed such patterns, arguing that there are distinctive male and female pathways of development. According to May, the prototypical masculine pattern is one of a heroic rise. However, since this "rise" reflects a rejection of part of the self – the earthly, embodied part – that rise is an arrogant one, involving hubris and self-inflation. Thus, this inflation of self is often compensated and followed by a sense of falling and humiliation. This pattern is exemplified by the story of Phaeton, whose mother has told him that his father is no other than Phoebus, the sun god. The boy, in doubt, visits his father and begs him to let him drive the chariot of the sun. The father, fearful of trusting so powerful and dangerous a tool into the hands of someone so young and lacking in wisdom, pleads with his son to give up his wish, but to no avail. As Phaeton steers the chariot, he is overcome by terror at the dizzying height and by fear of the monsters of the sky. Losing control over the chariot, he falls and sets the earth aflame. Only Zeus' intervention is able to save the earth and sea from scorching.

Phaeton's story is the story of the young man's rejection of what is associated with the "mother"–darkness, being limited by the body, being bound by the earth, and so forth–and his turning toward what is associated with the father–the sun, the limitless sky, light and abstract knowledge, and so on. Pride, drivenness, lust for power, and a denial of his own earthly limits motivate Phaeton's desire to drive the fiery chariot. The tale, thus, is one of heroic inflation. But, that inflation is eventually compensated by a demeaning and humiliating lesson: Falling back to earth, the hero is led to accept his human limitations.

In contrast, the archetypal myth of feminine development is one of descent, followed by a redemptive rise. An example of this pattern is the myth of Persephone's abduction by Hades. One day, as Homer relates in the "Hymn to Demeter,"[7] Persephone, the maiden goddess and daughter of the grain mother Demeter, is playing in the meadow when she encounters a narcissus flower. Homer describes this extraordinarily beautiful flower, the symbol of transcendent value and creative selfhood:

> It was a thing of awe whether for deathless gods or mortal men to see; from its root grew a hundred blooms and it smelled most sweetly, so that all wide heaven above and the whole earth and the sea's salt swell laughed for joy. And the girl was amazed and reached out with both hands to take the lovely toy.[8]

But just as Persephone reaches for this amazing symbol of self-realization, the earth yawns open, and Hades, god of the underworld, appears with his chariot and seizes the girl. She is abducted to the underworld and, through rape, becomes Hades' bride. Her mother, in the meantime, wanders over the earth in despair, searching for her beloved daughter. So great is her grief that she no longer attends to vegetation, and soon the earth turns barren and lifeless. But not until she threatens to keep the earth barren forever can she move Zeus to come to the aid of mother and daughter. He sends Hermes, the messenger of the gods, to free Persephone, who from then on returns to earth every spring, bringing bloom and abundant growth with every step.

Here we have a story of opposite structure, signaling a prototypical pattern of feminine development. Much as reaching for light and sun, development of intellect and reason, and creative pursuits are at the core of masculine development, so feminine development is depicted as the renunciation of these goals. Note, however, that in mythic language this renunciation is not at all voluntary. Rather, it is represented as a violent act: death, rape, or theft resulting from the appropriation of the feminine principle by the patriarchal masculine one.

Gender and relationship

What is the source of such patterns? Jung has suggested that this inner psychic equation between one set of attributes with the feminine and another set of attributes with the masculine may be a universal human tendency. Such a tendency, in the

Psyche and Eros

Jungian view, may result from basic, biologically based differences in instinctual patterns and emotive experiences between men and women. Some more recent followers and critics of Jung suggest, instead, that there may be a long process of cultural evolution that has led to this association.[9] According to the latter view, the pattern of attributes we associate with gender do not necessarily speak about characteristics that are masculine or feminine in some fixed sense. Rather, they result from a process by which gender is, in part, socially constructed. In this process, growing up in a culture requires that the self split off and repress parts of the self that are not congruent with what is considered sex-appropriate behavior. That part of the self, however, then becomes projected onto the other, to whom we then attribute that lost and abandoned part of the self.

This process by which male and female selves are thus defined in relation is referred to as "projective identification." The term was first introduced by Melanie Klein[10] who attempted to describe how the infant can cope with extremely negative affects such as rage and fear. She suggested that the infant does so by externalizing the "bad" and projecting it onto others; this process allows the infant to gain control over the other, to avoid painful feelings either of separation or of anger.

Since Klein's early work, the concept has been widely elaborated,[11] and applied to many other situations, including marital interaction patterns. Here, too, the emphasis is on the externalization of parts of the self that are felt to be unacceptable and frightening, although they may be neutral or positive in another (such as a person of the opposite sex). Once projected onto the other, the self then can maintain contact with the abandoned parts of the self in an indirect, interactional way; indeed, projective identification allows the self to feel at one with the recipient of the projection. Thus, the blurring of the boundaries between self and other allows the person to maintain a sense of closeness – even passionate rapture.

Another aspect of projective identification is that the person projects acts in such ways as to evoke the projected qualities in the person on whom they have become projected. In this way,

122

self and other continue to define each other in relation, in ways that allow both to split off the projected parts and to experience them through the other. Goldstein comments on this process:[12]

> For example, a husband maintains a desired image of himself as aggressive and competitive by projecting his unwanted passive and helpless qualities onto his wife. This is ideal for the wife, who is able to maintain her desired image of a passive and helpless woman by projecting her competitive and aggressive qualities onto the husband. Thus, the projective identifications are mutually rewarding and complementary.

Note that this example describes the culturally typical pattern of gender interaction; indeed, it also applies to the interaction between Psyche and Eros. Both partners collaborate in elevating and idealizing the image of the masculine, which is felt to be forceful, heroic, and active. Conversely, both partners also participate in keeping the feminine aspect in a hidden, restrained, and passive state. Thus, the idealization and inflation of the masculine and the devaluation of the feminine are considered "normal."

Indeed, the pattern of inflation of the masculine and suppression of the feminine is not only considered normal, it forms the very basis on which a relationship is built – even the basis of erotic attraction and desire. As a result, problems may arise if the woman does not submit to this pattern. Indeed, the myth of Psyche and Eros notes this danger. Thus, the girl Psyche revolts against her upcoming feminine fate by keeping aloof from men. Staying virginal promises escape from the death marriage for her. But Psyche eventually gives up her revolt and embarks on the prototypical female path of development. She, like women in general, needs to repudiate her desire for the more glorious masculine pathway of development. But, the myth tells us, even though this repudiation may form the basis of erotic and marital love, the unconscious points to its negative side: Part of the self experiences it as loss, as rape, as the theft of part of the self.

THE GENDERED MIND

Let us further explore the significance of the extraordinary mythic theme of the complementarity of the rise of the masculine and the descent of the feminine. Symbolically speaking, exactly what is being inflated, and what is being stolen? I suggest that this question can be answered by referring back to Chapter 2, where we discussed the emergence of the new way of speaking about the mind. That new language, I propose, allowed individuals to speak about new ways of creating: Creation was no longer just a physical act of procreation, but could refer to mental forms of creation as well. And, the new theories declared, these mental forms were not only far superior to the ones associated with the bodily realm but also were related to the masculine rather than the feminine.

Philosophers, of course, attempted to evolve a language of speaking about reality that was no longer dependent on the personifications of mythos. Hence, reference to gender came to be rather indirect and implicit, although, as discussed later in this chapter, some philosophers provided dramatic deviations from this rule. In general, however, it is fair to state that personifications of aspects of reality as gender-related remained much more explicit in such mythos products as art, poetry and other forms of literature, and religion.

Matriarchal and patriarchal principles

A particularly striking example of these personifications is offered by the great Greek tragedies centering around the myths of Agamemnon and Orestes. Here the struggle between older and newer models of reality is made concrete by the specific question of the value of a person's life. Is the value of a woman's life equal to that of a man's? Should the sacrifice or murder of a woman be punished to the same extent as that of a man? In general, the answer offered by these myths is that a woman's life is not as valuable as that of a man's. Thus, the sacrifice of a woman's life is not as morally objectionable as the sacrifice of a man's life.

This conclusion is exemplified in Euripides' *Iphigenia in Aulis*.[13] Agamemnon's ships lie ready to go to war against Troy, but there is no wind to enable the fleet to sail. Agamemnon consents to sacrifice his firstborn daughter, Iphigenia, so that a favorable wind might be granted to carry his ships to Troy and bring power and glory to Greece. At first, Iphigenia curses this decision and her murderous father, asking why "a thousand women are not worth one man?"[14] Nevertheless, eventually she agrees that her best service to her father and her country is the sacrifice of her life. Here again, we see the contrast between "masculine" heroic conquest and feminine adaptation through suffering and masochistic surrender when Iphigenia pleads with her mother:

> . . . O, mother, say I am right!
> Our country – think, our Hellas – looks to me,
> On me the fleet hangs now, the doom of Troy,
> Our women's honor all the years to come.
> . . . You who bore your child,
> It was for Greece you bore her, not yourself.
> Think! Thousands of our soldiers stand to arms,
> Ten thousand man the ships, and all on fire
> To serve their outraged country, die for Greece:
> And is my one poor life to hinder all?[15]

But while Iphigenia forgives her father's lust for power, her mother Clytemnestra does not. On Agamemnon's return from Troy, Clytemnestra prepares a bath for her husband and then murders the unsuspecting Agamemnon in revenge for her daughter's death. Orestes, their son, in turn murders his mother to avenge his father's death. The opposition between old, feminine values and newer, masculine ones is made concrete by raising the moral problem of which murder – male or female – is a more heinous act.

Note that the question of old versus new values here is translated into one of gender, just as it was in Aristotle's work discussed in the next section. This equation of the distant, mythical past with a feminine realm and matriarchal order and of the more recent, rational order with the masculine appears to be a very general feature of human symbolic life.[16] Freud, too, looked at human evolution in terms of this shift from a matriarchally controlled order to one that is controlled patriarchally. His theory of individual development, too, adopted that equation, since the core of the Oedipal resolution consists (for the boy) of a change from the primary attachment to the mother to an identification with the father.

Much recent work has appeared on this "change" from matriarchal to patriarchal images of creativity and divinity. Some authors have claimed from their research that these changes in mythic imagery probably reflect actual changes in social structure from matriarchal to patriarchal systems.[17] However, it appears from historical evidence that to believe that at some early time matriarchal social systems were predominant is questionable (for fuller discussion of this issue, see Chapter 6). What seems less controversial, however, is that the poets, just like the philosophers cited previously, were involved in building a conceptual structure in which the masculine and the feminine took on some precise conceptual meanings. It is quite possible that this conceptual structure merely elaborated and amplified an imagery that already existed in myth and ritual, translating that imagery into the more abstract language of the new concepts of human nature. According to those new concepts, the father realm represents mature reason while the mother realm represents its negation, the nonrational. The nonrational, in turn, was more and more believed to refer to archaic values; thus, the question of old and new orders was translated into a question concerning the value of women's and men's lives – the question that so fascinated Greek drama.

The victory of patriarchy

This opposition is also the subject of Aeschylus' trilogy, *The Oresteia*.[18] The last drama of the trilogy, *The Eumenides*, asks how Orestes' matricide is to be dealt with. The Eumenides, or Furies, represent the old, matriarchal order. They are horrifying women with serpents in their hair who accuse Orestes and who rage against Apollo, who aided Orestes:

Shame, son of Zeus! Robber is all you are.
A young god, you have ridden down powers gray with age,
taken the suppliant, though a godless man, who hurt
the mother who gave him birth . . .
You gave this outlander the word to kill his mother.[19]

Apollo, however, counters that the laws of matriarchy no longer hold. He reasons that the new patriarchal principle has come to assume more importance than the former matriarchal one. The reason this is so, he argues, is that fatherhood has come to replace motherhood as a principle of creation. Indeed, he claims that motherhood is not nearly so significant as fatherhood in the generation of offspring:

The mother is no parent of that which is called
her child, but only nurse of the new-planted seed
that grows. The parent is he who mounts. A stranger she
preserves a stranger's seed, if no god interfere
. . . There can
be a father without any mother.[20]

Another proof of the superiority of the new order, Apollo argues, is that patriarchy on its own can bring forth beings much more extraordinary than the old order could. As evidence of this claim, he points to Athena and says:

. . . There she stands,
the living witness, daughter of Olympian Zeus,
she who was never fostered in the dark of the womb
yet such a child as no goddess could bring to birth.[21]

Yet while he condemns other women, Apollo is not hostile to Athena because, as psychoanalyst Helene Deutsch puts it, "she represents *victory over motherhood*."[22] Apollo can rely on Athena's own hostility to the feminine to come to his aid. When Athena is called to cast the deciding vote to resolve whether or not Orestes is to be punished for the matricide of Clytemnestra, she declares:

This is a ballot for Orestes I shall cast.
There is no mother anywhere who gave me birth
and, but for marriage, I am always for the male
with all my heart, and strongly on my father's side.
So, in a case where the wife has killed her husband, lord
of the house, her death shall not mean most to me.[23]

The gendering of creativity

Athena here is a poignant example of the fate of the feminine in Greek society. In her comment on Apuleius' Psyche and Eros story, von Franz[24] points out that patriarchal Greek society did not recognize the positive value of the feminine, except as a highly purified and spiritualized version. Only that version was valued in the homoerotic circles of the philosophers, while the more organic aspects of the feminine were devalued and ridiculed. In a similar vein, others[25] also have pointed out that the thorough devaluation of the feminine was probably related to the inferior social status of women.

Athena here represents just such a figure who, like Iphigenia and like Psyche, has accepted that self-definition by sacrificing her feminine creative energies to the father. Greek culture had no means to deal with the intellectual and spiritual powers of this goddess of wisdom and of culture save by making her a masculine, war-loving, and women-hating figure. Thus, she surrendered her feminine self-identity and came to be identified with the father principle only.

Hesiod's story of Athena's origin and birth rather dramatically illustrates this relinquishment of feminine intellect and wisdom. Athena was the daughter of Metis, the ancient goddess of wisdom. When Metis was pregnant, Zeus feared the birth of a child of great power and to prevent that birth he transformed Metis into a fly and swallowed her. From her new place, Hesiod tells us,[26] Mother Wisdom continued to counsel Zeus. Athena, in the meantime, continued to gestate in Zeus' head, and soon was delivered with a mighty blow to the god's head by Hephaestus, the god of the forge. Wearing her golden armor, Athena sprang forth from Zeus with a mighty battle cry. Although often known as a war goddess, Athena was also associated with wisdom and culture, with pottery and music, with weaving and healing. But, as a sign of her own repressed femininity, she wore the snaked-haired head of Medusa on her breast plate. No longer aware that her mother, feminine wisdom, had been swallowed and appropriated by Zeus, she was completely identified with, and subservient to, the new masculine order.

Athena is one example of the many myths that deal with the theft of feminine forms of power, knowledge, and wisdom. For the Hellenic period, these attributes were completely masculinized, and, hence, the Hellenic Athena appears as a fearsome and unfeminine figure. However, some authors think that her gifts were not always considered masculine ones, but became so over time. Spretnak, for example, argues that this goddess was originally a Cretan goddess watching over the home and town, and associated with wisdom, arts, and skills. She was a patron of architects, sculptors, potters, spinners, and weavers. However, when the Mycenean princes of mainland Greece adopted her, she acquired the martial character of the Olympic Athena[27] – although, as a sign of her origins, she continued to be associated with healing, spinning, and flute playing, and as a sign of her superior knowledge, she retained the owl as her sacred animal.

Indeed, allusions to early versions of female creative powers permeate myths that predate the Hellenic period. They suggest that the gendering of creative powers may have proceeded along with the evolution of new theories of the mind, and that before those theories, creative powers were much more gender neutral, sometimes appearing as female, sometimes as male. According to the Pelasgian creation myth as reported by Graves,[28] for example, in the beginning there was Erynome, the goddess of all things. Rising from the Chaos, she divided the sea and the sky and began dancing on the waves. Her dance grew wilder and wilder, and out of her dance was created the universe. The first being created was the great serpent Ophion. Ophion coiled about Erynome and out of their union the Universal Egg was brought forth. Erynome and Ophion set up residence on Mount Olympus. But when

Ophion claimed to be the author of the universe, Erynome grew angry and banished him to the dark caves below the earth.

What is notable about this myth is that, like many (by no means all) ancient creation myths, it personifies the process of creation as a female act – in contrast to Apollo's claim. What is equally notable is that the myth raises the issue of female and male competition about claims to creation. Thus, Plato's language of competition between logos and mythos is specifically mirrored in gender-related language. Here, however, Apollo's creation imagery of the masculine replacing the feminine is reversed. The fact that the feminine imagery of creation prevails in this myth may be explained by its early origin – perhaps as early as the 5th millennium B.C.E.;[29] even so, the myth also introduced the theme of a threat to that claim. This theme of competition eventually evolved into one of subjugation and theft, and even of rape of female creativity. Hence over the course of time, as creation became more and more exclusively associated with the masculine, it also became associated with dominance over the feminine.

The superordination of the masculine creative principle over the feminine one is well reflected in the evolution of myths of creation and creativity. As Lerner[30] has pointed out, the earliest concepts of creation were purely mythic and equated creative processes organically. Often, as in the example of Erynome, creation was represented as the enactment of nature's fertility, and these organic processes were equated with feminine capacities and with the great mother goddess. With the gradual evolution of the differentiation between organic and mental-spiritual realms, a new concept of creation gradually evolved. From about the 3rd millennium B.C.E., creation often came to be represented as the cooperative act between a material, organic, and feminine principle and a spiritual and masculine principle. Thus, for example, Greek mythology represents creation as the mating of earth, represented as the goddess Gaia, with heaven, represented as the god Uranus.

Over time, however, the concepts of creation gradually became completely abstracted from any semblance of organic fertility and sexual procreation, and became purely symbolic and conceptual acts. No longer represented by a biological event, they were redefined as purely mental ones, subject to the willful and conscious conceptual activity of a male god figure. For example, Lerner shows, in a Mesopotamian creation myth, the god Enlil draws the shape of a dragon in the sky, and through this act the dragon subsequently comes to life. Similarly in the Bible, the planets and the life that populates them are created by god's verbal command. Logos has come to replace mythos as a prime creative principle.

Thus, creation has been reshaped from an organic activity to one that is primarily conceptual. That activity, moreover, no longer consists of the instinctive enactment of a concrete procreative force but has become the conscious act of a masculine mind. Here, then, we find a broad movement toward the symbolization of the capacity to create as a masculine, conceptual, and individual activity – away from one that is organic and symbolized by sexual reproduction. The new creativity becomes identified with an abstract and conceptual deed, associated no longer with birth but with "ideas," "concepts," and "names" – in short, with logos.[31]

Although the evidence on the issue involves a good deal of speculation (see Chapter 6), many authors think that, as the masculine principle of logos came more and more to represent the processes of creation and of authority, a systematic devaluation of the earlier powerful woman goddesses occurred. I already discussed this process of devaluation involving the goddess Athena. A similar process of devaluation is evident with the goddess Pandora, who originally was an earth goddess of great abundance. Her name meant "giver of all gifts,"[32] and in her jar she brought the riches of the earth. By Hesiod's time, however, Pandora had become degraded. No longer born of the earth, she is created when Zeus commands Hephaestus to craft her. She and her jar no longer represent earthly gifts but the evils of the female sex. Says Hesiod,

> . . . From her comes the fair sex;
> yes, wicked womenfolk are her descendants.

> They live among mortal men as a nagging burden
> and are no good sharers of abject want, but only of
> wealth.
> Men are like swarms of bees clinging to cave roofs
> to feed drones that contribute only to malicious deeds;
> the bees themselves all day long until sundown
> are busy carrying and storing the white wax,
> but the drones stay inside in their roofed hives
> and cram their bellies full of what others harvest.
> So, too, Zeus who roars on high made women
> to be an evil for mortal men, helpmates in deeds of
> harshness.[33]

Thus, in this particular goddess, female creativity emerges only as a dangerous attribute. Indeed, that connotation is maintained to the present day in the colloquial metaphor of Pandora with her box as a curious but silly figure who through her feminine lack of restraint brings untold troubles.

The significance of the Greek Pantheon, of course, declined dramatically with the rise of those Western religions that substituted a single male god for the old nature-based, polytheistic religions. This final superordination of the masculine principle over the feminine began to accelerate after the apex of the Hellenic period. This profound change began about 500 B.C.E., and was particularly notable in the Judaic and Christian evolution of a god who is outside nature and transcends it. This change did not evolve smoothly but usually was associated with an attitude of active war – of driving out and destroying evidence of the old religions.

How active this driving out was is recorded in the Old Testament. As Moses led his people out of Egypt back to their own land of Palestine, god was said to appear to him and tell him to lay down new laws for his people. As part of those laws, Moses was to make sure the old forms of religion were thoroughly eradicated. The Israelites were to give up all forms of nature worship. They were no longer to adhere to old nature religions, worshiping "graven images" such as "the likeness of any beast that is on the earth, the likeness of any winged bird that flies in the air, the likeness of anything that creeps on the ground, the likeness of any fish that is in the water under the earth. . . . For the lord your god is a devouring fire, a jealous god."[34] In Palestine, where goddess worship and nature religion prevailed, the Israelites were to destroy all evidence of that worship. Even the prophets and priests of these old religions were to be killed, those praying to idols (the idolaters) put to death, and their cities destroyed. Even one's closest friends and relatives were not to be spared:

> If your brother, the son of your mother, or your son, or your daughter, or the wife of your bosom, or your friend who is your own soul, entices you secretly, saying "Let us go and serve other gods" . . . you shall not yield to him, nor shall you conceal him; but you shall kill him. . . . You shall stone him to death with stones, because he sought to draw you away from the lord your god.[35]

Thus, all evidence pointing to the creative aspects of the organismic and the feminine were to be eradicated in a process of systematic, warlike destruction. Instead, only one single principle of creativity was to be admitted: that of a masculine god, one who was completely transcendent and outside of nature – a god of logos.

THEORIES OF GENDER AS STORIES

The differentiation between male and female forms of creativity, as well as the claim that the masculine form represents a more exalted one, not only characterizes mythical stories but also underlies many of the more "abstract" theories about the lives of men and women. Thus, even our modern theories of the development of gender differences are storied – that is, they ultimately are structured by the types of narratives we have discussed in the previous section.

Freud's theory

Of those "stories" perhaps the most widely known – and criticized – theory is that of Freud. Like Neumann's theory discussed in Chapter 3, Freud believes that early development is characterized by a state of undifferentiation. For him, that undifferentiation is, in part, one of gender. He believes that we begin our existence in a state of essential bisexuality, and that this relatively undifferentiated state only becomes differentiated and polarized in the process of individual development.

For the boy, this process is straightforward and follows the pattern already discussed in Chapter 3. Thus, maintains Freud, the boy begins to reject the feminine as "not me" and "other," and to define himself against it. But for the young girl, no such externalizing attitude is possible. She, instead, must turn the contempt of the feminine against the self, with the result that a degree of masochism and psychological self-mutilation characterizes the adaptation of many women.

Freud appears to have been quite unaware of the mythic and symbolic nature of the boys' and girls' way of dealing with the devalued condition of the feminine. He interprets this devaluation much more concretely as an actual lack. Thus, in his view, the psychological self-mutilation in which women engage results from the fact that the woman actually *is* biologically mutilated. Freud asserts that the little girl, discovering that she does not have a penis, is traumatized by this evidence of her physical inferiority:

> They notice the penis of a brother or playmate, strikingly visible and of large proportions, at once recognize it as the superior counterpart of their own small and inconspicuous organ, and from that time forward fall a victim to envy for the penis.[36]

For the boy, Freud states, the discovery of the mutilated state of the female results in a permanent attitude toward women: "horror of the mutilated creature or triumphant contempt for her."[37] But being female herself, the girl cannot so readily project outward the contempt for the feminine. Instead, she deeply identifies with her inferiority:

> After a woman has become aware of the wound to her narcissism, she develops, like a scar, a sense of inferiority. . . . She

begins to share the contempt felt by men for a sex which is the lesser in so important a respect.[38]

As a result, Freud believes that women harbor a deep envy of male sexuality:

Even after penis-envy has abandoned its true object, it continues to exist: by an easy displacement it persists in the character-trait of jealousy. Of course, jealousy is not limited to one sex and has a wider foundation than this, but I am of the opinion that it plays a far larger part in the mental life of women than of men.[39]

Another consequence for the woman's mental life is related to this process, according to Freud. For the boy, the results of the Oedipus complex are readily absorbed into the ego and the structure of the superego. But for the girl, her sense of castration persists and forms the basis for a presumed lack of conscience and morality:

I cannot escape the notion (though I hesitate to give it expression) that for women the level of what is ethically normal is different from what it is in men. Their super-ego is never so inexorable, so impersonal, so independent of its emotional origins as we require it to be in men. Character traits which critics of every epoch have brought up against women – that they show less sense of justice than men, that they are less ready to submit to the great necessities of life, that they are more often influenced in their judgements by feelings of affection or hostility – all these would be amply accounted for by the modification in the formation of the super-ego which we have already inferred.[40]

Freud also believes that there is a danger that the girl may not properly resolve this process and thus develop her femininity. She may revolt against her fate by developing a "masculinity complex," which consists in the girl's continuing to express an active orientation.

Male envy of the feminine

Freud's account of the formation of feminine identity has been sharply criticized for its mistaken and absurd conceptualization of feminine sexuality as a mere lack of masculine sexuality. Even in the 1940s, it was argued that Freud's own masculine bias caused him to distort the biological and psychosocial role of women. Indeed, the psychoanalyst Zilboorg claims that the symbolism by which woman is constituted as a mere negation of the masculine suggests that if women envy men, it is no less true that men envy women, and wish to "possess" feminine characteristics, too:

> When it is resolved not to overlook how much feminine there is in the masculine attributes of that which was heretofore mared as most primary and unquestionably most masculine, and when the fundamental envy with which man treats woman . . . is borne in mind, then I am certain that clinical observations will become enriched with new material which heretofore was obscured by androcentric bias.[41]

Thus, even though many of Freud's claims are absurd on an objective level, they have a rather compelling "logic" on the level of mythos processes. In his study entitled *Symbolic Wounds*, Bettelheim[42] suggests that male envy of the attributes of women is, in fact, an extremely pervasive phenomenon. He notes that "men stand in awe of the procreative power of women, that they wish to participate in it,"[43] and he goes on to suggest that evidence of such envy of female procreative powers can be widely found in Western societies, although on the whole, it may be highly repressed. But in less highly civilized cultures, these attitudes are freely expressed, though in highly symbolic form. This is evident worldwide in male initiation rites; such rites typically involve some symbolic wounding in which the initiate is made to bleed in imitation of female menstruation, or even has part of his genitalia altered to mimic female anatomy. Often, these aspects of bodily mutilations are followed by systematic instruction in sacred and secret teachings, part of which helps to define the role of men relative to women.

A stunning example of such a system of rituals and teachings is Herdt's description of male initiation rites among the Sambia in New Guinea.[44] The Sambia are highly polarized along sex/gender lines, and women are considered the inferior sex. However, the Sambia believe that this inferiority does not apply to biological and reproductive issues. In fact, women are considered to be more competent in the business of growing up, doing so naturally and competently without the support of additional measures. This is not true for Sambian men; in fact, the men are thought to be held back in their development by such female bodily substances as "womb blood" and "mother's milk" as well as maternal care. They cannot reach sexual maturity unless they are inseminated by men, whose semen is thought to substitute for mother's milk in prepubescent initiates. Thus, an elaborate set of rites initiates the young boys into a homosexual cult in which they are taught to perform fellatio on older adolescents. This semen cult is supported by an elaborate conceptual structure about the parallels between mother's milk and semen. Semen not only is the "milk" that makes boys grow into men, it is also the substance out of which fetuses are made through semen accumulation in the woman's womb. Once the baby is born, additional semen accumulation is necessary for transformation into mother's milk.

Bettelheim discusses a wide range of similar practices, all of which appear to be aimed at defining the unique nature of the masculine in contrast to the feminine. Yet in this attempt there is usually a defensive inversion in which the feminine is considered a lesser version of the masculine. Such a process of inversion appears to be basic to how gender is constructed in many cultural settings.

Psychoanalyst Robert Stoller[45] has discussed this process of inversion, arguing that far from indicating the primacy of the masculine, it results from the fact that femininity in actuality constitutes the primary state of human development, both biologically and psychologically. Psychologically, this state of "protofemininity" results from the mother's role in early development. For both boys and girls, the mother defines an early core of identity, which in the case of the boy's development becomes problematic. He, unlike the girl, needs to change his core identity from feminine to masculine, a change that leaves a lifelong vulnerability of self. In Stoller's words:

> I suspect that the problem boys have with creating their masculinity from the protofemininity leaves behind a "structure," a vigilance, a fear of the pull of the symbiosis – that is, a conflict between the urge to return to the peace of the symbiosis and the opposing urge to separate out as an individual, as a male, as masculine. Much of what we see as masculinity is, I think, the effect of that struggle. For much of masculinity, as is well known, consists of struggling not to be seen by oneself or others as having feminine attributes, physical or psychologic. One must maintain one's distance from women or be irreparably infected with femininity.[46]

More recently, Nancy Chodorow has reviewed similar evidence and pointed out that for the young boy, a unique (relative to the young girl) problem arises in development. Unlike the girl who can preserve a sense of continuity with the mother, the boy needs to push away from the mother and define himself against her. This is true, in part, because of cultural demands, but it also is a result, in part, of the unique bond the mother and her son share. Unlike daughters, sons to their mothers are an "other"; their maleness and oppositeness as sexual beings introduce a sexual and incestuous element into mother–son relationships. Thus, the boy is pushed to move away from that bond, to search for differentiation and independence, and to gain masculine identification in part by defining a realm of the masculine in opposition to the feminine.

Such processes of opposition may be inherent in early gender identification, particularly in a social context in which gender polarization is high.[47] In such cultures, argues Bettelheim, men "must repress the extent of their longing for the . . . potentialities of being a woman, whereas women are much freer to express their envy of males' equipment and roles."[48]

The feminine as negation

A result of the repression of the feminine mentioned by Bettelheim is the frequent construction of gender along a simple hierarchical dimension. This issue was addressed in Lacqueur's[49] discussion of historical changes in conceptualizations of male and female reproductive anatomy and physiology. As still evident in Freud's theory, such conceptualizations were often understood within a "single sex model" in which femininity was seen as a mere negation of biological masculinity, as negative space or void in contrast to the positive value of masculinity. Hillman notes in that regard:

> We encounter a long and incredible history of theoretical misadventures and observational errors in male science regarding the physiology of reproduction. These fantastic theories and fantastic observations are not mere apprehensions, the usual and necessary mistakes on the road of scientific progress; they are recurrent deprecations of the feminine phrased in the unimpeachable, objective language of the science of the period.[50]

One famous example is Aristotle's description of reproductive physiology. This model was an attempt, in fact, to map the duality of Plato's model of the mind onto issues of reproduction. Believing, like other Greek philosophers, that matter was of lower importance than spirit, Aristotle argued that this was evident in processes of sexual reproduction. He theorized that the woman contributed the more primitive and material principle to the embryo, but denied that the man's contribution also was of a material sort. Instead, he held that the masculine contribution was more spiritual and "divine." This superiority of the masculine principle was derived from the belief that the male principle is active, the female principle passive. In *De Generatione Animalium* he states:

If, then, the male stands for the effective and active, and the female, considered as female, for the passive, it follows that what the female would contribute to the semen of the male would not be semen but material for the semen to work upon.[51]

Indeed, Aristotle went on to argue, without the male spiritual principle, a predominance of the female principle would give rise to the birth of monstrosities:

> For just as the young of mutilated parents are sometimes born mutilated and sometimes not, so also the young born of a female are sometimes female and sometimes male instead. For the female is, as it were, a mutilated male, and the catamenia (female procreative substance) are semen, only not in the pure; for there is only one thing they have not in them, the principle of soul.[52]

This form of reasoning for Aristotle supported a very hierarchical view of the relationship between the sexes. Just as men and women were seen as hierarchically divided – men being rational, strong, endowed with the capacity for procreation, equipped with soul, and fit to rule; women being passionate and unable to control their appetites, weak, and bound to the mere material existence – so there is a natural order to existing hierarchies. In *Politics*, he wrote:

> The soul rules the body with the sway of a master, the intelligence the appetites with constitutional or royal rule; and in these examples it is manifest that it is natural and expedient for the body to be governed by the soul and for the emotional part to be governed by the intellect, the part possessing reason, whereas for the two parties to be on an equal footing or in the contrary positions is harmful in all cases. . . . Also, as between the sexes, the male is by nature superior and the female inferior, the male ruler and the female subject.[53]

Thus, women were on a level equal to animals and slaves – inferior beings without psyches whose nature was to serve their superiors endowed with a psyche:

Night and day

And also the usefulness of slaves diverges little from that of animals; bodily service for the necessities of life is forthcoming from both, from slaves and domestic animals alike. . . . It is manifest therefore that there are cases of people of whom some are freemen and the others slaves by nature, and for these slavery is an institution both expedient and just.[54]

Aristotle's construction of the feminine as a form of mutilation has served as a powerful image of femininity and feminine development in our cultural tradition. Like Aeschylus' Apollo, Aristotle suggests that the mental inferiority of women is directly related to some direct biological principle – an assertion that, as Daly[55] argues, was translated directly to prescriptions about sexual performance, as well.

Aristotle also argued that this results in the woman's inferior social position, thus carrying the metaphor of mutilation further. In later times, however, this principle of "mutilation" became more indirect, referring to attributes of mental rather than sexual functioning per se – although, as we saw earlier, Freud *did* maintain that women's mental inferiority derives from their sexual inferiority, as well. But more generally, many philosophical theories became concerned with an intellectual disempowerment of the feminine principle.

Richter has traced this disempowerment in his book on the god complex.[56] With the rise of science in the 17th century, with its predominantly rational image of human nature, many thinkers attempted to offer scientific proof that women were less evolved, less rational creatures than men. An example is the philosophy of Malebranche. He claimed that women's brains are constructed so as to allow but minimal rational functions. He did, however, admit that they may be capable of refined feelings. But, in the spirit of a time that completely devalued the importance of feeling, he went on to claim about woman:

But to discover truth, an ability that requires effort and thinking, is well beyond her capabilities. Everything abstract is beyond her comprehension. Her discrimination is unfit to untangle intricate interrelationships. She only apprehends the

141

surface of things. To explore depth and to compare all the inter-connections of things without becoming confused is well be-yond her powers or skills.[57]

This dualism between masculine rationality and feminine emotionality is also typical of the philosophy of Schopenhauer. This philosopher was remarkable for pointing to the power of emotions that underlie rational judgment in ethics. Critiquing a conception of morality based solely on an abstract, rationalis-tic conception of duty and justice, he suggests that an impor-tant source of morality is compassion, the "immediate, quasi instinctive participation in the suffering of another."[58] How-ever, his contempt of the feminine prevents him from develop-ing a truly new theory of morality. According to Schopenhauer, compassion and love of others are combined in women with stupidity and lack of will power, and these lacks are the reason that

> women are inferior to men. This is because, owing to the weak-ness of their mind, they cannot grasp general principles, nor hold on to them and adopt them as guidelines in the same way as men, who surpass them in the virtues of justice, honesty, and conscientiousness. Injustice and dishonesty are their vice, and lying is their element. Still, they *do* surpass men in the virtues of love of their fellow humans; this virtue they are capable of because it mostly requires concreteness and thus elicits com-passion, a feeling to which women are more readily susceptible.[59]

Like Aristotle, Schopenhauer thus thinks that the feminine is merely a degraded and inferior version of the masculine, and that social practices root in this inferiority:

> Women are well suited to be nurturers and educators of our earliest childhood, because they themselves are childish, mushy, and shortsighted. In a word, they are forever big chil-dren, sort of a halfway step between the child and man, who is the essence of a human being.[60]

Night and day

Women and eminence

With the rise of psychology as a science, many of these assumptions made their way into early psychological theories of the nature of gender differences in mental functioning. What was of particular concern to thinkers was the obvious fact that women showed very few extraordinary achievements in the arts and sciences. This lack was attributed to some deficits in female nature. Gould discusses these attempts in his book, *The Mismeasure of Man*, reviewing theorists that attempted to argue that women's brains were biologically unfit for superior achievement or even genius. Thus, LeBon, the founder of social psychology, also argues that women are biologically incapable of intelligent activity:

> In the most intelligent races . . . there are a large number of women whose brains are closer in size to those of gorillas than to the most developed male brains. This inferiority is so obvious that no one can contest it for a moment; only its degree is worth discussion. All psychologists who have studied the intelligence of women, as well as poets and novelists, recognize today that they represent the most inferior forms of human evolution and that they are closer to children and savages than to an adult, civilized male. They excel in fickleness, inconstancy, absence of thought and logic; and incapacity to reason. Without doubt there exist some distinguished women, very superior to the average man, but they are as exceptional as the birth of any monstrosity, as for example, a gorilla with two heads; consequently, we may neglect them entirely.[61]

Classing female excellence as a mere "monstrosity" does, of course, repeat the sentiment of numerous thinkers before LeBon – as well as anticipating Freud's disapproval of the woman who does not renounce her masculine powers. Apart from its blatant misogyny, however, the statement also touches on a problem that was and continues to be objectively real: namely, the relatively rare occurrence of exceptional female achievement throughout history and into recent times.

143

With the rise of psychology as a science, the problem of female eminence became a focus of vigorous study. In early scientific studies, however, the sentiment that women's brains did not permit them to think rationally became expressed in a less direct version. According to that version, women were not necessarily less intelligent than men on the average, but the range of women's mental abilities was more restricted. This "variability hypothesis" was based, in part, on the claim that fewer women were found in the extreme ranges of intelligence: Thus, there were fewer of them among those who have achieved eminence, but also fewer among the retarded. This claim supported early scientific views that women were constitutionally incapable of extraordinary achievements. Stated Thorndike in 1910:

> [In] the great achievements of the world in science, art, invention, and management, women have been far excelled by men. . . . In particular, if men differ in intelligence and energy by wider degrees than do women, eminence in and leadership of the world's affairs of whatever sort will inevitably belong oftener to men. They will oftener deserve it.[62]

With large-scale distribution of intelligence tests and the proliferation of research on intellectual capacities, however, many of these claims about brain size and intelligence were shown to be faulty. An early pioneer in dismantling the stereotype of inferior female intelligence was Leta Hollingsworth, a student of Thorndike's and an early leader of the study of the gifted. Hollingsworth showed that there was no actual difference among male and female retardates in terms of their test scores. However, large differences in social practices were evident in the treatment of male and female retardates. More male retardates were recognized and institutionalized fairly early in their life span, whereas more girls were simply kept at home to help with child care and household chores until they were older; only then were they referred to institutional settings. Thus, social customs rather than biological gender differences were the basis of the "variability hypothesis."

Hollingsworth was tireless in showing that the limitations encountered by women were sociological rather than biological:

Those who investigate eminence agree . . . upon the following facts. An overwhelming majority of illustrious persons have had fathers who were far above the average in social-economic conditions – nobles, professional men, or men successfully engaged in commerce. Very few children of manual workers become eminent in high degree. . . . Very few women can be included among those who in the world's history have achieved first rank for mental work. . . . One possible interpretation is that education and opportunity are the prime determinants of achievement, since nearly all the great men have been born in comfortable homes, of parents of superior circumstances. If opportunity were indeed the prime determinant of eminence, then we should expect those who belong to socially inferior categories to be virtually excluded from it. This is just what we do find, since the uncultured, the poor servants, and women are very seldom found to have achieved eminence.[63]

Thus, Hollingsworth began to unravel the circularity of the claim of female inferiority. As Noble put it recently in his book *A World Without Women,* that argument now must be seen as embedded in a complex psychosocial process in which our culture created masculine subcultures such as the religious and the scientific communities whose aim was not only to cultivate the depersonalized and disembodied language of logos, but also to maintain the "alienation from and dread of women."[64]

DISOWNING THE SELF AS CREATOR

The evidence just discussed suggests that most past theories about the nature of women's minds should hardly be taken as statements of fact. Rather, this evidence indicates that these "theories" have primarily symbolic value, statements about aspects of the self that have been rejected by a masculine perspective. Yet the value of such statements is not symbolic *only,* because they have become, through a process of projective identification, constitutive of a reality in which creative potentials – organic and mental – were carefully territorialized and assigned gender.

The achievement gap

The symbolic nature of these claims has become apparent as social realities have changed and as the rigid polarization of realities along gender lines has begun to break down. In that process, Hollingsworth's contention has been upheld. As education and subsequent labor market participation have become more accessible to women, overt differences both in actual achievements and in intellectual giftedness have been less and less evident.[65] Even as objective differences in intellectual status between men and women have been found to be groundless, many puzzling observations remain. Although female intellectual endowment does not lag behind that of men, women as a group continue to lag in achievement behind men. Moreover, this gender lag increases in the course of development. Indeed, in early childhood, girls *surpass* boys on most measures of school achievement. However, as they grow into adolescence, girls' superiority over boys begins to decline, and they tend to fall behind boys.[66] As they grow older, girls often are found to retreat from achievement-related challenges, and differences in achievement between adult men and women are profound.[67]

As research began to attend to this achievement gap, a popular hypothesis held that rather than suffering from gross anatomical or intellectual deficits, girls simply lack in motivation to achieve.[68] Girls were believed to be more oriented toward relationships and to be more dependent than boys; this dependency orientation, in turn, was thought to interfere with their intellectual strivings. Bardwick, a major researcher in the field, explains:

> For the adolescent girl, the interpersonal sphere is pivotal. Her sensitivity and skill in interpersonal relations express her

developing eroticism, and her efforts to gain popularity express her erotic needs and her skills in winning and maintaining love. . . . What the boy achieves through separation and autonomy, the girl achieves . . . through her attachment to others. . . . The girl's . . . goals were closely identified to the objects she identified with. This served to continue her tendency to be dependent, compliant, and conformist. An independent sense of self is not accomplished without the severance of old interpersonal ties, without the establishment of internal, individual criteria for achievement, without a sense of identity that is relatively independent of other people.[69]

In an early review of sex differences in intellectual functioning, Maccoby,[70] another preeminent researcher in the field, also had suggested that girls' dependency interfered with their striving for achievement. Thus, it appeared that it was primarily the more "feminine" girls who had conflicts with achievement. In contrast, the expression of intellectual competence appeared to be fostered by such unfeminine traits as assertiveness and activeness.

However, reviewing the development of gender differences in achievement nearly a decade later in her 1974 book with Jacklin, Maccoby concludes that these differences no longer held true. This change possibly occurred because of the rapid cultural changes that had affected the picture of sex differences in intellectual functioning. Thus, says Maccoby:

The 1966 Maccoby paper attempted to explain some portion of the sex differences in intellectual performance in terms of sex differences in personality structure. . . . These arguments have not stood up well under the impact of new evidence appearing in the intervening years. . . . there is now good reason to doubt that girls are more "dependent" in almost any sense of the word than boys. . . . girls are not more oriented towards interpersonal cues.[71]

Instead of pointing to major differences in personality and motivation, evidence began to suggest that girls may not be less motivated to achieve, but that they often have feelings of conflict about achievement and therefore retreat from it. Two major reasons are suggested to account for this finding. First, it appears that qualities of independence and intellectual striving are difficult to integrate into girls' sense of themselves in the same positive way that is possible for boys and men. For example, although objective differences in intellectual performances between the sexes are often absent, women are more likely than men to evaluate their abilities, performances, and the likelihood of their future success negatively,[72] especially in areas that are considered masculine. Indeed, to ward off the danger of appearing "masculine," women are more likely than men to reject personal authorship of their accomplishments, even to belittle and denigrate them. Thus, what for the boy or man appears to be a source of pride, for the girl or woman often becomes a matter of conflicted feelings.

Several women writers have recently pointed out that a different dynamic underlies the socialization of achievement in men and women.[73] Women's failure to achieve to levels equal to men often appears to be the result of a complex process of learning and internalizing social values. In identifying herself as feminine, the woman needs to learn to surrender those attributes that are culturally labeled as masculine, including her claim to knowledge and achievement. Interpersonally, and culturally, becoming feminine requires that the woman renounce her sense of agency and consciousness. Part of the self – the creator, thinker, questor – is thus experienced as monstrous, as outside of the self, and the woman attempts to cut it off from awareness altogether, to ban it into the unconscious. Indeed, she learns to feel a profound sense of shame at her competence. Instead, she idealizes herself as sweet, beautiful, and caring, while her agency is projected onto the man.

Indeed, just as Freud suggests, the process of socialization in women may require that they turn against themselves, actively suppressing evidence of superior intellectual achievement. Freud, of course, claims that this "turning against the self" resulted from the woman's biological inferiority. Instead, I am suggesting that the causes cannot be found in the woman's so-called nature, but rather in the cultural problem of how competition is regulated between the sexes. Within the competitive, vertical model of the mind, the problem was resolved by domination and submission rather than by cooperation, as we have seen. As a result, many women tend to "leave the field" to men when it comes to asserting intellectual and creative strivings.[74] Thus, the feminine retreat from achievement is hardly a matter of the girl's or woman's passive nature. Rather, it results from a most active and vigorous adjustment to a cultural reality, to which the girl adapts by inhibiting her achievement so as to avoid competitive conflicts.

Creativity and women writers

How actively this painful inner split is accomplished has been studied in many recent investigations of women's biographies. One example is the life and work of poet Sylvia Plath. In her novel, *The Bell Jar,* Plath describes the heroine Esther's fall into depression as she comes to understand the strictures against female creative powers.[75] Esther grew up a brilliant girl who wants to go for what her gifts seem to destine her: extraordinary creative achievements. Extraordinary achievements come to her easily indeed, but, paradoxically, she begins to experience deep conflicts about them. As a result of those conflicts, she falls into profound paralysis:

> All my life I'd told myself studying and reading and writing and working like mad was what I wanted to do, and it actually seemed to be true, I did everything well enough and got all A's, and by the time I made it to college nobody could stop me . . . and now I was apprenticed to the best editor on an intellectual fashion magazine, and what did I do but balk and balk like a dull cart horse.[76]

Threats to Esther's creativity are posed by many individuals of her outside world, including her friends and relatives. But more and more, these threats are deeply internalized and lead to an active process of self-victimization. She observes that women are systematically deprived of their self-confidence, of their sense of self as strong individuals. She feels that feminine powers are systematically taken over and destroyed by men –

and that, to be accepted as womanly, women need to learn to sacrifice cheerfully their creativity. For Esther, this process is starkly symbolized by a lesson she learns while visiting Mrs. Willard, her boyfriend Buddy's mother:

> Once when I visited Buddy I found Mrs. Willard braiding a rug out of strips of wool from Mr. Willard's old suits. She'd spent weeks on that rug, and I had admired the tweedy browns and greens and blues patterning the braid, but after Mrs. Willard was through, instead of hanging the rug on the wall the way I would have done, she put it down in place of her kitchen mat, and in a few days it was soiled and dull and indistinguishable from any mat you could buy for under a dollar in the five and ten.
>
> And I knew that in spite of all the roses and kisses and restaurant dinners a man showered on a woman before he married her, what he secretly wanted was for her to flatten out underneath his feet like Mrs. Willard's kitchen mat.[77]

Terrified, she realizes that growing up for a woman means learning to participate in her own slavery, to blunt her independence and creativity:

> I also remembered Buddy Willard saying in a sinister, knowing way that after I had children I would feel differently, I wouldn't want to write poems anymore. So I began to think maybe it was true that when you married and had children it was like being brainwashed, and afterward you went about numb as a slave in some private, totalitarian state.[78]

With alarm, Esther watches the bedazed women in her world. Mrs. Willard tells her that "What a man wants is a mate and what a woman wants is infinite security," and "What a man is is an arrow into the future and what a woman is is the place the arrow shoots off from."[79] A part of her rebels against this message; what she wants, she realizes, is not to surrender her dreams in feminine fashion, but "to shoot off in all directions myself, like the colored arrows from a Fourth of July rocket."[80] But her mother, too, warns her:

Nobody wanted a plain English major. But an English major who knew shorthand was something else again. Everybody would want her. She would be in demand among all the up-and-coming young men and she would transcribe letter after thrilling letter.

The trouble was . . . I wanted to dictate my own thrilling letters.[81]

Esther thus observes that the course of women's develop-ment becomes one of participating in the systematic destruc-tion of female creativity. Servitude, brainwashing, numbness, drugs that anesthetize the mind, docility are the words that for her characterize the feminine experience, which becomes sym-bolized in her stay at a mental asylum where women are given shock treatments, insulin injections, and lobotomies to quiet their creative hungers and their inquisitive intellects. Like one of her inmates, Valerie, Esther feels that growing into maturity for a woman means being lobotomized and having a bell jar permanently descend on her mind.

A similar conflict can also be observed in the poetry of an-other major woman poet, Adrienne Rich. In a series of poems, Rich has documented how difficult it is for a creative woman to accept a self-identification as creative. In her early work, this creativity is experienced as something dangerous, something outside, against which the self defends. In the poem "Storm Warnings,"[82] for example, it emerges as a dangerous storm, a metaphor for one's repressed creativity. Like a terrible storm, one's creativity cannot be completely denied; it continually threatens to resurface. So the feminine self shuts herself in, carefully closing the shutters against the onslaught of the ap-proaching storm – her dangerous desire to create.

As a result of this constant expenditure of energy attempting to restrain the self's longing to create, Rich experiences herself as fragmented, fractured into several selves. One, as in the poem "Orion,"[83] is the conventional self confined "inside" the house, a self experienced as "a dead child born in the dark." The other is the creative self who remains active and striving. But, to be experienced as less dangerous, this creative self becomes split off and projected onto a masculine world. As Rich stated:

> The poem "Orion" . . . is a poem of connection with a part of myself I had felt I was losing – the active principle, the energetic imagination, the "half-brother" whom I projected, as I had for many years, into the constellation Orion. It's no accident that the words "cold and egotistical" appear in this poem and are applied to myself. The choice still seemed to be between "love" – womanly, maternal love, altruistic love, a love defined and ruled by the weight of an entire culture; and egotism – a force directed by men into creation, achievement, ambition."[84]

Heilbrun, in *Writing a Woman's Life*, shows that this profound inner conflict is by no means the mere result of a profound pathology, as some biographers of Plath have suggested. Echoing Virginia Woolf's earlier study *A Room of One's Own*, Heilbrun agrees that highly creative women learn to experience their powers as dangerous and as outside the self. She goes on to examine the reason for this "blunted female destiny." Cultural attitudes belittle and ridicule the striving for power and creative expression in women: the voice of their creative self is likely to be called "shrill," "strident," "angry," "egotistical." Fearful of having these labels applied to them, and shameful of the creative strivings that lead to such labeling, extraordinary women are engaged in a constant struggle to suffocate their strong selves, to hide them apologetically. This dynamic is addressed in Spacks' essay entitled "Selves in Hiding," a study of women's own presentations of their lives in their autobiographies. The women discussed in this essay are profoundly active and powerful women, women like Emma Goldman, Eleanor Roosevelt, and Golda Meir. Yet it would be difficult to tell how extraordinary and exciting these lives were if one reads the women's own narratives of them. Notes Spacks,

> Although each author has significant, sometimes dazzling accomplishments to her credit, the theme of accomplishment rarely dominates the narrative. . . . Indeed to a striking degree

they fail directly to emphasize their *own* importance, though writing in a genre which implies self assertion and self display.[85]

Indeed, Heilbrun argues that well into this century, it remained impossible for women to admit in their own autobiographical narratives their claims of achievement, admissions of ambition, or the realization that their own accomplishments may be more than mere luck or the result of others' generosity. She notes that many autobiographies of women of the past indicate that women tend to describe their exciting lives in a flat and unexciting way, even though there is ample evidence – as can be gleaned, for example, from published correspondence – that this is a one-sided narrative:

> Their letters and diaries are usually different, reflecting ambitions and struggles in the public sphere; in their published autobiographies, however, they portray themselves as intuitive, nurturing, passive, but never – in spite of the contrary evidence of their accomplishments – managerial.[86]

In her book *Silences*, Olsen[87] also addresses this conflict. Women, argues Olsen, live under the agony that creation and femininity are incompatible. As an example, Olsen quotes from Anaïs Nin's diaries:

> The aggressive act of creation; the guilt for creating. I did not want to rival man; to steal man's creation, his thunder. I must protect them, not outshine them.[88]

Achievement conflicts in gifted women

These astonishing conflicts are also documented in the recent psychological literature, which suggests that these agonies of women over their achievement persist well into the present day. Evidence about these achievement conflicts began to accumulate after Terman's 1925 study of the "mental and physical traits of a thousand gifted children."[89] Although as children, the group showed small differences in intelligence, adolescence brought a rather sharp decline in IQ scores for girls. In her recent study of gifted girls, Kerr suggests:

> What was happening? It seems unlikely that inherited "male superiority" could explain differences at seventeen and eighteen years of age when these differences did not exist years previously. . . . Another possibility . . . is that the girls had decided *not to try* on the IQ tests. Though the girls may have felt it socially acceptable to continue to receive high marks in school and to achieve in extracurricular activities, they may have found the label "gifted" unacceptable, knowing this would be the price to pay for a high score on an IQ test. Since gifted girls are good adjusters, they adjusted – and may have begun to deny their giftedness.[90]

Kerr's own research supports this suggestion. Girls' paradoxical denial of their giftedness appears to result from the different personal meaning of giftedness for boys and girls. For the boy, giftedness is a source of pride for him and his parents; but for girls, being gifted becomes a source of profound denial and shame. Kerr's results suggest that this effect becomes more pronounced with increasing age. In the 8th grade, gifted girls had ambitious career aspirations, but by grade 12, this ambition had given way to profound confusion and denial. One girl's career aspirations changed from "start a career in international relations and help the revolution!" to "get a boyfriend."[91]

As a result of this denial, the later educational and employment history of girls, unlike that of boys, shows little of their early promise. In Terman's studies, for example, many differences in professional success were apparent between the sexes in adulthood – and they appeared to become more so over time. For example, while girls appeared to hold their own up to the time of college graduation, only 14% earned advanced degrees compared with 31% of the men. In 1955, while 86% of the men were employed in professional or managerial careers, only 11% of the women held similar positions.[92]

Kerr, too, observes how girls gradually gave up on their goals, noting that over time, "career goals were juggled, lost, confused, compromised, or downgraded, and only rarely pursued in a determined, progressive way.[93] Instead, these women had come to deny that they were gifted or special, and one finds a "cheerful insistence on normality." Thus, one woman said: "It's a well-known fact that IQ tests are inappropriate measures of intelligence; they mean nothing."[94] Another recounted her adolescent experience of her giftedness:

> You know, I think I was so afraid of the idea of being gifted that as soon as I got away from that crowd by attending college, I felt very relieved, as if the pressure was off and I could just be normal.[95]

That intellectual striving and the pursuit of excellence and knowledge take on completely different significance for boys and girls entering adolescence is also suggested by other research.[96] Poor academic performance for boys is related to emotional problems. For girls, however, *higher* academic performance predicts emotional problems: It becomes a predictor of depression. These girls, in order to improve their self-image and their emotional well-being, respond to the crisis of their giftedness by lowering their academic achievement. This trade-off is particularly pronounced in so-called masculine areas such as mathematics and science, where the pattern of trading grades for popularity and psychological well-being continues into the 12th grade.

More recently, several researchers[97] reported that for girls, high intelligence constitutes a risk factor related to depression. Such findings suggest that for a girl or woman, her agentic and intellectual strivings are experienced differently than for a boy or man: She is less likely to find them mirrored, and as a result to feel them to be "real" and to emanate from her own center. This conclusion is also upheld by research examining the relationship between actual intellectual performance and one's self-concept about these performances. Men and boys are more likely than girls to evaluate their performance positively in situations of performance achievement. That is, they are likely to overestimate their ability initially, and remain unaffected by negative evaluations. In contrast, women underestimate their performance and are more strongly affected by others' feedback. These patterns may be especially strong in gender-stereotyped areas such as mathematics or science, where girls are especially likely to disclaim their sense of agency, even though they may outperform boys.[98]

The work of Gilligan[99] and others also shows that girls who early in adolescence were confident and outspoken become increasingly confused and silent about what they know. They come to doubt that what girls and women know and experience has value in the adult world, because it too often "brings a message of exclusion – stay out; because it brings a message of subordination – stay under; because it brings a message of objectification – become an object of another's worship or desire, see yourself as you have been seen over centuries through a male gaze . . . keep quiet and notice the absence of women and say nothing."[100]

This pattern of relinquishing a sense of their competence primes the girl to emotional experiences of shame, depression, and powerlessness that are not equally prevalent in the boy. More generally, such core emotional experiences are related to different core senses of self as evidenced in different coping and defense strategies. Cramer[101] found that such differences increase with development. As they move through high school, males increasingly externalized conflict, while females increasingly use defenses that internalize conflict, turning aggression and assertiveness inward. In her most recent research,[102] "turning against others" remains a stereotypically masculine coping style, whereas women are more likely to use "turning against the self" defenses. These aspects were also found in our own research on adult coping and defense styles.[103] Women were more likely to utilize turning against the self, seeking social support, and escape/avoidance than men.

As a result of such gendered patterns, different patterns of vulnerability to disorders of self emerge for men and women.[104] These are minor prior to adolescence but intensify as children grow into adolescence, when boys experience more behavioral and acting-out disorders, while girls experience more emotional disorders such as anxiety and depression. Despite conflicting views on what constitutes depression and how it is measured, female prevalence of unipolar depression persists into adulthood and is generally twice that of males. Eating disorders are another example of internalizing disorders overwhelmingly experienced by the female population.

These gender differences in intellectual and emotional experience underscore the claim of gender differences in the core experience of self as an agent and subject versus self as an object. Girls begin quite early to relinquish a sense of their agency and desire to relational needs. Instead, these strivings become disconnected and repudiated as the "other," the bad or dreaded self. That disavowed self then is idealized in men and experienced vicariously in relationships. Boys, on the other hand, are encouraged from an early age to strive for and claim those accomplishments as their own.

CONCLUSION: THE SACRIFICE OF THE
FEMININE

In this chapter, I have suggested that theories and actual phenomena of women's lives often respresent the "dark" side of a masculine view of reality. The traditional model has been based on images of heroic ascent – of quest, of victory, of domination over primordial forces. As Jeanne Block[105] puts it, boys in our culture are encouraged to explore, to be independent, or to try difficult challenges. As a result, they tend to develop "'wings,' which permit leaving the nest, exploring far reaches, and flying alone."[106] In contrast, girls have been found to be less likely to develop wings and to take off in flight. Why should they fail to do so, unless nature has failed to equip them for the task?

157

I suggest that to answer that question, it is necessary to realize that the images of ascent and victory logically, and mythically, also imply their opposites. Ascent entails its opposite, descent; victory requires defeat; the slayer needs a victim; domination implies submission. In Chapter 3, we applied this dialectical opposition toward an examination of traditional images or models of development. We saw that the image of ascent is usually associated with the rise of such masculine powers as conscious decision making and abstract thinking. By contrast, this rise implies the "slaying" of female stereotyped powers; women are made "feminine": passive, pliant, yielding.

In this chapter, I suggest that the sacrifice of the feminine has become a concrete consequence of such a model. Much as in the myth, Eros implores Psyche to be passive, to surrender her curiosity as a precondition for their passionate encounters, so in early development the girl often learns to relinquish her sense of creativity, her dream of quests, her aspirations to heroism. Since these attributes are labeled masculine, women often engage in a vigorous process of psychological self-mutilation in which authorship of the creative self is disowned and surrendered to men.

I have also noted, however, that this process may be specific of a particular phase in historical and in individual development. The masculine model of domination of logos over mythos is gradually being dismantled and we are now observing marked deviations from this prototypical pathway of development. With these recent cultural changes, opportunities have been opened for many individuals – male and female – to go beyond the simple polarizations of early development, and to work out a new form of balance between the masculine and the feminine. Indeed, the sequel to the myth of Psyche and Eros suggests that the marriage of death with its union in the dark is but a preliminary and yet immature form of adaptation. Let us return, then, to the myth and its lessons about continued development in mature adulthood.

Part II

The mind restored

Chapter 5

Knife and lamp: Mythos rediscovered

Finally, Eros surrendered to Psyche's passionate pleas and told Zephyr to carry her sisters down the crag. The sisters, beholding the marvels that surrounded Psyche, felt anger rising in their heart. Jealousy burned like a fire inside them, and – though secretly and to themselves – they began to bewail their own fortunes. "Why should she live here as a Goddess, while I, poor wretch, have a husband older than my father, balder than a pumpkin, and feebler than a child, and who keeps the whole house under lock and key?" They left to plot evil, and returning, they said to their young sister:

"Psyche, dear sister, we are torn with anguish for your misfortune. He that lies by your side in the night is a huge serpent, a fierce and ugly beast who only has lured you to devour you. You must act quickly to save yourself. Here, take this two-edged blade and hide it in your bed, and when night falls, light a lantern and hew off the serpent's head."

The sisters departed again. Night fell and trembling, Psyche rose and lit the lamp. But as soon as the light fell on the bed, Psyche beheld the fairest, most beautiful youth, Eros himself. The blade slid from her hand as, trembling, she watched the glorious sight. She took an arrow from Eros' quiver, but her hand shook and the arrow's point pricked her skin. Soon ecstasy filled her heart and she bowed down to kiss him on his lips.

All of a sudden the lamp sputtered, and a drop of oil fell on Eros' shoulder. Her husband leapt from the bed and tore himself away from Psyche's kisses and lamentations. "Ah, simple-hearted Psyche," he cried, "so do you betray my love. I, neglecting the commands of my mother, wounded myself with my own arrow so that I might be your lover. I wished our child, who you carry this very moment, to be of divine nature, but all has come to ruin. You listened to your sisters' false admonitions, and now I must leave you." And thus flew Eros away.

This section of the story introduces a major turning point. Psyche enters into a new sphere, a new era of her development. The blissful union, the comfort of not knowing and not seeing, the "ecstasy of darkness"[1] comes to an end. Psyche chooses to disregard Eros' warning that she is not to look at him. By moving out of her state of darkness and striving for conscious knowledge, Psyche violates the implicit contract of the death marriage and as a consequence, Eros leaves her.

Psyche's straining to leave the bliss of unconsciousness here represents the striving for a model of mind and self that transforms the vertical and hierarchical model that has so far determined her actions. I have discussed how in that hierarchical model, parts of the self are pushed into darkness and inactivity by that part of the self that is often referred to as the ego. But here the myth suggests that such a hierarchical relationship, successful though it is for youthful adaptation, eventually proves limiting and oppressive. Thus, Psyche begins to yearn for a more balanced union, one in which her darkness ends and she, like Eros, is able to "see."

Examining darkness and shadow

Jung[2] has suggested that this striving to expose to the "light" what has been hidden by darkness is a major theme of mature development, a process happening around the middle of life. According to his theory, the individual around midlife begins to reevaluate those parts of the self that so far were pushed underground. Having forged a quite successful adaptation to life according to the norms and rules of one's culture, the individual begins to experience the loss of abandoned and devalued parts of the self. Jung thinks that this sense of loss initiates a search for a new way of being – a way that is no longer dictated by the individual's obedience to the norms and rules of logos, but one that establishes a dialogue between two modes of being and two ways of knowing. Psyche's emerging curiosity here represents the beginning of just such a transformation. Eventually, as a result of that transformation, self and mind will be represented within a new, lateral model. In that model, parts of the mind and self are no longer represented as a competition between different aspects of the self, but rather as a cooperative union between equal partners.

It is significant, however, that Psyche's decision to move from a state of blissful darkness to one of knowing is not an entirely active and conscious decision. In fact, it is not experienced as a decision at all, but rather as the intrusion of evil outside forces. We encounter these evil forces as Psyche's sisters, thus far forgotten and in the background, who return to the scene to inflame Psyche's curiosity. Even though her husband has implored her not to seek knowledge of his identity, Psyche in the end approaches Eros and his identity is revealed to her. But, with that act, the bond between Psyche and Eros is broken – or, rather, altered in a decisive way, leading to a transformation of both individuals and their relationship.

In that transformation, Psyche's sisters play a major role. At first, that role looks hardly helpful. The sisters are gripped by the most blatant, crass, rageful envy of Psyche's great fortune. "Oh! cruel and unkind, unprofitable Fortune!"[3] exclaims one of them when she sees the magnificent dwelling in which Psyche lives, and when she realizes that Psyche's husband must be no less than a god, "I cannot any longer endure that such wealth and fortune should have fallen to one so unworthy. . . . If I am a woman and have a spark of life in me, I'll oust her from her fortune."[4] Feigning concern for Psyche, her sisters tell her:

> Ah! you are happy, for you live in blessed ignorance of your evil plight and have no suspicion of your peril. But we cannot sleep for the care with which we watch over your happiness and are torn with anguish for your misfortunes. For we have

learned the truth, and . . . we may not hide it from you. He that
lies secretly by your side at night is a huge serpent with a
thousand tangled coils; blood and deadly poison drip from his
throat and from the cavernous horror of his gaping maw . . . as
soon as your time has come, he will devour you with the ripe
fruit of your womb.[5]

But for their apparently evil nature, the sisters present a
paradox, because it is they who determine the subsequent
development of the story. They represent not only envy and
rage, but also a drive to consciousness – or, at least, the germ of
such a drive. Says Neumann:

Not that the sisters represent this consciousness, they are only
its shadowy, that is, negative precursor. But if Psyche succeeds
in attaining this higher level, it is only because she starts by
subordinating herself to the negative directive of her sisters. It
is only by breaking the taboo that Eros has imposed on her, by
responding to the seduction of her sisters, that she comes into
conflict with Eros.[6]

Indeed, the sisters do point out to Psyche a fact she has not
yet been able to face – namely, that she is in Eros' bondage:

For with all its rapture, is this existence in the sensual paradise
of Eros not an unworthy existence? Is it not a state of blind,
though impassioned, servitude, against which a feminine self-
consciousness . . . must protest, against which it must raise all
the arguments that are raised by the sisters? Psyche's existence
is a nonexistence, a being-in-the dark, a rapture of sexual sensuality which may fittingly be characterized as a being
devoured by a demon, a monster. Eros as an unseen fascination
is everything that the oracle of Apollo . . . has said of him, and
Psyche really is his victim.[7]

However, Neumann also notes that Psyche's living in the
"dark paradise" of Eros is not a uniquely feminine predicament. In stories of men's individuation, too, the danger of
"engulfment" and arrest at still immature levels of development occurs frequently. This danger is represented as a dark

and regressive, seductive though sensual paradise. An example is the gingerbread house of the tale Hansel and Gretel whose inviting sensuality hides a devouring monster in the form of the witch – just as for Psyche, Eros is the seductive devourer.

Indeed, the fact that men, too, are in danger of "being devoured" is evident in Eros' relationship with his mother, Aphrodite. This relationship is no less one of bondage than is the one between Eros and his bride. It is a relationship characterized by the goddess' possessive, incestuous hold on her son. Sending him out to ruin Psyche, the mother "with parted lips kissed her son long and fervently";[8] throughout the story, she remains full of jealousy toward the woman who would claim her son for herself; and calling him a "matricidal wretch," she berates the son who would separate from her by taking a woman of his own choosing.

For both Psyche and Eros, then, the task is to extricate themselves out of their bondage. Both need to evolve a more differentiated self, one that is no longer fused with the primary, parental, and institutional structure. As far as Eros is concerned, the story leaves it to the reader's imagination just how this differentiation is to be accomplished. But for Psyche, the story is quite specific.

Psyche must learn to be able to hold consciously the opposites that Eros combines in himself. For Eros is not only an ideal masculine figure, symbolized by light and sky and gold, but he is also an embodied being who partakes in the realms of earth and nature. In her state of darkness, Psyche attempts to deal with the tension of that opposition by a process of dissociation: "In the same body she hated the beast and loved the husband." She has not yet integrated the dual nature of her husband as man and god. Thus, the aspects of Eros that do not fit her idealization – his beastliness, his dragon nature – are split off and driven into unconsciousness.

As a result of this dualism, Psyche's love of Eros is not really a love of Eros the individual man but of the idealized figure. Psyche needs to give up that idealization and accept her husband as a person who unites in him paradoxical opposites.

Ultimately, this will permit her to emerge from her captivity and to develop a more individualized encounter with the masculine and with "otherness" – just as Eros must develop a more individuated relationship to Psyche.

The encounter with envy

At this juncture, the story delves into a vivid portrayal of envy, suggesting that this problematic but rarely discussed emotion is one of the major barriers individuals confront in their search for a more individuated self. In turn, it also suggests that one of the major mechanisms by which individuals extricate themselves from the prison of idealistic denial is to confront the dynamics of their envy.

For Psyche and Eros alike, that encounter with envy occurs in the form of the sisters. The sisters here really represent an aspect of the self. Since this aspect is too threatening for the developing self to integrate, however, it is split off and imaged as "otherness." In Chapters 3 and 4, I discussed this process of shadow formation and projective identification in Jungian theory. Here, the sisters are such shadow figures in which an unsavory feature of the self is represented as somebody other than the self.

How, then, does envy enter into the process of development? In their penetrating study of envy, Ann and Barry Ulanov[9] build on the work of Melanie Klein[10] and suggest that as the individual abandons aspects of the self and projects them onto others, he or she feels not only empowered but also, to an equal extent, diminished in the most painful way. That sense of diminishment has two seemingly paradoxical aspects. On the one hand, there is a sense of idealization: The other seems to be in the possession of all the "good" the self strives for. But on the other hand, rather than experiencing joy or admiration for these good qualities, the individual experiences them as a painful reminder of the good that the self has renounced. To ward off the painful feelings of being diminished, the self attempts to "spoil the goodness of the other" by hateful attacks on the individual imagined to possess the good the self has relinquished.

Envy is a plight for the envying person, but it is no less a plight for the person being envied. The envied person, too, may suffer from a "dread of the good." In an attempt to ward off the attacks of the envying one, he or she may withdraw from pursuing the good, instead turning against the self through guilt and self-blame. In either case, envy imposes powerful limits on positive self-expression, with the devastating result that further development may be halted.

Often, these two experiences may co-occur in the same individual, as they do in the myth of Psyche and Eros. Psyche's plight of finding herself in the attacked position of the envied person hides the fact that she herself is in an envying position: Her envy is the envy of the woman who is, or believes she is, disempowered in a masculine world. Freud has written widely on the problem of woman's envy of the masculine, arguing that it is a natural result of the realization of her physical and psychological state of mutilation. But although he has been perceptive about the phenomenon, he was less so about the exact dynamics that cause it to come about. In actuality, as suggested in Chapter 4, those dynamics are more complicated, and the results tragic not only for the development of women but of men as well. Seeing herself deprived of the possibility of expressing the full range of her abilities and her desires, the woman is forced to idealize in the man what she cannot acknowledge in herself. State Ulanov and Ulanov:

> Feeling so empty of goodness in themselves, they lunge violently at the men outside them or the [masculine] figures inside them, trying to fill up that emptiness. The envious woman seizes on a male to substitute for her own unclaimed femaleness. She wants what he has, or what she thinks he has: his power, his position, his sexual organ and whatever it may represent. She reduces him to a part-object – his penis and the symbolic meaning he assigns to it – and fails to see him as a man, or herself as a woman, either of them as a whole person in his or her own right.[11]

CRISIS AND INTEGRATION

Paradoxically, the only way out of this depersonalizing situation is to deidealize the masculine and to claim for the self the powers that belong to it. In the story, that situation is symbolized by Psyche's exposing Eros to the light. Thus, the relationship is no longer to take place in the dark. Even more, Psyche is to affirm her new emerging consciousness by cutting off Eros' head – the very seat of all those qualities of reason, mindful control, and willful self-assertion that culture associates with the masculine. Paradoxically, that act of self-assertion plays a profoundly transformative and beneficial role in the subsequent turn of the plot.

Note that the process of transformation here is represented as deidealizing the masculine. Since (as discussed at length in Chapter 4) the traditional model of reason is based on an inflation of the masculine features with a deflation of feminine ones, the process of rebalancing must involve a compensatory countermovement. The masculine must be dethroned from its heavenly seat and reconciled with earth, while the feminine must be upgraded and idealized. Indeed, the story suggests that, in the end, the feminine must rejoin the masculine as an element that is no less divine. This marriage between the divine feminine and the divine masculine, then, represents a necessary balancing in cultural and individual development.

Since such rebalancing requires that the masculine be deidealized, it is often thought to be typical of no more than a vengeful "matriarchal" consciousness, in which the feminine turns hatefully toward the more powerful masculine element. Indeed, Freud believed that envy is primarily a feminine problem, but the story of Psyche and Eros suggests that is by no means the case. Because if the sisters represent split-off self-aspects of Psyche, they also represent split-off aspects of Eros. Indeed, Eros' attacks on the sisters are no less vicious than those of the sisters on him. He warns his bride that the "wicked ghouls" and "false she-wolves are weaving some deep plot of sin against you";[12] he calls them "those hateful women, . . . your monstrous sisters, . . . those wicked women – sisters I may not call them – for they have conceived unnatural hate for you."[13] Thus, he vigorously opposes Psyche's emergent striving toward a more conscious way of being.

I have already commented on the paradoxical duality of envy, and that dual nature can turn into a blessing what is a peril to the further process of development. On the one hand, its intention is "spoiling the good"; on the other, it can be reflected back on the self as self-affirmation. This is possible as the individual allows himself or herself to feel the pain of loss consciously. Thus, though shadow material can be destructive if not assimilated to consciousness, it can be redemptive if it is brought into awareness.

In the Psyche story, the beneficial effects are symbolized by the light. Once she is allowed to see, Psyche is no longer enraged with hate and envy. Rather, these feelings are transformed into love and admiration as she gazes

> upon the beauty of that divine face and her soul drew joy and strength. She beheld the glorious hair of his golden head streaming with ambrosia, the curling locks that strayed over his snow-white neck and crimson cheeks, some caught in a comely tangle, some hanging down in front, others behind; and before the lightnings of their exceeding splendor even the light of the lamp grew weak and faint. From the shoulders of the winged god sprang dewy pinions, shining like white flowers, and the top most feathers, so soft and delicate were they, quivered tremulously in a restless dance. . . . His body was smooth and very lovely.[14]

Now, Psyche's love is no longer one of darkness, but one of knowing and consciousness.

But such knowledge carries its own dangers and painful moments. No longer "protected" by the distorting buffer of envy, the individual may feel cast out into a new and terrifying reality, one in which all the old comforts abandon him or her. This is why Jung associates the emergence of a new form of consciousness with a crisis. Similarly, Dabrowski[15] talks about a process of "positive disintegration," of dismantling the primary structure of development in such a way that a more mature secondary structure can emerge.

The myth of Psyche and Eros deals with this positive disintegration primarily through the symbolism of gender relatedness. I will examine this aspect in the chapter to follow. In the present chapter, however, I will emphasize the implications of that symbolism for our descriptions of the mind, thought, and self. Thus, just as Psyche's task is to deidealize the elevated view of the masculine, so a rebalancing of those functions of the mind that are often associated with the masculine and the feminine is characteristic of a move to a new sense of consciousness. Thus, the task is to reconcile the exalted dimension of logos – transcendent, unchanging, and abstract – with the devalued dimension of mythos – change and relatedness, symbolic meanings and organismic groundedness. I will examine in this and the following chapter how the individual turns this crisis into an opportunity for continued development.

TOWARD THE LATERAL MIND

Psyche's yearning for light and knowledge, I have argued, represents the emergence of a new model of mind and self in the individual's process of development. But the evolution of such a model is not just an individual task. It is also a broader, cultural task. Culturally, the search for a new, less competitive model of reality has become a wide-ranging enterprise spanning many disciplines. As a consequence, many have become interested in understanding how (and if) the individual can emerge out of the primary developmental structure and go on to develop more mature, autonomous, and balanced functioning.

Deconstructing logos

Up to nearly the beginning of this century, the model of the individual was framed in terms of the ideals of logos. The hope was to build knowledge on axiomatic foundations that seemed indisputable, and this ideal was captured in its most pure form by the language of logic and mathematics. In ancient times, the prototype of that model was the work of Euclid. When Euclid systematized all of the geometrical knowledge of his predecessors in the *Elements,* his work became not only the major text of mathematics and geometry, but the very model for scientific and objective thought. The importance of his work lay in the fact that here one dealt with a body of knowledge that was indubitably true and firm. It was not inductive knowledge, not derived from empirical generalizations, and not, therefore, subject to the "imperfection of the senses."[16]

The pursuit of geometrical knowledge – and the kinds of thought processes it permitted – subsequently was identified with rational thought, per se. Descartes believed that the ability to discern laws of geometry attested to the mind's power of rational insight. Kant, from a somewhat different angle, believed that the mind was endowed with Euclidean spatial forms and that to describe those forms was to gain insight into the mind's very sensibility. Thus, it was widely held that Euclidean statements spoke to any truth imaginable at all. According to the German logician Frege:

> The truths of geometry govern all that is spatially intuitable, whether actual or a product of our fancy. The wildest visions of delirium, the boldest inventions of legend and poetry, where animals speak and stars stand still, where men are turned to stone and trees turn into men, where the drowning haul themselves up out of swamps by their own topknots – all these remain, so long as they remain intuitable, still subject to the axioms of geometry.[17]

The core conviction was that the objective laws of logos would reveal ultimate truths, truths that were completely neutral and untainted by subjectivity. Therefore, for about 2 millennia the history of human thought was, in essence, the history of logic; that history, in the words of the philosopher Lakatos, was "essentially the history of criticizing and improving the deductive channels and destroying the inductive channels by making logic formal."[18]

Early in this century, however, the notion that thinking could be described in terms of completely universal and decontextualized truths began to be completely overhauled. That overhaul, to be sure, had begun with the claims of the 19th-century romantic philosophers, foremost among them Nietzsche and Schopenhauer. It was these individuals who pointed out that our views of what is rational also contain their shadow side: the contempt of vulnerability, the pursuit of power, the competitive fight of all against all. However, shortly after the turn of this century, the deconstruction of rationalism became not "merely" a romantic enterprise, but moved into the very bastions of rationalism.

It is not without a degree of irony that the erosion of the objectivist, logos-oriented view was initiated, in part, by the field of mathematics itself. A decisive blow to the rationalist doctrine was dealt, for example, in the form of the so-called limitative theorems of, among others, the mathematicians Skolem, Goedel, and Church.[19] These theorems pointed out that only relatively basic and perhaps even trivial matters could be framed in the closed deductive form that had been the hope of past philosophers. Once one moved into domains that were empirically richer, it was necessary to accept less formal, less deductive, more uncertain systems of thinking. In general, these theorems were interpreted as stating that truth is not a static and universal thing, but that it is best understood as a dynamic process, something that evolves, that is being constructed, and that is being continually redefined. Truth has, therefore, an explicit historical and developmental perspective, and is moved out of the realm of axioms and ideals into the very context of human practice. DeLong commented on this:

> The analogy of a game is useful in explaining [this notion]. . . .
> It often happens that a game is invented (and the rules are laid
> down which define that game), but at a later time a circumstance occurs for which the rules give no guidance. At this

point a decision has to be made as to what will henceforth be the rule concerning that circumstance. The decision might be made on the basis of fairness, whether it makes it a better spectator sport, whether it increases the danger, etc. . . . We are thus forced to define the notion of arithmetical truth historically; that is, it cannot be explicated once and for all but must be continually re-defined.[20]

This realization instigated a revolution. Some of this century's most famous philosophers went through this revolution, changing from the old form of the paradigm to a new one. One of those was Alfred North Whitehead who in his youth had, together with Bertrand Russell, set out to erect a logical system that once and for all would exclude individual sources of error by a rigorously axiomatized system of logic. Yet later in his life, he asserted that "an abstraction is nothing more than the omission of part of the truth."[21]

Ludwig Wittgenstein underwent a similarly dramatic change of mind – so much so, in fact, that it is customary to differentiate between the "early" and the "later" Wittgenstein. In his early work, the *Tractatus Logico-Philosophicus*, he had attempted to develop a completely formalized language from which all complex relationships could be reduced to their basic constituents. However, just when he was celebrated as one of the founders of this turn to formalism, he turned away from it. He now thought that words cannot be explained or understood in such an abstract context. Rather, he viewed them like tools that changed their meaning depending upon what one did with them. He introduced this notion in a celebrated passage:

It is like looking into the cabin of a locomotive. We see handles all looking more or less alike. (Naturally, since they are all supposed to be handled.) But one is the handle of a crank which can be moved continuously (it regulates the opening of a valve); another is the handle of a switch, which has only two effective positions, it is either off or on; a third is the handle of a brake lever, the harder one pulls on it, the harder it brakes; a fourth, the handle of a pump: it has an effect only so long as it is moved to and fro.[22]

Wittgenstein and other philosophers began a systematic deconstruction of the classical view of the nature of reason, which had held that there was a basic chasm between logos, the language of truth and rationality, and mythos, the language of desire. By purging rationality of the elements of mythos, these philosophers hoped that we would be able to assure an inevitable march toward progress and enlightenment.

But now, that fervently held belief gradually was revealed to harbor, if in hidden form, the very elements of mythos it had attempted to censor. Just as Freud had pointed out that rationality if used in excess turns into its opposite, irrationality, so the roots of the fervent idealization of logos were revealed to speak a language of desire. This is so because the prohibition of desire is itself an act of desire; the denial of community is itself an interpersonal attitude; and the belief in the inevitable emancipative power of logos is itself a myth.[23] All of these beliefs display, in fact, the exact structure of the hero myth I discussed in Chapters 3 and 4: The orientation toward power and competition and the denial of the body, the emotions, and the feminine – all form an integral part of that myth.

Rationality as myth

Plato's own allegory of the nature of reality and knowledge, the allegory of the cave,[24] reveals the basic elements of that heroic mythic narrative. In that widely quoted allegory, Plato suggests that humans are bound to remain in ignorance as long as we take as reality the play of shadows on the walls of the cave; only if we are freed from the darkness by force and dragged into the light will we be able to partake of an absolute reality of which the world of shadows is merely an illusory image.

In contrast to that view, however, a more modern evolving view gives up the notion that we can ever train our sight on the images of light and logos; instead, it might be better to say that these images, at best, are *only* revealed in the play of shadows. Rather than banishing those shadows to darkness and forgetfulness, like Psyche the modern individual must turn toward them and examine them to see if they, after all, contain redemptive features. Thus, quite like Psyche in our myth, it has become a critical task for contemporary culture to "dethrone" the exalted heroic view of reason by exposing its dark, shadow side. What, then, is that shadow side of reason? If the classical view had attempted to erect a language of reason that was free of the distortion of power, the influences of social experience, and the stirrings of bodily desire, modern analyses have begun to point out that the language of reason is often one obsessed with power and control. Consider this statement by George Boole, whose logic served as a model for Piaget:

> Were, then, the laws of valid reasoning uniformly obeyed, a very close parallelism would exist between the operation of the intellect and those of external Nature. Subjection to laws mathematical in their form and expression, even the subjection of absolute obedience, would stamp upon the two series one common character. The reign of necessity over the intellectual and the physical world would be alike complete and universal.[25]

On the one hand, one may read this statement (as intended by Boole) as an ode to the perfect harmony between thought and reality; on the other, one may also discern here a language of dominance and submission, of coercion and obedience.

Nozick has similarly argued that the language of traditional philosophy thus is permeated with coercive terms. He maintains that philosophy has tended carefully to select and prearrange its premises so as to lead the thinker to the conclusions intended:

> The language of philosophical art is coercive: arguments are *powerful* and best if they are *knockdown*, arguments *force* you to a conclusion, if you believe the premises you *have to* or *must* believe something, whether you want to believe it or not. A

successful philosophical argument, a strong argument, *forces* someone to a belief.[26]

Lakoff and Johnson,[27] in their important study of *Metaphors We Live By,* also suggest that metaphors of competition and even of war structure the ways in which we approach knowledge claims. Lakoff and Johnson think that such ways of speaking about knowledge are not "mere" metaphors, but that they reflect the way in which we actually tend to feel when engaging in discursive and argumentative activities. Thus, when we say that we win or lose an argument, or that we plan the strategy or attack of our argument, or when we feel our arguments are shot down, this is evidence that the basic experience of attack or surrender underlies the notion of dialogue. Further, our perception of reality is suffused with spatial metaphors in which reality is structured in terms of up and down, "up" being associated with fortune, power, and luck, and "down" with misfortune and lack of power. Even the envy and competition about claims to creativity discussed in Chapter 4 are evident when we see that knowledge is structured in terms of metaphors related to sexuality and birth: Thus we may talk about a seminal idea, about having incubated a thought, or given birth to a theory! And, this basic structuring of logos in terms of competition and envy has its parallel in the tendency to think of knowledge as a fixed entity: Often, that tendency is reflected in metaphors that speak about knowledge as a container, something that is not responsive to the interchange of individuals participating in communication.[28] Thus, knowledge often is viewed as a tool, an instrument rather than a process of communication.

Contemporary views of the mind have begun to return to the dimensions of mind and self abandoned by the classical view. This contemporary confrontation with the shadow elements of rationality is often referred to as a postmodern attitude.[29] If the earlier attitude was structured by a myth of the heroic ascent of reason, postmodernism, according to Lyotard, is characterized by a skepticism of that enlightenment narra-

tive. As a result of that incredulity, the dogma of the insep-
arability of the domains of logos and mythos is being
deconstructed. A view is emerging that holds truth to have
inferential elements that are located in the domain of mythos:
the discourses unique to a culture,[30] conventions that have
ritualized what we imagine,[31] the rhetorical and practical,[32]
the mythic and symbolic,[33] and the organic and emotional.[34]
In fact, so thorough is this deconstruction of the dogma of the
primacy of logos that the result has been a widespread relativism in which any unitary concept of reason is completely
denied. In fact, as the title of one recent compendium of the
thinking of major philosophers suggests, some individuals feel
that we have reached "The end of philosophy."[35]

Toward new narratives of the mind

Not all writers, however, see the concept of rationality as a
relic of the past and want to give it up completely. There continue voices in search of new standards of rationality. According to those voices, giving up the narrative of heroic rise and
its ideals of objective certainty and control does not imply that
we are left without a narrative altogether.[36] To assume that we
have lost all narrative structure is only a negation of the classical paradigm. As negation, it remains completely steeped in
that paradigm, rather than transcending it. A bit akin to
Dabrowski's[37] notion of "positive disintegration" discussed
earlier, these views imply that a necessary phase of
deconstruction must be followed by a phase that is oriented
toward reconstruction.

What, then, might a new narrative look like? I propose that
the story of Psyche and Eros gives a suggestive answer. Psyche
and Eros' old union fails because the heroic narrative provides
its main structure, and the feminine structure of surrender is
merely molded around that structure as its negation. But this
relationship of negation is not the only possible one. The relationship needs to be transformed into one of mutual affirmation, and thus Psyche feels driven to expose the contract of the

symbiotic relationship to light. How this traumatic gesture eventually leads to transformation is more fully outlined in the next chapter.

In the meantime, one example of such mutual affirmation is the example of play we discussed in Chapter 3. In play, there is no sharp boundary between subject and object. Instead a self and an other come together to create a new structure; that structure arises out of the cooperation between self and other, but cannot be reduced to either. Such a view involves a restructuring of our metaphor for knowledge: Rather than using core metaphors of control and competition, we can employ metaphors of playful cooperation. Indeed, Lakoff and Johnson suggest the metaphor of a dance, and note:

> Try to imagine a culture where arguments are not viewed in terms of war, where no one wins or loses, where there is no sense of attacking or defending, gaining or losing ground. Imagine a culture where an argument is viewed as a dance, the participants are seen as performers, and the goal is to perform in a balanced and aesthetically pleasing way. In such a culture, people would view arguments differently, experience them differently, carry them out differently, and talk about them differently.[38]

Is such a playful model of knowledge possible? One example of such a model of knowledge is a position that has been elaborated over the past decades in continental philosophy and that is known under the notion of hermeneutics. The term *hermeneutics* has its origins in biblical study, in particular in questions relating to how the Bible is to be interpreted. In the past century, Schleiermacher and Dilthey expanded the scope of the hermeneutic method, applying it to symbolic structures such as social practices, norms, and values – domains that, with their need for interpretation, appeared to be distinct from more "objective" approaches such as the natural sciences.[39]

With the realization in contemporary philosophy that issues of interpretation are not unique to the investigation of social norms, practices, and institutions, but also extend to the "natural" sciences, the hermeneutical method was further extended

as a method to deal with questions of truth claims most generally. One philosopher who has offered a particularly cogent
defense of the hermeneutic position is the German philosopher Gadamer. In *Truth and Method*,[40] Gadamer completely
rejects the notion that there is, in principle, a different method
that should orient the study of the sciences of meaning and the
objective sciences, since interpretation and norms are inherent
in the latter no less than they are in the former. Gadamer notes
that the problem with the classical paradigm is that such notions as objectivity and subjectivity, logos and mythos were
seen in dualistic opposition. In this way, the notion of truth
and objectivity was completely removed from the domain of
mythos, which as a result appeared as a mere subjective chaos.
But, notes Gadamer, play has structure, too – a structure, however, that is larger than any one player. It is a structure, in fact,
that emerges out of play, when individuals submit themselves
to the interpersonal process of play. In that process, old notions
of control no longer work. Rather, the image is one of process
and emergence, of something new and unpredictable being
created. Here, the core structure is that of a dialogue, not that
of a monologue in which one is in complete control:

> Now I contend that the basic constitution of the game, to be
> filled with its spirit – the spirit of buoyancy, freedom and the
> joy of success – and to fulfill him who is playing, is structurally
> related to the constitution of the dialogue in which language is
> a reality. When one enters into dialogue with another person
> and then is carried along further by the dialogue, it is no longer
> the will of the individual person, holding itself back or expos-
> ing itself, that is determinative. Rather, the law of the subject
> matter is at issue in the dialogue and elicits statement and
> counterstatement and in the end plays them into each other.[41]

Note that such a conception of knowledge gives up the opposition on which the heroic narrative of knowledge is based.
No longer at issue is a division of reality into active and passive, spirit and matter, masculine and feminine. Play requires
that we adopt an attitude of surrender, of pathos, of being
receptive. We open ourselves to change, to being changed. Yet

this receptivity is not merely passive; it requires an agent solidly centered in his or her viewpoint. In the words of Gadamer again:

> But do not make me say what I have not in fact said; and I have *not* said that when we listen to someone or when we read we ought to forget our own opinions or shield ourselves against forming an anticipatory idea about the content of communication. In reality, to be open to "other people's opinion," to a text, and so forth, implies right off that they are *situated* in my system of opinions, or better, that I situate myself in relation to them.[42]

Gadamer's view here integrates two notions that until now have been held to be in opposition: the notion that, on the one hand, truth is inevitably linked to different perspectives and that, on the other, it is possible to maintain faith in a rational enterprise. To accept such an integration, we must accept however, that there is no *ultimate* truth, but that truth really cannot be separated from the process of communication. The basic metaphor becomes that of cooperative play, subjective engagement, and trust rather than the old metaphors of envy, objective certainty, and control. In Gadamer's view, the old split between objectivity and subjectivity is completely rejected. Instead, objectivity becomes a form of intersubjective engagement. That engagement gives up individual claims to truth, relying instead on a supra- and transpersonal principle.

Gadamer's hermeneutical principle has not gone without criticism. Both Habermas[43] and Apel,[44] point out that the process of communication does not necessarily result in objective consensus. It is possible that the very process of communication is systematically distorted, for example, when discussion takes place under conditions of force and coercion. In fact, many forms of discourse are performed under ideological commitments to repression, such as those related to race, gender, and social class. Moreover, such commitments may exist on a fairly unconscious level, side by side with a conscious commitment to undistorted communication. Hence, a theory of truth must also supply an analysis of how discourses become systematically distorted.

However, Gadamer's position would not deny that distortions are possible, and that not all communication is *ideal* communication. But it is also consistent with his views that if individuals have an attitude of mutual respect during the process of the discourse about truth, then they will be able to reflect on distortions that may have entered the discourse. Hence, I suggest that to enter into the process of communication with an attitude of openness and playful exploration implies that individuals are also able to remove gradually whatever barriers to such open communication become evident.

The notion that an open attitude toward communication will gradually change the very process of communicating is similar to Piaget's position. Piaget maintains that there are certain self-correcting features about the process of communicating, and that these self-correcting features over time will eliminate systematic distortions from the communication process. Entering a dimension of time, here, becomes important. Truth is never final and determined; it is not a product, but an ever-evolving process. It is a dance of interacting subjectivities, performed under objective rules of mutual tolerance and respect. Individuals surrender to that dialectic of interacting subjectivities and permit themselves to be changed in the process.

Individuals entering into this "hermeneutical circle," then, exemplify an altogether new approach to rationality. As I pointed out elsewhere,[45] individuals operating within that model are able to function with maximum integrity within an environment of high epistemological certainty. Their standards of "objectivity" are based, not on a concrete product, but rather on a more abstract process through which they strive for truth. That process is oriented not only by a vision of transcendent ideals but also by a deep understanding of the constraints under which all individuals function in reaching for those ideals. Hence, the resulting concept of rationality is a truly dialectical one: Individuals realize that only by working with the tension between objective and subjective factors can they engage in the search for truth.

In many ways, a hermeneutical view of mind and knowledge leads us full circle back to the discussion in Chapter 2. If classical theories of the mind were based on a process of dissociation of functions and of disenchantment, modern theories are based on a reversal. This reversal, however, is not at all regressive. Instead, the dualities are rejoined on a more complex plane, and on that more complex plane, such polarities as self and other, objective and subjective, and reason and desire ultimately are no longer logical opposites, but support each other.[46] They play off each other and mutually influence and transform each other; they are no longer vertically related in a model of control, but laterally within one of creative transformation. Thus, a bit like the ancient thinker, the individual can partake in a reality that is evolving and animated. However, that "reenchantment"[47] is no longer opposed to a rational view of life. Now, the self integrates the tension between "rational" and "nonrational" poles, and that tension is understood to be a precondition for creative transformation. If previously the dualities of objectivity, self and other, mind and body were put in opposition, now the individual realizes that reason bridges the tension between the concrete and the abstract, the emotive and the cognitive, the time-bound and the eternal, the immanent and the transcendent.

ADULTHOOD AND THE TRANSFORMATION OF REASON

This discussion of the notion of rationality suggests that we are in the middle of evolving an altogether new concept of rationality, one in which the ancient dualites of objectivity and subjectivity and the associated ones of self and other are being transcended. Such a new concept of rationality and human nature is not an enterprise of philosophy only. Indeed, it is an enterprise that characterizes a far-reaching change of worldview that is affecting our culture at large. We can find many individuals elaborating such dialectical structures. Indeed, I suggest in this section that the attempt at such elaboration forms a normal component of continued development in adulthood; many individuals have found fault with traditional views of reason and maturity and are evolving a new concept of mature functioning.

The growth of relativism

I have discussed in Chapter 3 evidence to suggest that the hierarchical, vertical, and objectivist model of reason may be quite suited to understanding what youth can do. But as individuals move from youth into mature adulthood, many begin to question that model and its dualisms between objectivity and subjectivity. One of the first studies to address this issue was one by William Perry.[48] Perry selected undergraduate men who had just entered Harvard and followed them through college. He was interested to find out how these individuals made sense of the vastly diverse information they confronted when coming to a college environment: How did these youths understand what they were going through?

Perry suggests that, when they entered college, these individuals had a particular view of the nature of knowledge that fit quite well with the traditional concept of rationality. They believed that they were in college to learn what was "right" or "true." There was little awareness of the fact that thinking often involves gray areas, or that what we are told often is filtered through the perspective of a particular teacher, expert, or other authority figure. Instead, these students believed it was their task to learn the "right" facts and to repeat those facts to the professors. The self was not understood to have an active role in this process, but a rather passive one of recording what is expected. Perry calls that perspective "dualist" because these individuals sharply polarized between "right" and "wrong" knowledge. That dualism further led to dividing individuals into those who were on the "right" or the "wrong" side of knowledge, too.

That dualist view soon became a source of stress, however.

Typically, a youth would discover that professors expected something other than the concrete mirroring back of facts. Or he might realize, with a sense of alarm, that different professors in no way agreed about what was the "right" way to describe facts. At first, these individuals thought that perhaps they were being tricked; perhaps the professors did not convey knowledge in a straightforward manner, obfuscating it so that they, the students, would figure it out on their own. However, they soon began to understand that the problem was not the professors, but their own dualistic view of the nature of knowledge. Thus, the view that there were safe, "objective" facts that were somehow outside the realm of human subjectivity began to crumble, giving way to a position of *relativism.*

In contrast to dualists, relativists give up the view that there are safe and objective ways of knowing. Instead, they assert that all knowledge is subjective, and that it is impossible to say anything for certain unless one understands the subjective viewpoint from which it is said. Perry notes that this relativist position greatly expanded the sense of active involvement in the learning process. Now, the individual could examine facts and theories, weigh and compare different points of view. These youths now began to realize that the self is not a passive, voiceless entity who merely absorbs "objective" knowledge, but that knowledge is a human activity in which each subjective self is involved.

Relativism, however, confronts the individual with a new dilemma. How, in the face of diversity and subjectivity, can one make choices? How can we decide, reach closure, take a committed stand? At first, individuals would deny that commitment was a possible choice, but eventually, they would reach a position in which choice was possible again. This, according to Perry, reflected a new and transformed model of rationality, in which the old notion of objective knowledge was wedded to subjective engagement and commitment:

> Reason reveals relations within any given context; it can also compare one context with another on the basis of metacontexts established for this purpose. But there is a limit. In the end,

reason itself remains reflexively relativistic, a property which turns reason back upon reason's own findings. In even the farthest reaches then reason will leave the thinker with several legitimate contexts and no way of choosing among them – no way at least that he can justify through reason alone. If he is still to honor reason he must now also transcend it; he must affirm his own position from within himself in full awareness that reason can never completely justify him or assure him.[49]

The advantage of this realization is that the individual now can become a much more active participant in the process of knowledge. There is vastly increased tolerance for diversity, yet the self can be securely anchored in an own viewpoint that is understood to have strong subjective elements. Thus, subjectivity in self and other are understood to be valid and necessary.

Beyond relativism

Perry's work has been of extraordinary influence in the study of adult cognitive capacities. However, not all have agreed with his implications that the mark of true maturity is a return to a new, if more educated, form of subjectivism – the very stance of postmodernism we discussed already. Rather, several individuals suggest that once someone has confronted subjectivism and relativism, he or she often begins to wonder again about the nature of objectivity – though a notion of objectivity that is expanded and transformed.

An example of this search for a new concept of objectivity is the research of Kitchener and King.[50] These authors worked with individuals ranging in age from 16 to 34. The research participants were given problems that required making judgments about controversial issues. One problem, for example, asked that they take a stand on the controversy of religious versus scientific accounts of evolution: Did they believe the religious claim that God had created all life in a single instant, or did they believe the scientific account of gradual biological evolution?

Kitchener and King observed that the youngest individuals behaved very similarly to what Perry had found: They thought dualistically, believing that there was only one possible truth. For example, a subject might say:

Subject: I believe in my religion. God created man as a person. We did not evolve.
Interviewer: On what do you base that point of view?
Subject: On my religious background, what I've been told.
Interviewer: Can you tell me more about how that happened, the process of learning about that?
Subject: I was taught by my parents and the church. Its worked into me that way.[51]

What is characteristic of beliefs at this level, according to Kitchener and King, is that the individual does not admit of doubt and uncertainty. Knowledge is assumed to simply exist; beliefs are firm and unshakable and the individual does not see any need to justify them. He or she thinks they are objective, yet they really are completely rooted in the individual's subjective background. Thus, even though the individual believes in an objective truth that is not contaminated by his or her subjective beliefs, in fact objectivity and subjectivity are completely fused.

That sense of fusion and certainty gradually opens, however, as individuals mature. For example, individuals first begin to realize that knowledge is not always firm. At first, they cope with that problem by assuming that even though the self may not know the truth, legitimate authorities do. Soon, however, comes the awareness that not even legitimate authorities may know the truth. That realization ushers in a period of relativism where individuals completely deny the possibility of any objective truth. Here, for example, is the response of one subject:

Interviewer: Can you say one point of view is better and another worse?
Subject: No, I really can't. . . . It depends on your belief, since there is no way of proving either one.

Interviewer: Can you say that one is more accurate than the other?
Subject: No, I can't. I believe they are both the same as far as accuracy.
Interviewer: Would you go so far as to say your opinion is the right one?
Subject: No.
Interviewer: But yet you believe so strongly in it – that's why I am asking . . .
Subject: I am the type of person who would never tell anyone that their idea is wrong – if they had searched, well, even if they hadn't searched, even if they just believe in it – that's cool for them.
Interviewer: Can you say that one opinion is better and one is worse?
Subject: No, not at all. It's better for them and like their opinion would probably be worse for me.[52]

From this position of quite radical relativism and subjectivism, individuals begin to wonder again, however, about whether there may not be truths that are more objective than others. Even though they realize that nobody, not even legitimate authorities, actually know what is the objective truth on most issues, these individuals realize that nevertheless they can tell more from less objective evidence by the way it has been gathered and evaluated. Here, for example, is what such an individual might say:

Interviewer: When people differ about matters such as this, how does one make a determination about what is correct?
Subject: Again, how well thought-out the positions are, at what level one chooses to argue and support the position, what kinds of reasoning and evidence one would use to support it, how it fits into the rest of one's world view or rational explanations . . . how consistent the way in which one argues on this issue is as compared with other issues.[53]

Here, then, truth becomes a much more tentative idea: an ideal that we work toward, that always has subjective elements, but that nevertheless can be judged by a set of prescriptions and procedures. It has not so much to do with objective "facts" but with an attitude of critical thinking, careful evaluation, openness to falsification and change.

Kitchener and King found that with increasing age, individuals tended to move from the less to the more mature (i.e., less dualistic and absolute, and toward a reflective notion of objectivity) positions. This finding was repeated in follow-up research separated by 3-year intervals, resulting most recently in 9-year longitudinal data. Overall, this research demonstrates progressive development of reflective thinking at least into middle age (the highest age level sampled thus far in that research).

Since Perry and Kitchener and King, a number of researchers have developed similar tasks and shown that as individuals develop beyond adolescence and youth and into mature adulthood, they become less dualistic and better able to think in terms of change over time, comparisons of contrasting viewpoints, and the relationship of thinking to context. Such changes in thinking are referred to as *dialectical thinking*.[54] This form of thinking can have implications for many everyday kinds of tasks.

One form of dialectical thinking that has been studied is the ability to understand that opposites can stand in a complimentary rather than contradictory relationship.[55] For example, before this century, physicists thought that light had the properties either of a wave or of matter, and tried to find out which was the "true" description. In this century, however, physicists proposed that such descriptions can form opposing though complementary ways of describing physical reality. Such thinking is of great importance in everyday life, as when we ask whether something is due to biology or culture, whether our behavior is determined by free will or by circumstances out of our control, or whether something is "in the mind" or "in the body." Reich did research on such questions and found that older individuals are better able to think in terms of complementarity. For example, Reich asked children, adolescents, and adults whether a pianist had achieved her level of skill as a result of her genetic endowment or of her diligent practice. A child aged 8 years claimed that "inborn is important!" An adolescent aged 15 suggested that either practice or endowment could be the cause. But an adult aged 66 asserted that no either-or answer was possible: "None is right. To me, it is like a very complex computer program; it takes different kinds of input at different points, but still it is only one program . . . practice or endowment do not add up, and one cannot replace the other."[56]

Kitchener and King's work suggests that as individuals mature from young to mature adulthood, they develop a dialectical relationship between such concepts as objective and subjective. At first quite polar and dualistic, these notions gradually become integrated into an understanding that subjectivity is always involved in so-called objective enterprises. However, there is a critical difference between the individual who is "merely" subjective from the one who can embrace both subjectivity and objectivity. The latter knows something the former is not aware of: Objectivity requires that one present one's subjectivity in a particular way. One must be willing to accept certain procedures, to be open to criticism, and to accept that by engaging in the process of inquiry one becomes changed.

Hermeneutical thinking

This same suggestion also comes from a study conducted by myself and my collaborators, in which we were interested in how adolescents and adults made sense of the subjective elements that are involved in many apparently "purely" objective and factual problems. For example, in a study examining problem solving in preadolescents, adolescents, and adults through their 40s, we[57] presented individuals with a simple logical problem that was embedded in a brief narrative. The problems were such that individuals could respond literally by only considering the problem's logical dimensions, or by focusing on the problem's interpretation, or both. Consider the following problem:

> John is known to be a heavy drinker, especially when he goes to parties. Mary, John's wife, warns him that if he gets drunk one

more time, she will leave him and take the children. Tonight, John is out late at an office party. John comes home drunk. Does Mary leave John?

Our preadolescents and most adolescents adopted a purely logical approach. They were not aware that what one concludes from such a problem depends on how one has interpreted it in the first place (e.g., if Mary is likely to follow up on a threat or not). Instead, they simply affirmed that Mary would leave – and asked to justify their answers, they merely stated, "because it says so." Thus, they were extremely literal and text-dependent. They behaved as if conclusions sprang automatically from the text, rather than requiring the interpretation of a reader. Indeed, when asked to provide a rationale for their answers, they seemed perplexed at being asked to justify the obvious. They simply pointed to the text, stating, "it says so right here!"

Older adolescents, in contrast, *did* have a beginning awareness that conclusions are related to the self's interpretation. Now, individuals realized that there was a degree of ambiguity to the problems. Their reaction to that realization was, however, an attempt to eliminate it. They seemed to feel that the ambiguity was merely a result of an error they had made rather than inherent in the problem's structure. As a result, they increased their effort with enhanced attention and concentration.

Many young adults *did* realize that interpretation entered into the problem. Even so, however, they were not able to provide an integrative solution by which both interpretation and a logical argument mattered. Instead, they erected a dualism that talked about the problems in terms of two kinds of opposing strategies. One strategy was based on an approach called "logical," "objective," "mathematical," or "rational," while the second was called "subjective," "emotional," or a matter of "opinion." These strategies were seen as antagonistic, often suggesting a struggle between two inner voices. Consider this answer of a man in his 30s:

The key is "one more time." Mary's simple statement – if she meant it – is weighted off of John's drunkenness. The logic is clear, clean – if you choose to ignore human dimensions. If A happens, then B will result – a gross simplification of cause and effect, or event and result – again, when my creative urge is not suppressed, I can misfire, hear what I want, distort the story and place a wrong answer, firmly convinced that it is correct.

In this man, the inner struggle discussed by Neumann remains quite stark and cannot be integrated. Only a very few individuals, indeed, were able to give up the dualism between the objective and the subjective and assert that solving problems depends on a combination of both.

I suggest that such attempts to integrate notions of objectivity and subjectivity are examples of just the kind of hermeneutics discussed in the previous section. Here, the individual recognizes that knowing is not just a matter of making logical conclusions from propositions, but also requires knowledge about how adults communicate. That knowledge includes those things that motivate adults from outside the domain of propositions, yet structure their interpretation of a problem so that, even if both people are equally competent logically, they nevertheless can come up with different solutions, given their different subjective viewpoints. Yet at the same time, hermeneutics also suggests that individuals nevertheless do not remain locked in these subjective perspectives. Rather (and perhaps a little paradoxically), coming to know objectivity requires that individuals be able to coordinate their subjective perspectives. It is this knowing – that objectivity is not something outside of subjectivity, but consists of the way in which subjectivity is expressed – that is a precondition for objective inquiry. In this way of knowing, it is possible to commit ourselves to cooperative and dialogical ways of approaching inquiry. Thus, ultimately, we realize that objectivity is not at all outside the arena of subjectivity; rather, it is a way in which we coordinate our subjectivities, following particular methods and disciplines in doing so.

I propose, therefore, to call that kind of thinking, and the kinds of actions it supports, *hermeneutical thinking*. I propose, too, that such a hermeneutical level constitutes the hallmark of mature thinking. This proposal is in line with a growing body of research literature indicating that, as they become more aware of issues of interpretation and subjectivity in the process of knowing, adults are better able to integrate the subjective dimension of rationality with what thus far has been believed to be objective.[58]

Thus, I suggest that many adults evolve a model of knowing in which rationality and the subjective partake in a most intimate relationship. Yet they also come to understand that this ideal, though a rational requirement, is often violated in reality. But this very awareness can be held as a paradoxical tension; and this tension constitutes a dynamic force that motivates the individual to examine such distortion, with the goal of removing it from the process of inquiry. Thus, adults begin to realize that the business of rationality is always intertwined with a language of affect and desire. Still, it is possible to unravel and reweave this fabric of intertwined strands if one continually aims to differentiate the notions of valid rational dialogue from distorted dialogue. In so doing, individuals elaborate a deeper and deeper view of the nature of subjective selves and, correspondingly, a richer view of how these selves can interface in objective inquiry. This view is truly dialectical: As the understanding of subjectivity deepens, so it also can be related to more powerful rational structures and, thus, presented in a more "rational" form.

THE REENCHANTMENT OF ADULT THOUGHT

But are the changes in concepts of the subjective and objective just discussed not perhaps rather abstract; are these issues debated by philosophers really of concern to the fabric of our daily lives? To these questions I would reply that such changes are of concern not only to the philosopher but saturate the lives of the layperson as well. In everyday life, they find expression in terms of what Broughton[59] has called "naive epistemologies" – commonsense theories of knowledge held by all of us, and giving structure to our daily interactions.

In adulthood, then, such naive epistemologies become restructured. What once appeared to be nonrational becomes integrated into our notion of what is rational. This process, then, reverses the process of disenchantment we discussed in Chapter 2. The result is a "reenchantment" of adult thought, and this reenchantment has several dimensions.

Selves in transformation

One consequence of the onset of hermeneutical thinking is that it breaks the isolation of the traditional, logos-identified thinker and relates him or her back to a sense of place, history, and community. The self emerges out of a sense of static universalism and moves into a view of reality that embraces diversity, change, and transformation. Such a process of reorganizing a sense of reality was first identified by Kohlberg[60] and Riegel.[61] Both point out that while young adults often are concerned with the stability of conventional structures of thought, more mature adults are more interested in how to critique and possibly transform them. Kohlberg, in particular, shows how these issues are played out in the area of moral dilemmas. In their youth, adults often reason out moral issues in terms of a conventional logic that is aimed at the maintenance of the traditional order. But some years later these same adults are concerned that conventions are not necessarily moral, and that one needs to evolve a broader perspective within which to judge issues of morality. Thus, these adults have developed a sense of morality as something more than a mere faithful replication of what is generally considered moral; instead, they have become concerned with how to create transformation that is aimed at fostering more general levels of moral functioning.

Kohlberg's notion of postconventional thought and morality has been criticized as widely as it has been applauded, since it easily leads into the slippery waters of how to legislate what is "really" objective, and who is to legislate such judgments. Thus, there is sometimes a fine line between an individual who moves on to a more mature concept of what is "objective," and one who simply claims to possess such understanding! Nevertheless, as Loevinger has recently pointed out, the notion of postconventional thought captures an important folk understanding of the nature of an individual with a mature morality. That understanding is reflected in such terms as "conscientious objection" or "civil disobedience." Like the concept of postconventional thinking, it suggests that the mature individual does distinguish what is merely a convention from what seems to correspond to some more general laws of human nature.[62]

Kohlberg's notion of postconventional thought was primarily developed in the area of morality. Since Kohlberg's early work, however, it has become apparent that the processes Kohlberg outlined are much broader than morality per se. Kohlberg had assumed that part of the progression in moral values was due to the fact that, as the individual grows to maturity, he or she becomes less dependent on others for self-definition. This decrease in dependency for Kohlberg was relative, however. It implied that the individual became less dependent on immediate others whose values defined the self, and better able to relate to more abstract agencies: groups, communities, institutions, societies, and even humanity in general. Thus, Kohlberg dealt, in effect, with an expanding definition of the self in terms of a more and more abstract and broad social radius.

To say, however, that this self-definition becomes broader and more abstract is not to say that it is not somehow deeply felt or real in a personal sense. Erikson, in his theory of the life course, has suggested a somewhat similar movement. Erikson maintains that, as the individual grows into mature adulthood, he or she becomes less concerned with the immediate survival of the self and more with that of others. For example, major concerns of young adults may be to establish careers and a level of success, and to find the love and emotional security provided by intimate relationships. However, the older adult, at least ideally, becomes better able to invest the self in the well-being of others: of the younger generation, of society at large, of a vision he or she holds about a possible future for other generations.

Erikson's concept of "generativity" dovetails nicely with the studies we have reviewed in the previous section. Perry's work, for example, suggests that young adults, far from having reached the epitome of wisdom, still very much rely on the guidance and authority of those more knowledgeable and mature. Thus, there is a need for a generation of mature adults who can parent a generation of more youthful ones. In turn, Erikson's work also suggests the damaging and even catastrophic consequences for society of a generation of adults who grow old without necessarily gaining in maturity; as he put it, not every individual ages into an "elder," but many become merely "elderly."[63]

Despite their importance, Erikson's notions have not stimulated much research. One reason may be that continuities from stage to stage of life were not well enough articulated in his theory to lend themselves to measurable observations. But Kohlberg's concepts have influenced several writers to attempt to flesh out how the self evolves through these successively broader circles. For example, in his book *The Evolving Self*, Kegan proposes such a theory of an expanding self. For Kegan, increasing cognitive development has the result that the individual gradually differentiates from a primary attachment relationship that provides an original holding matrix within which all cognitive and organic activity is regulated. Eventually, he or she acquires the ability for more autonomous self-regulation. Before the conventional level, the child can control impulses but still is lacking in his or her ability for social coordination. The strength of the conventional level is that a more genuinely shared reality, based on the coordination of social perspectives, emerges. However, the self remains fused with an interpersonal and then institutional matrix, and the ability to experience distinctness and an individuated self remains limited. That capacity to maintain a more autonomous sense of selfhood emerges at the final stage, when self and other can be understood as entities that transcend interpersonal and institutional meanings. Thus, both a more authentic sense of selfhood and a deeper capacity for intimacy can result.

Other authors have pointed out that such changes in the self also affect the kinds of values the self affirms. For example, Armon[64] studied adolescents' and adults' responses to such questions as how to live an ethical life, and how to find meaning in one's work. In her study, conventional individuals think that ethical values are those that promote mutuality and a sense of happiness and success in the immediate social environment. Postconventional individuals, however, think that values must be rooted in something deeper than our immediate well-being and relationships to others. These individuals are concerned with defining a wider, more principled conception – one that has to do with a larger view of human nature and is rooted in a view of universal human interrelatedness and humanitarian concerns. A similar progression happens when individuals are asked to judge about the meaning of "good" work. For the conventional individual, the meaning of work derives primarily from personal enjoyment, financial security, and social utility. But for the postconventional individual, the meaning of work derives from achieving a balance of creative self-expression and the value one's work has in terms of its impact on society or humanity.

In my own ongoing study of changes in individuals' conceptions of self and others,[65] we find that younger or less mature individuals frame self and others in terms of a conventional perspective. In that perspective, self and others can be described in terms of an organized, codified, and abstract set of role expectations. Such role expectations are important for smoothly functioning institutions, such as family, work, and community. Conventional individuals see others from a static perspective – a perspective that becomes transformed in older and/or more mature adults. At that more developed level, the institutional values become susceptible to doubt and criticism – for example, such values can be "carried too far." Instead, a dynamic perspective evolves in which descriptions of self and others convey in vivid language the unique and evolving experience of individuals within the context of their particular life histories. Lives now are understood in the context of multiple frames – cultural, social, and psychological, for example. There is keen insight into the psychological dynamics that are at the root of human diversity, yet an understanding that such diversity appears to be regulated by a common human heritage.

Fowler[66] has also extended similar concepts to his study of religious thinking. Fowler shows that before they reach conventional thinking, individuals have an exceedingly magical and concrete conception of god. At the conventional level, the conception becomes more abstract, and the individual understands that god exemplifies relatively abstract values such as love, mercy, justice, and so forth. However, the orientation is based on acceptance of cultural values with only little critical evaluation: Religion now is oriented toward maintaining dogma and interpersonal validation. At this level, individuals also may become invested in their view of their own religion as having a "right" and privileged perspective on life. In contrast, the postconventional individual becomes critical of conventional religion. Instead, she or he evolves a perspective that is broader, that examines what different religious paths may have in common. Thus, many individuals come to realize that individual conventional religious frameworks form separate though equivalent paths toward more universal spiritual goals. At the highest level, such individuals may often appear to be saintly; yet, they also can become the target of violent fundamentalist hatred, because they seem to embody heretical attitudes. An example is Gandhi, who was dedicated to teaching a universal spiritual message but eventually was shot by a religious fundamentalist.

All of the various theories discussed emphasize that, as an ideal of maturity, individuals expand their view of the relationship of the self to the community. At first merely personal, that community becomes more and more extended and finally encompasses all of humankind. Overall, these various theories have spawned an impressive body of studies to support their claims. Whether one examines moral thinking or ego development, evidence suggests that before they reach adulthood, individuals tend to think in terms of conventional standards and ideals. Thereafter, some (but not all) adults move on to develop more encompassing forms of judgment. Even though not all adults move on to this level, it is interesting to note that those who do tend to be relatively mature adults, individuals over the age of 30.[67]

Why should some but not all adults move on to transcending narrower convention-based systems of thinking? One reason is that this is a complex form of thinking that itself appears to be related to levels of intelligence and education.[68] Thus, only those with relatively high levels of intelligence may be capable of the kind of complex processes that go into postconventional thinking. In a related vein, whether an individual displays this form of thinking will depend on whether there is a supportive culture that fosters it. Traditionally and currently, for example, many business organizations and many educational and religious institutions themselves may have fostered conventional and closed forms of thinking. Indeed, we have seen throughout this book that the notion of conventional values amounted to a cultural and philosophical ideal. Such closed cultural ideals may well set limits on what most adults are capable of achieving.

There are also more personal reasons why individuals may not move on to more advanced levels of thinking. As noted in Chapter 3, as individuals move along in their process of development, the result is not inevitably an increase in flexibility. Sometimes, enhanced cognitive powers are put in the service of increased defensiveness, as when we build more and more complex systems of rationalization (amounting, even, to elaborate theories!). Thus, an increase in rigidity rather than flexibility can be the result of growing older. We will deal with this issue of barriers to development in Chapters 6 and 7.

Symbolic thinking

Kohlberg's approach to morality and values has remained primarily guided by a search for rational universal principles. By such principles, the individual, as it were, searches further and further outward in an attempt to come up with a broader and more flexible base on which to base his or her thinking. However, as noted in the previous section, that "outward" movement of necessity goes along with an inward shift in which the individual becomes more and more concerned with the conditions of human subjectivity. Hence, the individual learns to see through and beyond the "objective" to encode underlying conditions of human subjectivity. As a consequence, an epistemological shift is necessitated in which the organismic and inner dimensions are successively upgraded, permitting the individual to evolve a lateral or dialogic structure between rational and nonrational ways of processing.[69]

In my own research, I have applied this notion of an epistemological shift to an examination of how individuals of different ages process information, for example, when reading texts or stories. This work follows up on the earlier view by Neugarten that middle and later adulthood bring a turn inward,[70] and expands on that view by adding that such an inward turn brings specific cognitive consequences. For the young adult, information is seen as an outer given that one attempts to reproduce with a minimum infusion of one's own self. Hence, young adults are apt to have a literal, text-dependent bias. In contrast, middle and older adults relate to text in a more interpretive and psychological mode. As the individual realizes that information is not independent of an interpreter – a self who reads and who infuses self into a text – the individual turns more to the landscape of human motivations and intentions that determines how texts are generated and interpreted. Hence, these adults may become experts at the processing of information relating to subjective processes and inner dynamics. Although this processing style will result in deficits in tasks that require more objective and formal ways of processing, it may be an advantage to ones that specifically require more psychological ways of processing.

This shift from a more text-dependent mode to one that is more interpretive and subjective was shown in a series of studies about individuals' rendition and interpretation of narratives.[71] For example, in one study adults in their 20s and their 70s were told to provide either a detailed recall or a summary of a fable about a crane who put its neck down a wolf's throat to dislodge a bone stuck there, but who, when asking for the promised reward, was told to be glad to have gotten away with its life. The young adults in both conditions produced detailed, almost verbatim, reproductions of the fable. But the older adults only did so if specifically instructed to recall as much as they possibly could. When asked, however, to provide a summary, they were concerned with a completely different kind of recall. One older adult, for example, gave this response:

> The moral of the story as I understood it was that people should not seek a reward for their well doing, but to be content with having done a good deed. It also depicts a certain shrewdness as noted by the wolf who sought help in time of need but was unwilling to give of himself, even in a small way, to show appreciation of the help he had received from the crane. Many times people who do good deeds receive only a spiritual reward for their well doing.[72]

What was interesting about this style of responding was that it reflected little of the actual detail of the story. Yet, the essential meaning was coherently conveyed and meaningfully related to the actions of the story protagonists. Moreover, meaning was framed in terms of an overall moral or spiritual meaning. Thus, these older individuals were not so much interested in the specific actions of each protagonist but in what these actions had to say about the human condition in general.

Similar results were also found in a study by Adams, who gave her sample a Sufi story about a stream that was about to run dry in the desert and its encounter with the wind that saved it from drying up. The adolescents focused primarily on literal renditions. For example, here is what a 13-year-old said:

> Once there was a stream. The stream made a journey and was stopped by the desert. When the stream tried to pass the desert it was absorbed by the sand. A voice said that the wind had to carry the stream over the desert. The stream doubted it but later agreed to let the wind carry him over. The wind carried the stream over and the stream never forgot what the voice said.[73]

Middle-aged adults were less interested in the text's literal base, but instead focused on the implied psychological meanings as illustrated by the response of a 39-year-old:

> I believe what this story was trying to say was that there are times when everyone needs help and must sometimes make changes to reach their goals. Some people may resist change for a long time until they realize that certain things are beyond their control and they need assistance. When this is finally achieved and they can accept help and trust from someone, they can master things even as large as a desert.

The oldest adults produced protocols similar in spirit to those of the middle-age adults, though highly condensed, as shown in these responses from a 65-year-old and a 70-year-old, respectively:

> The essence of the story is that in order to accomplish one's goals, one sometimes has to sacrifice one's individuality and join forces with others moving in similar directions.

> Do not be afraid to venture out of your original and present form for you will retain your true identity.[74]

That research suggests that adolescents and college students in reading text primarily attend to the structure of actions and events depicted in the text. However, for mature and older adults the primary interest is not in this literal action-event structure, but rather in what it reveals about underlying aspects of the human condition. To that extent, the mature adults' interest in text becomes more abstract and symbolic: A narrative does not refer to the concrete here and now of protagonists and their actions, but rather is taken as indicative of human actions in general.

On the basis of this and similar evidence, my collaborators[75] and I suggest that adulthood may bring a return of a symbolic style of processing. On that view, mature adulthood brings a symbolic processing style that emerges in a uniquely adult form. This is in contrast to Piaget who held that symbolic ways of processing, along with their tendency to animism, are immature. Instead, we propose that these ways of processing also may show a developmental line. For example, a Nobel laureate of biochemistry, Jacques Monod,[76] has argued that vitalism, a tendency to experience nature as animated and conscious, has always constituted a major alternative to determinism for scientists. And many discussions of creativity in science abound with examples of such animistic thinking being a catalyst for major breakthroughs.[77]

The notion that a uniquely mature form of symbolic thinking characterized mature adulthood also forms the cornerstone of Jung's[78] theory of adult development. Like Piaget's theory, Jung's is also structured around the opposition of sign and symbol. Unlike Piaget, however, Jung argues that human experience always remains intimately tied to the symbolic. For him, mature adulthood brings the ability not merely to live out these symbols but to enrich them with rational understanding. Indeed, Jung believes that out of the dialogue between the rational sign and the nonrational symbol, individuals can activate the "transcendental function" that constitutes an essential dynamic force for continued development in later life.

As already mentioned, the adult's need for mythic and symbolic forms of experience is also the topic of the essay by novelist Thomas Mann[79] on "Freud and the Future." Mann rejects the view that mythic thinking is a primitive form of thought. Instead, he proposes that it helps the adult to anchor his or her sense of self in more than abstract ideals of right and wrong. This is because the mythic offers a medium directly and concretely experienced. In this way, the individual can experience his or her individual life as part of larger, perhaps universal patterns. Myth, therefore, helps the individual to ground his or her sense of individuality in broad and transpersonal patterns.

That a return of the symbolic and mythic may be one of the critical features of adult cognition has also been suggested by Fowler.[80] Fowler argues that the basic contrast between knowing on the basis of reason and knowing on the basis of faith is resolved by stage 4 individuals in a demythologizing mode. The individual may be motivated to show that faith and myth can be reduced to structures of reason – a motivation that also dominated the philosophy of the Enlightenment era. In contrast, for the postconventional individual, religion is less concerned with reinterpreting myth in the light of reason. This level of thinking involves an integration in which "symbolic power is reunited with conceptual meanings"[81] – a "second naivete"[82] or "emancipated innocence"[83] in which one opens one's self to the nonrational in a way that is not precritical, but rather postcritical.

Organismic information

What I have reviewed here involves rather complex notions about how adults reorganize their view of the nature of knowledge. However, these reorganizations can take place in rather everyday kinds of problems. Take, for example, a situation in which individual A says to individual B, "You are angry at me!" Is A to conclude that B felt angry but did not know it, or that A was incorrectly accused of an anger that B projected on her, or that the problem somehow lies in the interaction? In such organismic contexts, assumptions about knowledge become expressed in a most direct and vital way. For this reason, my collaborators and I turned to a cognitive-developmental investigation of how individuals reorganize their understanding of the regulation of emotional processes over the life span.

It is by now well accepted in the area of child development that the understanding of emotions develops along with other dimensions of how we understand reality. Following Piaget,[84] many researchers[85] have proposed that as the cognitive system evolves, so does the individual's emotional repertoire. Specifically, that repertoire could be said to evolve along two epistemological dimensions.

The first of those is a mind–body dimension. Younger and/or less mature individuals express emotions externally in terms of actions, physical processes, and their concrete social consequences. This physicalistic, impulsive language is replaced in older and/or more mature individuals by an understanding of emotions as inner, cognitive, or "mental" processes that are symbolic and that emanate from one's memories, wishes, and other inner states. Similarly, processes of coping and defense also come to be more dominated by more complex intellectual and interpretive processes.[86]

Second, the standards or norms by which the individual references and regulates his or her behavior also become more complex. The young child depends for the regulation of behavior on the identification with concrete reference persons such as parents and, later, peers. By adolescence, a somewhat more autonomous self emerges that is no longer in need of such direct supervision but has internalized more abstract, conventional, and collective standards.[87]

By adolescence, therefore, individuals master a set of rules that permit them to regulate behavior in accordance with cultural dictates. However, that outward movement carries with it certain disadvantages, as well: In the process of adaptation to outer reality, youths need to be able to dissociate impersonal, abstract, and collective meanings from ones that are more concrete and personal and that carry a great deal of organismic significance. In contrast to the outward movement, adulthood may bring a compensatory movement inward. A focus on inner dynamics, on private experience, and on rich organismic experience and emotive content now comes to the fore – a process Gutmann refers to as the "greening" of the mature individual.[88]

Our own research shows this progression from adolescence to middle adulthood.[89] Younger or less mature individuals used a language of emotions that was almost entirely devoid of felt sense. Feelings were described not in terms of inner feedback, but in terms of an outer conventional language (e.g., "Things were bottled up"). Formal and technical processes and distant, static terms were used as descriptors (e.g., "Your blood pressure rises"). In addition, feelings were described in terms of how one *should* feel; external rules and standards of conduct rather than the felt experience characterized individuals' expression of emotions (e.g., "I was really scared, because I knew that if I didn't play good, that they'd tease me about it").

Our mature adults – those around middle adulthood – gave evidence of a significantly reorganized emotional language. Feelings were described in terms of a vivid felt process (e.g., "My heart felt like bursting," or "I felt a rush of energy"). Their language was inner and personal rather than outer and technical. Metaphors became dynamic, dealing not with static states, but with process and transformation. At the same time, individuals began to differentiate an inner realm of emotional experience from an outer realm of convention. The conflict between these realms was acknowledged, and the individual was concerned with accepting impulses and thoughts that previously seemed too overwhelming to accept.

This progression in how individuals describe their emotions was paralleled by the control strategies mentioned. Young persons or less mature adults often controlled emotions through active mental strategies such as forgetting, ignoring, and redirecting one's thoughts. The primary end of emotion control appeared to be repression of emotional tension and freedom from emotional conflict. The individual also looked to others to affirm the self's feelings.

These controls contrasted with the language of the mature adult who was open to acknowledging periods of intense inner conflict and rumination. Aware that emotions have a lawful regularity of their own that may oppose our concepts about them, these individuals evolved means of control that allowed a fuller acknowledgment of their emotional experience. For example, realizing that "you can't paper your emotions over," individuals often made an effort to examine their felt experience rather than inhibiting it under a layer of "shoulds" and

Psyche and Eros

"oughts." Emotions were accepted as motivating energy to assist the self in either acting upon or accepting the prevailing situation. Others were no longer blamed for the self's emotional state but were viewed as part of a more complex system of interaction and communication.

All of these various results, I suggest, indicate that mature adult development, may bring a reconnection of splits that are part of normal development – what I have called "primary development" in Chapter 3. If primary development often is built on the suppression and dissociation of private and organismic meanings, later development just as importantly demands that such meanings be reintegrated with abstract ideals. Thus mature adults are able to reembody the abstractions of youth in stabler, more universal patterns of immediate human experience. In this way, they transcend the traditional splits between abstract and concrete, mind and body, transcendent and immanent.

CONCLUSION

In this chapter, we have begun to examine the process of development past young adulthood. Early development was based on the establishment of a primary structure in which the individual develops an outward orientation. This outward orientation implies that the self is idealized in terms of "objective" and conventional truth criteria. It also implies a degree of negation of inner, "subjective" parameters.

In contrast to that outward movement, later development tends to bring an inward movement, what Neumann has called a process of "centroversion." In that process, individuals move away from the earlier hierarchical model and establish a way of thinking in which the two poles of mental functioning are seen as interactive and as dialectically related. As a result of the process, such categories as objective and subjective, self and other or self and society, and mind and body are no longer in dualistic opposition. Instead, the individual understands that each mutually affects the other, mutu-

206

ally defining and deepening each other. I propose to call the resulting structure "hermeneutical thinking."

The evolution of hermeneutical thinking in many ways brings us back full circle to the forms of "enchanted" thought discussed in Chapter 2. Now, however, thinking is no longer based on a lack of differentiation of the polarities of thought. Instead, the mature individual is able to hold the tension between those poles and work with it. This "reenchantment" of thinking brings, then, a new form of rationality that aims at reconnecting with the organismic, evolutionary, and spiritual-communal ground of life. It also brings a new sense of self and reality, in which the individual evolves a deeper sense of self that is more attuned with the symbolic and affective dimensions of life, yet able to adhere to a vision of objective conduct under a new concept of "passionate rationality."[90]

Chapter 6

Psyche's trials: The transformation of desire

Eros flew away to his mother's temple, lying in her chamber and groaning from the wound the lamp had dealt him. Psyche, however, began to wander in search of her lover. At length she arrived at the temple of the enraged Goddess, and to satisfy her vengeful spirit, Aphrodite set Psyche several impossible tasks.

In the first task, Psyche was to sort a heap of different grains – corn, barley, millet and poppy seeds, chick peas and lentils and different kinds of beans – and sort it out all before day's end. Next, Aphrodite asked her to gather some fleece from the golden rams. Next, she was to bring some water of life from the holy river Styx.

Now Aphrodite had designed each of those tasks to plot the ruin of Psyche, and the young woman despaired at being able to do the impossible. But first, the ants came and sorted all the grains into different heaps, each after their kind. When she came to the river close to the rams' grazing place, the reeds told her to wait till sundown when the rams go to sleep, then to gather some wool from the bushes. Finally, Zeus himself sent an eagle who filled Psyche's urn with the holy water.

But still the Goddess was not appeased, and invented yet another task. Psyche must descend to the Underworld, there to gather some beauty ointment from Persephone. Now, a tower instructed her to be firm on her way: Psyche should steel her heart to the pitiful cries of the miserable souls who ask for her mercy and help, and thus obtain the box with the ointment from the Goddess of the Underworld. Grave though the perils were, Psyche was successful and quickly returned to the world above. Just then, she was overcome with desire for her lover and wanted to adorn herself with divine beauty. But no sooner had she lifted the lid off the box, than a deathlike sleep possessed her.

THE ROOTS OF DESIRE

This section of the story expands on the previous chapter and details Psyche's journey toward a more passionate mode of thinking and being. The present section of the chapter adds a specific gender dimension to this journey, however. We have noted in Chapters 3 and 4 that the model of development as ascent to rationality is based on an imagery of gender relations and their polarization. In contrast, Psyche's progression through a series of tasks suggests that for the mature adult, that polarization begins to reintegrate. Thus, as the individual evolves a more genuine sense of self and a more integrated structure of the two modes of knowing and being, he or she also confronts the imagery of gender with which the polarized modes have been associated. Again, since the development of that polarization has somewhat different consequences for boys and girls, so it also has somewhat different aspects for the maturation of men and women.

The story continues as Psyche, alone and pregnant, sets out to find her lover. But the old bond has been breached irreparably, and before Psyche and Eros can become reunited, they need to experience a series of transformations. These transformations are described in the four tasks Aphrodite poses to Psyche.

The story was set in motion with Aphrodite's rage, and on hearing of the new turn of the story, the goddess breaks out in rageful incrimination again. "Oh!," she yells when hearing that Eros has wounded himself intentionally with an arrow so as to fall in love with Psyche, "you seducer, you worthless boy, you matricidal wretch."[1] When Psyche finds Aphrodite, the goddess calls her a "worthless slut" and vows that Psyche will pay for her disobedience.[2] She drags Psyche off by the hair, tears her clothes and her hair, and beats her cruelly. Finally, she gives her four seemingly impossible tasks.

Going beyond the parents

Before turning to a discussion of the tasks, it is worthwhile to ponder the meaning of Aphrodite's rageful behavior. On the surface, Aphrodite appears to embody no more than the stereotype of the jealous mother-in-law. But if seen in terms of the inner dynamics of an individual's development, her role is more complex. It indicates several challenges the developing individual needs to confront.

Psyche has set out to transform a mode of relating built on convention. That task can confront a person with frightening inner dynamics and social forces. Thus far, the individual like Psyche has moved, with a degree of protection, within the channels firmly set up by the culture. But as she begins to develop, she often moves beyond what culture has categorized and systematized, and into the domain of that which has not yet been structured and made familiar. If individuals are to continue to develop in a creative fashion, they need to push out into that domain of the not-yet-mastered and attempt to master it. As suggested in Chapter 5, this requires that the individual confront the "Shadow" dynamics so far repressed.

Neumann[3] suggests that this pushing out of the boundaries of cultural domains of mastery is often experienced as the confrontation with forces that are experienced as transpersonal and divine. Moreover, the task on which the individual set out is experienced as fraught with danger. Mythologically, this striving for mastery is often represented as the theft of divine powers. A familiar example of such a theft is the story of Prometheus, who stole fire – symbolic of knowledge and mastery – from the gods. For his action, he was confronted with divine vengeance and chained to a rock for eternal torture.

Aphrodite then represents such a power against which human consciousness struggles in the move toward postconventional thought. It is a power that may be felt to be supraindividual, divine, and transpersonal. It may also be experienced as a force that is terrible and punitive, and that will turn vengefully on the individual who reaches for his or her dreams.

Followers of Jung, such as Neumann, would claim that whenever the individual ventures into the new and aims creatively to transform reality, he or she is probably confronted with this archetypal layer of associations. But there are more personal dynamics, as well, that make the move beyond the normative a difficult task. One reason the individual may be fearful of developing beyond the conventions of culture can reside in the actual dynamics between the parental generation and the offspring. I have noted Erikson's view that ideally, adults are able to nurture and foster the well-being of the new generation, but such "generativity" remains an ideal and has its limits. Rather than feeling supported by the older generation in their creative quests, many adults instead may fear "going beyond" their parents' accomplishments, or breaking the rules and values the family represents. To do so may seem disloyal, and the individual may fear that he or she risks being outcast into the wilderness like Psyche.

Even worse, the wish to go beyond the parents may unconsciously be represented as a mythological killing of the parent, as a death wish against the parent. Freud,[4] indeed, argues that this myth of the killing and overthrow of the parent represents an eternal dynamic between generations of fathers and sons. Jung[5] also believes that the desire for individuation often is linked to imagery of parental death. Thus, the individual, not aware of the deeper symbolic meaning of such imagery, may feel guilty and frightened and defend against it by not attending to the important messages contained.

Another reason the parent can be seen as vengeful and dangerous is that the parent usually stands not just for the individual biological parent, but is symbolic of the social system or of culture. In the individual's relation to the social system, pressures toward conformity are a reality to be considered – as a Japanese proverb has it, "a nail that sticks out gets pounded back." Further, the individual who moves beyond conformity is often perceived as deviant: a rebel, a heretic, a revolutionary, or, perhaps, a fool. Even though such an individual may embody special wisdom and integrity, these qualities are not necessarily universally cherished. Rather, they may unleash hate and rage, as the example of Gandhi's assassination discussed in Chapter 5 shows. For these reasons, the types of transformations we are discussing can often be stillborn. As the individual is confronted with powers that are not only beneficial but also dangerous, he or she may give up the quest for further development, a problem that will occupy us later in this chapter.

Aphrodite represents, then, a set of dynamics the individual confronts as she or he breaks out of the confines of a system of cultural traditions. Paradoxically, even though the story emphasizes the negative aspects of that condition in the image of the hysterically raging Aphrodite, the goddess becomes a driving force and catalyst for Psyche's further development, as well. For it is Aphrodite who has set Psyche a series of tasks that are extraordinarily difficult.

Aphrodite's tasks

What Aphrodite gives Psyche is no less than a series of heroic tasks or developmental challenges. Neumann believes that these tasks are uniquely feminine, but I think that in actuality, they constitute universal symbols of the individual's journey toward wholeness. Since our culture has superimposed an imagery of gender on the development of men and women that may not at all do justice to the complexity of individual selves, the task of the individual is to somehow deconstruct that imagery and find the roots of the true self.

The first task is a mythologically familiar one. Aphrodite shows Psyche a huge heap of corn, barley, millet and poppy seeds, chick peas, lentils, and beans and says to her:

> I cannot conceive that any serving-wench as hideous as yourself could find any means to attract lovers save by making herself their judge; wherefore now I myself will make trial of your worth. Sort that disordered heap of seeds, place each kind of grain apart in its own place, and see that you show me the work completed before the evening.[6]

Psyche at first despairs of the sheer impossibility of the task, but soon she is helped by the ants who sort the seeds for her. Order in this confused mess of potentialities is thus represented by the ants, who as a force of nature and the instinct of life are "feminine" powers. But what is interesting here is that it is these "feminine" powers that begin to classify the seeds, to separate them and put them into orderly categories – all activities associated with the "masculine." The story thereby suggests that it is necessary for the individual to transcend conventional definitions of what is masculine and feminine and to realize that the activity of ordering, at its best, results from a combination of both aspects. Thus, the ordering activity of reason needs to be wedded to the wisdom rooted in intuition and organic knowledge.

For her second task, Psyche is to go to the mountain and gather a wisp of wool from the fleece of the sheep who roam there. As Psyche crosses the river that leads to the mountain, a reed warns her not to approach the sheep in the light of day, because they are extremely fierce and dangerous and likely to destroy anybody they see approaching. Thus Psyche is to wait until nightfall, when she can find the wool of the sheep clinging to the bushes.

Here, Psyche encounters a more direct confrontation of "masculine" and "feminine" principles. Psyche is to confront the golden rams who with their fierceness and association with the daylight and sun clearly represent a solar masculine principle. She is to disempower this powerful principle by a kind of taking possession, of symbolic castration, of theft of divine powers. The masculine principle as embodied by the rams – artificially elevated in the first place as discussed in Chapter 4 – needs to be reduced in power just as the feminine is correspondingly increased in its significance by taking the fleece. The result is a balance of the two.

This task expands on the first one, but it is more explicit about what kinds of danger can come from a failure to balance these principles. The fierceness of the rams here connotes the danger of an "unmitigated" action of the masculine principle.[7] To balance that principle, Psyche consults the reeds, a spiritual principle that belongs to the feminine realm. Neumann argues that this represents a special task for the feminine. But the task for men is complementary, though, as argued later, for men the primary experiential quality is quite different from the prototypical feminine experience.

Psyche, in the meantime, has passed this further trial, only to find that she still has not satisfied Aphrodite. Aphrodite gives her another task, one that seems even more impossible and frightening. She gives Psyche a small jar carved out of crystal and tells her to gather water from the river Styx. Neumann argues that this task is a variant of the quest for the water of life. It is an impossible task because Psyche is supposed to capture the very flow of life itself – something that since ancient times philosophers have claimed to be a sheer impossibility.

Psyche, however, is able to come up with the seemingly impossible. Now she is helped by the eagle, the bird of Zeus, a masculine spiritual principle, the ultimate symbol of logos. The eagle takes her crystal vessel and fills it with water. The eagle here already indicates that masculine and feminine principles are integrated, the urn, as Neumann states it, receiving "like a woman," and the eagle "apprehending and knowing like a man." Thus the unconscious situation of the marriage of death with its splitting of masculine and feminine has been transcended. The two poles have become integrated within a single individual.

Still Aphrodite is not satisfied and gives Psyche a fourth task. She is to journey into the underworld and get some of Persephone's beauty ointment. Now Psyche is instructed by a tower – a symbol of logos, of the masculine, of accumulated cultural knowledge, of the power of reason. But again the emphasis is on integration: The tower admonishes Psyche of the dangers of her journey. There are four specific dangers of which she is warned, and all of these dangers have to do with refusing to become involved in the agendas of others, and instead to concentrate on her own path. As Houston[8] notes, this ability to voice a creative no to others may be a particularly feminine predicament, since women have been raised to become strongly concerned with the issues of others, often to the detriment of attention to their own self-development.

But at the very end, Psyche's long trials almost come to naught. Even though she was warned not to open the box with the ointment, she gives in to her curiosity. As she opens the box, she is overcome with a deathlike sleep. The meaning of this event has puzzled many interpreters. Some suggest that Psyche here engages in a typically feminine act of vanity, but I think the issue is more complex.

It is significant here that the beauty ointment that so attracts Psyche's consciousness is that of Persephone. Persephone is the goddess who like Psyche was abducted into the under-world; yet there, she became a queen on her own, a knower of the dark side of life. Her beauty represents a beauty unlike that of the young Psyche, a beauty enriched by suffering and depth – a beauty of the mature feminine that does not enchant by its maidenlike innocence, but that lies in its depth of knowl-edge, in its wisdom, in its independence, and in its passionate rootedness.

But "stealing" beauty from this regal figure of deep wisdom is not enough. Psyche must explore it, experience it, fall into its spell. Sinking into the deep sleep of unconsciousness, Psyche must revisit her own woundedness and, thus, become one with the goddess of suffering and victimization, Persephone. Paradoxically, that regressive act becomes the source of Psyche's transformation. Revisiting her woundedness, falling into the core of her feminine passivity and paralyzed agency, Psyche recovers the secret of her true desire. Thus, she shows that ultimately, the growth in consciousness must be wedded to the realm of mythos desire. However, desire has become profoundly transformed. It is no longer immature desire, the desire driven by a sense of an incomplete self searching for completion in another individual, but a new form of desire. This new form is one in which the traditional boundaries be-tween logos and mythos, between discipline and freedom, be-tween reason and emotion, between masculine and feminine fall completely away.

The story of Psyche and Eros describes this integration, and the steps that lead to it, from the perspective of the feminine. But the process is likely to be a little different from a masculine perspective. For Psyche, the task is to balance her earlier emphasis of suffering and surrender with that of heroic rise; but for Eros, it is to encounter suffering, surrender, and compassion as a principle complementing his heroic adaptation. This principle is not well developed in the tale, though it is alluded to by Eros' burning wound. However, the masculine path to wholeness is the topic of many myths and fairy tales.[9]

One of those is a Russian fairy tale, "The Frog Princess."[10] In this story the tsar sends out his three sons in search of wives. Ivan, the youngest of the three, finds a frog and marries it. Though Ivan is despondent at first, the frog proves to possess invaluable knowledge and comes to his help as the father puts three challenges to his sons' wives. First, she sheds her skin and reveals herself as Wassilissa, the "all-wise, the one who is more beautiful than the sun and the moon and the stars." Wassilissa bakes a delicious bread, then sews and embroiders a magnificent shirt; but after each task, she puts her skin back on again and returns to being a frog. Finally, Wassilissa shows up at the tsar's ball in the most regal of attire. Ivan rushes home to search for the frog skin and then burns it. When his wife returns from the ball and finds Ivan has burned the skin, she is horrified and tells him she must leave because she is still under a magical spell.

Desolate, Ivan begins to search for Wassilissa who, he learns, was turned into a frog by her father who resented his daughter's wisdom and power. On his journey, he encounters a number of trials. Encountering first a bear, then a hare, a duck, and a fish, he must contain his urge to kill them and instead is kind to them. Then he finds the witch, Baba Jaga, who shows him the way to the castle of Wassilissa's father. On the way, the animals he previously let live return to help him in resolving the secret of the powers of the evil man. Ivan destroys him and is rejoined by his wife.

This story repeats all of the themes of the Psyche and Eros story: the disempowerment of the feminine by male envy, the initial marriage of masculine and feminine principle in an unconscious marriage of darkness, the liberation of the contrasexual element through a series of trials. But now, the journey is recast in a specifically masculine form. Whereas from the feminine perspective, the task is to see that activities of ordering and so forth can be accepted as part of the self, from the masculine vantage point the goal is similar, but the route may be different though complementary. Now for the male, it is necessary to accept that the so-called feminine qualities in no way characterize women only, but are an enriching aspect of mature masculinity. Thus, these stories show that the same goal is reached by men and women but by a different pathway.

THE RETURN OF THE FEMININE

Even though masculine and feminine routes to the achievement of wholeness and maturity may differ, they tend to reinforce a similar message. In each case, the loss of wholeness has resulted from a devaluation of the feminine principle. In evolving a lateral and dialogical concept of the mind, I suggest that confronting the polarity of masculine and feminine requires a reevaluation. Since, as discussed in Chapters 4 and 5, at the core of the classical model of reason is the heroic narrative of masculine ascent and feminine surrender, it is critical that any new model of rationality that is developed restructure this traditional imagery of gender. Such a restructuring involves deidealizing the traditional notion of the masculine and grounding it in the material and concrete, while elevating the feminine and enriching it with mind and spirit.

Changing images of the feminine

In Chapter 5, we discussed the return of mythos, of a language of desire, in formal and informal theories of mind and human nature. Congruent with the main tenet of this book, that return also brings an awareness of the gender-related images that undergird our theories of mature adulthood. In her book, *Reflections on Gender and Science*, Evelyn Fox Keller examines historical aspects of that gender-related imagery. She argues that the exclusion of a language of desire from theories of the mind actually was not a total exclusion, but involved specifically an exclusion of female desire. To demonstrate, Keller discusses Plato's theory of the mind that, as elaborated in Chapter 2, involves an asymmetry between mind and body and also implies an asymmetry between reason and desire. But, argues Keller, the exclusion of desire in Plato's theory is of a specifically feminine form, whereas a more masculine form of desire is a necessary part of the process of knowing.

To the question, How can we know? Plato answers that our journey to knowledge is guided by Eros. On the surface, this would posit a unity of desire and knowledge, but Plato's conception of Eros contains specific limits. First, he draws a distinction between the homoerotic and spiritual love between men; this love, he claims, forms the true pathway for the philosopher. It is contrasted with the love of a man for a woman, which is merely "material" love. Thus, in the *Symposium* Plato says:

> Those whose creative instinct is physical have recourse to women, and show their love in this way, believing that by begetting children they can secure for themselves an immortal and blessed memory hereafter forever; but there are those whose creative desire is of the soul, and who long to beget spiritually, not physically, the progeny which it is the nature of the soul to create and bring to birth. . . . If you ask what that progeny is, it is wisdom and virtue in general.[11]

Plato's model thus sets the stage for a model of knowledge that is based on a specifically unique masculine union between knowledge and desire. That basic model was carried over into the Enlightenment era, though there it appeared in the specific form of a more modern concept of knowledge. As Keller suggests, that model was no longer purely formal and abstract, but aimed at mastery of nature and the concrete world. In fact, according to Bacon the new view of knowledge marked a new "birth" of time – a birth he thought was uniquely masculine because it characterized not purely theoretical inquiry but a form of marriage between mind and nature. Thus, the main metaphor remains sexual, and is specifically framed in terms of the satisfaction of male desire. Man's task of understanding nature is framed in terms of metaphors of control and submission, as when Bacon says that "I am come in very truth leading to you Nature with all her children to bind her to your service and make her your slave."[12]

During the Romantic Age, that masculine imagery underlying knowledge and inquiry underwent a systematic reevaluation, as philosophers often attempted to upgrade the importance of feelings. Rousseau, for example, is well known for celebrating feeling rather than rationality as a source of knowing. Nevertheless, his theory did not really change the competitive nature of the two modalities. It merely attempted to stand the dualistic metaphor on its head, and thus it retained the images of competition. Certainly, his theory's attempt to upgrade the feminine was not applied to women. Says Richter:

> The passionate defense of feeling in no way is aimed at a new view of gender, certainly not at an emancipation of the feminine. In fact, . . . [Rousseau] is not at all concerned with an emotionality that has communication as its goal, but rather with the triumph of a narcissism whose aim is that of throwing off all fetters.[13]

The romanticizing of the emotive as feminine, then, in no way abolished the competitive motivation underlying the claim of basic differences in the mental natures of men and women. Richter shows this in the case of the 19th-century philosopher, naturalist, and physician Carl Gustav Carus. This thinker is notable because he anticipated Freud in developing the concept of the unconscious and in developing a psychology based not on rationality but on an emotion-oriented internality. Equating emotion with the feminine and with divine inspiration, Carus nevertheless was not concerned with an emancipation of femininity in a larger sense. Rather, his concern was with an emancipation of the masculine. He wished to enrich the masculine with feminine qualities, opening up avenues that were closed to men in the past. He did not envision, however, a symmetrical process in women, for whom such enrichment must be limited due to their inferior natures:

> Women rarely can step out of mediocrity and map their own course of life with decisiveness; with few exceptions, it is not possible for them to focus their lives on singular, noble goals; and never has sprung from their mind a great discovery, the genius of which has opened up new avenues for mankind.[14]

Thus, the romantic thinkers, although in some sense beginning a project in which the feminine element began to be upgraded and included in a model of knowledge, also remained steeped in the classical dualism and opposition between the masculine and the feminine. Battersby, in her book *Gender and Genius*,[15] suggests that this resulted in a new rhetoric of sexual exclusion: What was praiseworthy in a man was considered undesirable in a woman. Feminine qualities were thought to enrich the male mind, to give it a creative and androgynous cast, to animate it with feeling and intuition. But such enrichment was not acknowledged for women, whose participation in masculine forms of creativity was not looked at with favor. Rather, the feeling of most thinkers continued to echo Kant's assertion that women who knew Greek or mathematics "might as well even have a beard."[16] Knowledge makes them grotesque, freakish, even "loathsome."

Nevertheless, I believe that the romantic writers slowly began changing the nature of discourses about the mind. Even positing an androgynous mind began blurring the more rigid concept of masculinity associated with classical notions, and also began to expose the inevitable association of our theories of the mind with gender imagery. However, that imagery remained rather implicit until close to the turn of this century, when it was introduced more explicitly into discourses about the nature of the mind and of human nature. However, since most of these discourses were conducted in the domain of mythos, their relevance for changing concepts of mind and human nature still have not fully been realized.

The return of the feminine

One of the first individuals to address the topic of the imagery related to mind and gender was the Swiss jurist Jacob Bachofen,[17] who in the 1860s anticipated the main thesis that the prehistory of the human race was one in which not a patriarchal, but a matriarchal principle reigned. Bachofen's assertion was strongly based on Plutarch's *Isis and Osiris*,[18] a treatise on the mythology and rituals surrounding the ancient Egyptian twins and lovers. Isis, as already noted, was associated with the birth of culture. Together with her brother and husband Osiris, she brought agriculture, beer, and breadmaking to her land. Her association both with fertility and authority is indicated by the dual meaning of her name. Isis means "black soil," referring to the rich, fertile soil of the Nile Delta; but her hieroglyph, a part of her headdress on many of her statues, also is the form of a throne, indicating her royal authority.[19]

Unlike many later goddesses, Isis represents an extremely powerful figure, and the frequent occurrence of such powerful figures in ancient times suggested to Bachofen that there must have been, in prehistoric times and before the rise of the major patriarchal societies, the reign of a maternal principle. This thesis has had wide popularity[20] and has stimulated a great deal of scholarship in the area of mythology and religion. However, its historical accuracy has recently been doubted. True, there may have been *some* early societies in which gender was less polarized than it came to be, quite universally, with the rise of major patriarchies. Still, most historical and anthropological evidence[21] does not support the view that earlier and/or less civilized societies granted women more power *universally*.

This is true even though matriarchy myths exist in many societies. However, as Bamberger[22] argues, such myths often can be seen as part of a social order that belittles and demo-

nizes power in women. They usually talk of the dire consequences of letting women handle power. Thus they become
part of a cultural code distinguishing men from women in
terms of morality and authority and granting men more power
in social life. Even though they talk about a time before the
current social order, they fix that order as invariant and in-
alienable. In this way, they constantly reiterate that women are
not capable of handling power – that they represent the rule of
chaos and trickery.

Nevertheless, Georgoudi[23] suggests that Bachofen's work
has had an important function. Even if not based on historical
fact, it shows important evidence about how, throughout history, the feminine was constructed *symbolically or mythically.*
Thus, Bachofen pointed out that to think of the "female element" as a "primitive, chaotic, obscure, undisciplined, and
dangerous"[24] force was by no means a historically universal
phenomenon. Rather, it appears to have happened at a particular historical juncture, whereas before that juncture that construction was not so universally true. States Georgoudi:

> Some Greek myths placed this fearsome female element at the
> beginning of time and endowed it with venerable primordial
> power. To relegate woman's power to the remote past, to assign
> it in a place in "prehistory," to associate it with the barbarian,
> "gynecocratic" regimes characterized by the absence of law
> and morality – to do these things was no doubt to write women
> out of the picture, to exclude them from Greek history, indeed
> from all history. Bachofen and his followers clearly saw this
> legendary "reality." Their error was to take the Greeks at their
> word, to mistake myth for history. In so doing, they unwittingly
> created a myth of their own, itself a worthy object of study.[25]

Although it is worthwhile to be wary of this myth of matriarchy, Bachofen began the inquiry into the specific symbolism associated with the gender-related dualism that is part of
our concepts of mind and human nature. Thus, he realized that
basic to this dualism is the clash between male and female:
"nature versus culture, darkness versus light, east versus west,

Aphrodite versus Apollo, left versus right, death versus life, and so on."[26]

The importance of Bachofen's work, then, lies in the fact that by elaborating that dualism, it stimulated a process of rewriting history into a new type of narrative – one no longer based on the polarization of the old myths of heroic ascent versus victimization and surrender, but one based on mythic notions of the complementarity of masculine and feminine principles. In that process, there is a danger that we merely reverse the old dualism we wish to reject, projecting into the past our desire for lost unity. Nevertheless, in this process what may emerge is a new set of guiding images or archetypes.

One feminine archetype that appears to hold much fascination is that of the woman deity who combines in her leadership and erotic abundance. Isis is one example; another, related one is the principal deity of the first civilization from which we have texts. Of her, Kramer, the decipherer of the Sumerian texts, states:

> Female deities were worshipped and adored all through Sumerian history . . . but the goddess who outweighed, overshadowed, and outlasted them all was a deity known to Sumerians by the name of Inanna, "Queen of Heaven," and to the Semites who lived in Sumer by the name of Ishtar. Inanna played a greater role in myth, epic, and hymn than any other deity, male or female.[27]

The hymns and stories of Inanna not only show her to be a figure of exuberant sexuality, but also one who gives her culture civilization. The gifts of priesthood and ritual and the gifts of political power, craft, and husbandry all are associated with her. Yet she not only symbolizes the masculine values of power and culture, Inanna's stories also tell of her journey into the underworld to acquire suffering and self-knowledge.[28]

One figure that has claimed much recent interest is that of the biblical Sophia, or Wisdom. According to Engelsman's *Feminine Dimensions of the Divine*,[29] Sophia was a personification of the divine attribute of wisdom. She grew in stature and importance from the 4th to the 1st century B.C.E., and her power was enormous. In the Hebrew scriptures, she emerges as a figure of great importance – only God, Job, Moses, and David are treated with more depth.[30]

In the Proverbs, Sophia was associated with a feminine creative principle, a cocreator with God of the universe. She was considered a feminine form of intelligence or spirit, knowledgeable not only of such masculine forms of learning as the law, but also of the workings of nature, the heavens, and living creatures from beasts to plants. In the Gnostic Gospels,[31] she emerges as a figure of extraordinary power, uniting in her paradoxical opposites:

> For I am the first and the last,
> I am the honored one and the scorned one,
> I am the whore and the holy one.
> I am the wife and the virgin.
> I am [the] mother and daughter.
> I am the members of my mother.
> I am the barren one and many are her sons.
> I am she whose wedding is great,
>   and I have not taken a husband.
> I am the midwife and she who does not bear.
> I am the solace of my labor pains.
> I am the bride and the bridegroom,
>   and it is my husband who begot me. . . .
>
> I am the silence that is incomprehensible
>   and the idea whose remembrance is frequent.
> I am the voice whose sound is manifold
>   and the word whose appearance is multiple.[32]

Isis, Inanna, and Sophia are just three examples of the recent resurrection of ancient goddesses[33] that are said to exemplify the emergence of a new way of thinking about the feminine. That new way of thinking has begun to reverse an ancient process, in which the feminine has been emptied of its divine and spiritual dimensions as it became associated "merely" with matter. Thus, we can discern here a process of counterbalancing. As projections of the organismic, the emotive, the instinctual, and so forth are withdrawn from the concept of the feminine, it is spiritualized. In fact, Psyche will be raised to a goddess at the end of the story.

Some writers on the topic have sharply criticized this notion of the restoration of the feminine dimension of the divine, arguing that the notion of feminine divinity is irrelevant and even absurd.[34] However, while in some sense it may be true that ultimately, a gendered notion of divinity is an absurdity, the debate is not just about an abstract concept but about a psychological process. As I have argued in Chapter 3, our notions of the abstract are most effective if they are under-girded by concrete imagery capable of rendering rich and vital personifications. Thus, these recent writings, I believe, reflect a dimension that adds richness and depth to the more abstract philosophical discussions of Chapter 5. They elaborate, in oth-er words, in the domain of mythos what I have attempted to show in Chapter 5: We are in the midst of evolving a new concept of reason and human nature, one that bridges the old tension between the "immanent" and the "transcendent" that has been the cornerstone of classical philosophies and models of men and women. Only by developing new images can such concepts as divinity and what they exemplify be changed.

This recent trend to spiritualize the dimension of the femi-nine is only one aspect of the evolution of a lateral and cooper-ative model of the mind. Another, and complementary aspect, is a parallel reevaluation of the concept of masculinity. Here, however, the movement is in the opposite direction: If the traditional concept of the masculine has placed excessive em-phasis on "mind" and "spirit," now we observe a widening discussion of the material and organismic aspects of mas-culinity. Thus, just as the feminine principle is raised and spir-itualized, the masculine principle is despiritualized and grounded in earth and feeling.

An example of this grounding of the masculine principle is found in recent discussions of the mythological figure of the "green man."[35] The green man is a masculine divine figure of pagan origin, a figure occurring widely in northeastern Eu-rope and the Mediterranean basin. Unlike the transcendent god of logos and disembodied spirit, it is an earth and fertility figure. It derives its name from the form in which it most often occurs: a male head formed out of a leaf mask or surrounded by leaves or other vegetation. This composite of leaves and a man's head symbolizes the union of the organismic plant and the human world, especially its mental and spiritual aspects. It is a symbol of renewal and rebirth.

The green man, like the powerful mother goddesses, is not a new figure but an elaboration of an ancient and pervasive theme. He was considered a remnant of pagan religions but has remained extremely pervasive. Anderson and Hicks, in *The Green Man*,[36] document its wide existence in the folk habits of Europe as well as its architecture. It is a prevalent symbol occurring throughout the churches and cathedrals of Europe, where it is an integral part of the intricate stone and wood carvings of most cathedrals. Although the green man is a specifically European figure with its concentration on the head, similar masculine deities representing the union of the plant and the human world were pervasive in other cultures. Sometimes, as in the Aztec corn god, they occur as the god of spring from whom new growth arises in the form of corn shoots.

The Egyptian Osiris, twin brother and husband of Isis, is another such corn or green god figure. As we saw earlier, according to Egyptian legend, Osiris brought the arts of civilization and agriculture to Egypt. He taught his people to cultivate wheat and barley, to pick fruit from the trees and train vines on poles, and to make wine and beer. Through trickery Osiris eventually was killed by his jealous brother Set who tore his body into pieces which he dispersed over the land of Egypt. The murdered Osiris was resurrected by his sister-wife Isis. Osiris' cycle of death and rebirth came to be associated with the cycle of changing seasons. Each spring, his body was thought to be reborn like the planted earth and to sprout forth new life.

Dionysus is another vegetation god associated with the cycle of death and rebirth. Dismembered and resurrected, he was called the "twice-born," a symbol of the path of development from dying to cultural dictate to birth of a new, genuine self. Dionysus was associated with the ecstatic; adorned with grapes, he was the god of drunkenness, of emotional excess, and of deep inner knowledge. He is a figure who suggests that to develop, one must expose one's self to the dark, unconscious, feminine side of life. Indeed, as Bly notes, these ancient figures, and modern awareness of them, suggest that to attribute that dark side to the feminine has been a grave error in human history, one that can be corrected as we realize that the masculine is no less part of the organic, earthly, and concrete order than is the feminine![37]

THE HERO'S DESCENT INTO DARKNESS

A discussion of the balancing of feminine and masculine elements might be of academic interest only, if it were not a very part of the psychological development of men and women in middle life. The notion that maturity requires a rebalancing of masculine and feminine was first explicitly proposed by Jung.[38] Jung suggests that the first half and the second half of life are aimed at quite different goals and involve quite different mechanisms. Jung compares the first half of life to an individual's learning to wear a mask or "persona" – just as in classical Greek theater, actors wore a mask to typify the characters played. In later adulthood, however, Jung believes that the individual needs to confront a deeper sense of selfhood, to search, as it were, for the wearer of the mask, and to lay open the potentials of this original structure. Jung refers to this deep structure of the individual as the Self.

According to Jung this process represents a major crisis in the lives of individuals; he, in fact, coined the now popular notion of a midlife crisis. Here, we immediately need to specify just in what sense the word crisis is to be used. Jung believes that often this new search for the self brings with it a "turning inward";[39] energies that previously had been invested in the pursuit of outer goals are withdrawn, and the individual focuses those energies toward an examination of his or her inner life in an attempt to rebalance the life structure. This turning inward, according to Jung, often can have a depressive quality, but should not be confused with clinical depression. Rather, it represents a necessary redirection of one's attention and energies. To be sure, in that process of redirection the individual confronts emotions that he or she has defended against so far. Thus, a degree of pain and suffering is, for Jung, a normal and necessary part of the crisis.

The notion of a midlife crisis does not necessarily imply major upheavals of a quasi-pathological kind. Rather, there may be subtle shifts in how individuals understand their inner world. As a result of this individuation process, individuals become so renovated or transformed that they have fuller access to their potentials. Rather than repressing part of that potential in the interest of maintaining the persona, they bring all of their faculties into conscious play. This may involve "renewal without any change of being, inasmuch as the personality which is renewed is not changed in its essential nature, but only its functions, or parts of the personality, are subjected to healing, strengthening, or improvement."[40]

Reclaiming the inner feminine

One major way in which this renewal happens is that an individual confronts the images he or she holds of the masculine and the feminine. Jungians[41] believe that the split-off elements are usually encountered most profoundly in the contrasexual images – the individual has to begin realizing that these are inner constructions and that the split-off elements must be reclaimed and integrated into the self.

What is the evidence that men do encounter such a crisis? The issue is quite controversial, but evidence does suggest that midlife is a problematic period for many men. Alcoholism is at its peak, and so is depression. At the same time, such stress-related diseases as peptic ulcers, hypertension, and heart problems are on the rise. Also, men often judge this time as an especially difficult one.[42] About their sample of men, who, in their youth, had been selected for their exceptional promise of health and successful adaptation, Vaillant and McArthur have noted:

228

Around forty a change occurred in the men. They appeared to leave the compulsive calm of their occupational apprenticeship, so reminiscent of grammar school days . . . Most subjects consciously perceived their forties as more tumultuous than they had their adolescence. . . . Just as adolescence is a time for acknowledging parental flaws and discovering truths about childhood, the forties are a time for reassessing and reordering the past.[43]

Levinson has outlined his process in his study of *The Season's of a Man's Life*. Levinson maintains that around midlife, the men of his sample engaged in an examination of the polarities of life, such as good–evil and young–old. One polarity that is of particular interest in this context is that of masculine and feminine. In youth, that polarity is somewhat of a precarious issue, and much of what the young man experiences as feminine entails unresolved remnants from his childhood experience with women, especially his mother, and/or aspects of himself that he has not integrated into the self. In both cases, that sense of otherness emerges as his concept of the feminine.

As far as the man's relationship with his mother is concerned, even though he has set out into the adult world and begun to establish a measure of worldly success, (unconscious) aspects of his experience with his mother continue to determine his life profoundly. Thus Levinson believes that even in early adulthood,

a young man's efforts to establish an intimate marital relationship are complicated by his continuing sense of himself as a little boy in relation to a powerful maternal figure. He is engaged in a struggle both to express and to control his various fantasies of this figure as devouring witch, feeding breast, sexual seducer, humiliating rejecter, willing servant and demanding master. His wife attracts him in part because she seems to lack these qualities he fears and resents in his inner maternal figure. Yet their relationship may actually contain these and other aspects of the mother–son interaction (such as her indulging or admiring him), which in time are likely to become more problematic.[44]

As far as his female age peers are concerned, Levinson argues that the young man often is attracted to women whose primary function is to mirror his sense of being a hero and thereby to support and animate his life's dream. This kind of woman serves to help him shape his dream by sharing in it, believing in him as a hero, giving her blessings, and helping sustain his inner life so as to nourish his images and hopes.

At midlife, however, a man typically confronts these inner constructions of the masculine and the feminine, and examines how they have limited his life structure and narrowed his dream. Now, he is more likely to confront an inner split in these two images. For example, he is likely to recognize that masculinity for him has connoted such things as achievement, ambition, getting ahead, being successful. The woman experienced as feminine was the kind who would support these strivings: the kind who as a wife furthered his advancement rather than pursuing her own dream, and who, if she turned to employment, did so in a subordinate and noncompetitive way.

As he matures, however, a man often needs to confront the fact that he has constructed the feminine in a delimited and delimiting way. This is especially true if he wants to branch out from a life structure that he experiences as limiting and confining and move into one that may bear greater potential for creativity and self-expression. One of the men in Levinson's sample, for instance, yearned to give up his career as a business executive and turn to novel writing. Yet his feelings that artistic activity was not a useful enterprise like business, that it was somehow "feminine" and queer, proved to be a considerable stumbling block – although one that, once he negotiated it, expanded his life in a creative fashion.

Many men like the executive just cited find themselves limited by the fact that they have come to associate the feminine with being weak: submissive, unassertive, and easily victimized by those given to abuse positions of power. At midlife, however, these inner representations may come to haunt the self who then feels compelled to reexamine them and to work toward healing the split.

One of the ways the split is healed, argues Levinson, is through a reexamination of the relationship to the mother, and an exploration of the inner figure of the mother within a man's psyche. That examination prepares him to gradually upgrade his image of the nature of femininity, causing not only a richer, more integrated and mellow self-structure, but also less conflicts about power in women:

> He is then less afraid of a woman's power to withhold, devour and seduce. He can give more of himself, receive more from her, and accept her greater independence. He is more ready to work collaboratively with a woman or to work as a subordinate under her without feeling emasculated.[45]

The result of this shift is often not only a creative expansion, but also a change in relationships to women, who can then be accepted as peers with dreams of their own.

In his classical article on "Death and the Mid-Life Crisis," Jaques[46] also suggests that a reevaluation of the nature of femininity is at the core of creative reorganization in later life. Jaques begins with the observation that in the lives of many creative men, midlife appears to mark a kind of watershed. For some, this is a time when youthful creativity dries up, whereas for others, it marks a first burst of creativity. In many creative men, however, it is a time when the nature of creative production becomes transformed. Jaques argues that the creativity of young men is often marked by an impulsive, "hot-from-the-fire" quality. For example, a young poet writing about love is likely to emphasize either the positive or the negative aspects of love, exulting in its ecstasies or lamenting its despairs. He is, thus, likely to display a degree of idealization, which has a certain one-sidedness, whether positive or negative. In contrast, the writing of later life often shows enormous complexity not only of cognitive integration, but also of affective balance. Aging artists appreciate the paradoxical and the tragic, and incorporate them into their work. Jaques terms this shift a transformation from a "precipitate" to a "tragic" style, where musicians, artists, and poets show an appreciation for the full range of human complexity and emotion.

Jaques argues that a central aspect of this creative transformation is the working through of those aspects men have come to split off as "otherness" in early development. As is true of Levinson, Jaques suggests that this otherness often confronts the man at first in terms of the feminine, especially the mother. Early idealizations are beginning to crumble, and one aspect of that crumbling is that the man discovers the "bad" mother. That is, he begins to give up his (conscious) idealization of the mother and explore the fact that the mother not only was a source of support but also one of frustrations, disappointments, and failures. Thus the man discovers that she is not only a symbol of love, but also of its denial – feelings of yearning, of denied love and of being lost, deserted, and powerless all are associated with this split-off, "bad" mother. Of course, eventually the man is able not only to concentrate his sense of disappointment on the mother but to marshal it toward evolving a less idealized and more mature view of life.

Jaques focuses primarily on the role of the mother, whose importance looms large because of her primary role in very early development and the adaptations it has fostered. But midlife is no less an opportunity to examine the role of the father and the internal models of reality he has created. A vivid display of such an examination is given by Noam,[47] who discusses the case of the poet Franz Kafka. About a year before his death, Kafka wrote a letter to his father, addressing difficult feelings about the relationship that he located in the early interaction between father and son. Kafka describes his lifelong fear of the father, a fear that emanated out of arbitrary strictness and rejection. He struggled with his own sense of self-hatred and futility, which he traced to these early difficulties. Noam traces how this sense of self-rejection pervades the adult son's life, not only in his interaction with his father, but in his relationship with women, and even his ominous sense of impersonal, senseless, and unforgiving institutions. Perhaps tragically, Kafka's letter never reached his father: Kafka had given it to his mother, in the hope that she might pass it on to the father. The mother, however, returned the letter to the son, lending credence to the earlier discussed notion that parents may vigorously resist their grown children's efforts to individuate.

Jaques believes that the midlife reexamination forms a crisis that, though it is confronted by all adults, is not necessarily resolved successfully by all. Instead, adults may retreat from the crisis:

> the compulsive attempts, in many men and women reaching middle age, to remain young, the hypochondriacal concern over health and appearance, the emergence of sexual promiscuity in order to prove youth and potency, the hollowness and lack of genuine enjoyment of life . . . are familiar patterns. These are attempts at a race against time. And in addition to the impoverishment of emotional life contained in the foregoing activities, real character deterioration is always possible. . . . Increase in arrogance, and ruthlessness concealing pangs of envy – or self-effacing humbleness and weakness concealing fantasies of omnipotence – are symptomatic of such change. . . . These defensive fantasies are equally as persecuting, however, as the chaotic and hopeless internal situation they are meant to mitigate.[48]

The greening of men

Another theorist who has focused on the man's internal reorganization of the meanings of masculine and feminine is David Gutmann.[49] Gutmann argues that young men's imagery in general displays an enjoyment of assertive and aggressive striving. Gutmann believes this to be a universal aspect of masculine development, which in many societies is regulated in such a way that the young man comes to be the vessel for the collective aggression in the group. Young men are expected to be industrious and enterprising, to push out energetically into the mundane and pragmatic world, to pursue success vigorously. But older men show a different pattern of concerns and strengths. They are expected to give up aggression, to withdraw their competitive concerns from the outer

world, and instead to deflect these concerns into other channels. In some societies, this shows up as a prescription for a
religious life in which older men refocus their attention to the
spiritual world and their relationship with god.

Men now may discover, sometimes with a sense of shock,
their "tender feelings." Gutmann terms this process the
"greening of men" and presents a variety of data. One set of
data deals with changes in masculine–feminine imagery of
artists. For example, in the life of cartoonist William Steig,
Gutmann observes a definite sequence:

> As a younger man, though doubting his own credentials, Steig
> tries to gain acceptance in the world of men from the big guys,
> the gatekeepers already established there. However, by early
> middle age, though aggression is still an important variable,
> Steig appears to have turned against his own assertive striving
> and now disparages masculine qualities in cartoons of power-
> ful but pretentious or stupidly destructive men. In his young
> manhood, Steig gently ridicules his own wish for acceptance by
> the big guys, but in his middle years he turns against those who
> have made it as men, and instead mocks the aggressive mas-
> culine ideal that he once emulated. . . . But even as he rejects
> the aggressive versions of masculinity, in his middle years Steig
> also seems to be troubled by an emerging femininity . . . that he
> seems to recognize, uncomfortably, as part of himself. In other
> words, having put aside the idea of aggressive masculinity,
> Steig discovers – like his age mates around the planet, and with
> a kind of horror – a hidden quality of softness and femininity at
> the very core of self.[50]

By the time he has reached his 60s and early 70s, this artist's
drawings show a marked change in content and style. Now,
says Gutmann, the drawings show an

> idealization of bounteous, queenlike women – Venuses at-
> tended by diminished men. . . . The aging Steig, like the gener-
> ic men we have been studying, divests himself of aggression, or
> uses it to obliterate the masculine rather than the feminine
> principle. Older now, he tries to please the mothers rather than
> the fathers. When he was more interested in masculinity, the

younger Steig wanted the affirmation of men; but when the older Steig has come to terms with, and even relishes his more feminine side, his wistful men try to link themselves to a "good mother," but one who forever eludes them.[51]

Gutmann emphasizes that this turn from the idealization of masculinity to the elevation of femininity has many positive and adaptive aspects. In many societies, the elder men can take over caretaking functions such as mentoring – the generative pursuits Erikson talks about. No longer interested in proving their aggressive potentials, they can become interested in peacemaking and in symbolic leadership. Nevertheless, one senses in Gutmann's interpretation also a profound sense of loss and fear – note the difference of this interpretation from that of Jaques. These men, in Gutmann's description, have not fully integrated a sense of femininity. Rather, they seem to be haunted by a sense of diminishment vis-à-vis the feminine, of feeling disempowered by women they have come to experience as powerful and even dominant. In fact, for some men this sense of diminishment persists in a pernicious form in which evil is projected onto these larger-than-life female figures. For these men, the ascendancy of female power, far from leading to an integration, causes them to perceive women as "witches," as carriers of evil and dangerous powers. Thus, they turn powerful women into "hags," into hostile forces that the self evades by escaping into a sensual isolation. Rather than creating a cooperative and loving relationship, the self retreats into a kind of war in which "men can gain some version of victory by creating their own supplies, the belly pleasures and eye pleasures of booze and boob tube."[52]

Although brilliant in many ways, Gutmann's analysis still remains embedded in the tendency to view the feminine as dangerous, and to devalue it accordingly. It contrasts to that of Jung,[53] who has gone further and suggested that the successful resolution of this issue can be measured by the extent to which a man is able to accept the feminine as a force that is entirely positive. In her study of masculine symbolic imagery, Dougherty[54] addresses this issue and describes the dream themes of one particular man undergoing analysis. Early in the process of analysis, this man has many dreams in which the feminine appears as a dark and demanding force, putting the dreamer into a trance and into bondage. Over time, however, that imagery changes. The feminine begins to appear as a figure of light, as a guide and Muse, to which the dreamer responds with awe and respect and whom he accepts as a leader to transformation and wholeness.

Dougherty's observations underscore findings from an ongoing study of dream themes along the life span.[55] In dreams, men too can experience a new relationship to the feminine. Here is a dream of a 38-year-old man:

> The dream begins with me delivering some supplies to an office within a hospital. After knocking on the door, a beautiful nurse answers and begins to take the packages from me. As I stand there watching her place these boxes on a shelf in a closet, I suddenly find myself becoming embarrassed because I am staring. I then leave and find myself lying in a room which oversees a patient corridor. In this corridor lies an elderly terminal gentleman on a hospital stretcher. As I lie there, I notice this same gorgeous nurse walk up to this man and begin to comfort him. Before you know it, almost as an act of mercy, she begins to unbutton her uniform to reveal her white breast to this expecting fellow. All while this is happening I remember thinking to myself, what an unselfish act.

This dream becomes interpretable if one accepts that in the language of mythos, temporal ordering often represents a causal relation.[56] Moreover, in Jungian dream interpretation same sex figures usually represent aspects of the self that are not integrated into consciousness. Thus, the dying old man is part of the self, and what has depleted the self is the giving of part of himself to the feminine. Moreover, the gorgeous beauty of the nurse indicates that this giving up of the self is erotically toned. Lying on a stretcher and close to death, however, the self needs to reverse this process. At first sight, the woman's baring her breast might appear no more than a sexual overture, but the dream with its allusion to the whiteness of the

breasts and to mercy suggests a deeper message, almost spiritual and redemptive, for the restoration of the self. The
depleted self now needs to accept the feminine as a nourishing
part of the self.

This theme of revisiting the feminine can occur in ways that
are quite innocuous and seemingly insignificant. For example,
in our sample one man aged 50 had the following dream:

> I went to visit my sister. I stayed at her house, we took her car
> and went into the local town and went shopping and had
> something to eat. I spent the hour sightseeing. Upon returning
> we had dinner and spent the evening conversing.

Here, the theme of developing a more "nourishing" relationship to the feminine is embedded in an apparent everyday
interaction with a sister. Jungian dream analysis, though,
would hold that dreams are rarely just about such personal
relationships, but point beyond the personal to something
more general and archetypal – here a type of relationship with
the feminine that the dreamer is yearning for. The dream, thus,
signals that the dreamer is ready to integrate these aspects into
the self.

However, not all men discern such signals. Instead of becoming integrated, these feminine aspects may remain split off
and perceived as hostile and dangerous. Here is the dream of a
48-year-old man:

> I dreamt I visited an old friend's house, and thugs lived there. A
> woman was shaking a broom at me.

Here, the dreamer encounters the split-off elements as men-
acing individuals. The most specific of these is the figure of the
witch, signaling to the man that it is time to reexamine his own
inner construction of the feminine as dangerous and
threatening.

In our study of dreams across the adult life span, we find
that individuals rarely are cognizant of the meanings of these
dreams. Even so, the emergence of such themes of integration

is a significant trend around the middle of life. Nevertheless, it appears that few individuals take such signs as an encouragement to begin an exploration of their representations of gender. This is why I believe, along with others, that the achievement of integration in middle adulthood is perhaps an ideal. Literature suggests, as well, that behaviors may not change dramatically during midlife. Even though older men may report a desire for closeness, they actually spend most of their time alone, while their wives continue to complain about their inability to communicate.[57]

Moreover, some of the sex-role changes observed in older people may be due to other factors. Troll and Bengtson[58] report that sometimes they may occur because of failing health. For example, postmenopausal women are often healthier than they were before, and are healthier than their male age cohorts. Further, since many women continue to work after their husbands retire, the balance of power may change significantly, with the woman increasing in power and dominance.

Before closing this discussion of men's changing experience of the feminine, a brief discussion is in order about the notion of a crisis around midlife. Some researchers [59] claim that there is no evidence of major upheavals and pathology surrounding midlife. However, it is not necessary to find major problems to allow the notion of a crisis. In fact, in Rosenberg and Farrell's[60] study a state of dramatic crisis characterized only some subgroups of men that apparently had a long history of ongoing problems. One subgroup, called "punitive-disenchanted," were in crisis, felt restless and irritable, unhappy with their families; another, called "anti-hero," felt alienated from the community and mass culture, from their marriages, and their lives in general. Yet the one subgroup apparently most developed, called "transcendent-generative," did not show any major symptoms of crisis.

Research by Livson[61] also suggests that full-blown crisis may be characteristic of only certain subgroups. She identified two groups of men who had high levels of mental health at midlife. One of the subgroups, which included men who had appeared angry, hostile, defensive, and ruminating, had considerably improved mental health over the previous decade. Another subgroup had remained stable, showing a picture of good mental health throughout the whole period. Livson suggested that perhaps the degree to which an individual encounters a crisis depends on the degree to which he is able to conform to traditional gender stereotypes. For the younger adult, a mismatch between those stereotypes and one's inclinations may be very difficult to integrate. But in later adulthood, the individual may be better able to integrate the resulting tension between inner inclination and outer demands.

THE WOMAN'S "ESCAPE FROM INTERIORITY"

If the masculine route to maturity consists of the relinquishment of the heroic attitude that is balanced with compassion, the feminine route, we noted earlier, involves balancing compassion with a heroic and more self-centered attitude. That theme is central to the well-known Grimm fairy tale, "The Frog Prince."[62] Interestingly, however, the end of the tale is typically distorted, both in popular translations of the Grimm tale in children's editions and in the recollection of many adults. According to that distorted ending, the spell under which the frog prince has lived is broken as the princess overcomes her distaste and kisses the frog, causing its transformation into a beautiful prince. But the original Grimm version hardly ends with such a "typically feminine" gesture of self-sacrifice. Rather the princess, gripped by disgust and fury at the frog's insistent demand to share her bed, picks him up and in anger throws him against the wall. It is this act of self-assertive self-knowledge that transforms the frog into a prince. Thus, liberation comes to the woman – and the man to whom she relates – by expressing her anger rather than by engaging in the youthful pattern of holding it in.[63]

Hildegard of Bingen

The history of women's life course occasionally provides dramatic examples of that theme. An example is the life of Hildegard of Bingen, a 12th-century abbess, political figure, physician, and musician living near Bingen, Germany.[64] Born in 1098, she was educated by a Benedictine anchoress. When her teacher died, Hildegard, then 38 years of age, took over the leadership of her small female community. Within four years she had a profound spiritual awakening that decisively altered her vocation and her creative life. Eventually, a young monk was appointed as her scribe and secretary, and from her 42nd to her 52nd year, Hildegard recorded her visions in word and picture in her famed illuminated book, *Scivias* (Ways of wisdom). After this major work, Hildegard completely transformed what had been a secluded life and went on to write many books on physiology, plants, healing, and theology. She was also a major figure of musical history, writing many hymns as well as an opera. Her correspondence was tremendous and encompassed many of the major intellectual and political figures of the day, including the pope and Emperor Barbarossa, whom she castigated for his lack of compassion.

Hildegard's breakthrough stands as an example of what many writers associate with the midlife crisis. For her, the before and after of this crisis were profoundly different. She described the before as a condition of passivity, of being without a voice, of being frustrated. Her powerful visions did not correspond to traditional teachings, and out of "humility" and "obedience" she refused to write. But, she reports, this creativity-turned-against-the-self caused her severe suffering and illness: "Not in stubbornness but in humility, I refused to write for so long that I felt pressed down under the whip of God into the bed of sickness."[65] She stated that "because of doubt and erroneous thinking and because of controversial advice from men,"[66] she had refused to write. But once she followed her inner voice, her suffering ended and she experienced a profound surge of creativity and spiritual growth. "Beaten down by many kinds of illnesses," she says, "I put my hand to writing. Once I did this, a deep and profound exposition of books came over me. I received the strength to rise up from my sick bed, and under that power I continued to carry out the work to the end, using all of ten years to do it."[67]

Jung[68] has claimed that for the man, later life brings a transformation of the inner guiding image (or figurative representation) of the feminine. Similarly for the woman, later life brings a transformation of the inner image of the masculine. For the man, the task is to accept that not all that is associated with the body and the senses, with nature and the imaginative, is feminine, and that logic and reason are just as much a part of womanhood as of manhood. For the woman, I suggest, the compensating movement is of the opposite sort: She needs to reclaim for herself the mental and creative gifts she hitherto has projected onto men.

For a woman like Hildegard whose life was organized around religion, that image would naturally focus on her conception of God. Fox [69] argues that her mature concept of God spells out a vision quite opposed to the patriarchal fall–redemption theology of Augustine, who emphasized a vengeful God whose wrath was directed toward the feminine. Instead, states Fox, Hildegard suggests that we accept our bodily existence as a way of celebrating the universe. She emphasizes the interconnectedness of all beings, and believes in nature and cosmos as a place that is hospitable. Moreover, humans can help make the universe a more hospitable place by accepting and celebrating their creative gifts rather than suffocating them under the weight of guilt.

Women's "growing down"

We often discuss changes along the life course in relation to heroic masculine patterns, but the feminine perspective constitutes a parallel and complementary narrative of the life course. That narrative is discussed by Pratt in her important study, *Archetypal Patterns in Women's Fiction.*[70] Pratt notes that novels by women about women suggest woman's struggle for wholeness and to regain control of her body, her intellect, and her sexuality. That struggle, she notes, is often expressed indirectly, because women fear the consequences of their struggle for authenticity. In a woman's earlier life such authenticity may be quite impossible. Instead, she becomes invested in proper feminine conduct, constantly suppressing subversive desires for self-expression and development. To pursue self-development means to transgress social taboos. However, for the woman in her prime, such authenticity and selfhood may come more easily than to the younger woman or to the woman who is overly concerned with being socially established.

Just as we discussed in Chapter 4, Pratt states that novels of early female development often are models for "growing down" rather than "growing up." The goal of the story is the suppression of intellect and eroticism, and the ideal, the suppression of individuality and anger, even when the result is injustice. As a consequence, development often is experienced as a form of entrapment, themes of suffocation and dwarfing are frequent, and a sense of claustrophobia and enclosure prevails. But as women mature, argues Pratt, novels often portray a more integrated vision of self – a self that, like Psyche, rejects the cultural view of proper masculinity and femininity and that goes on to form an integration of the two. Pratt thinks that this process is usually portrayed as following a particular course.

First, the woman begins to have a conscious awareness of her situation. She perceives its confining limits and its sense of entrapment, and she decides to split off from family, husband, or lover. Like Psyche, she turns away from a model in which masculine and feminine are experienced as split, as arranged in terms of an inner or outer marriage of death. Of course, that "leaving the marriage" here is primarily an inner event, not an outer one, though Jungian authors[71] would point out that many individuals may mistake this inner signal as a stimulus to change their outer life structure.

At a later juncture, the woman often encounters, whether as an actual figure or a reverie, a new type of masculine figure. If previously the masculine figure was one that entraps and suppresses, now it becomes one of liberation. Pratt calls this figure the "green world lover." This is akin to the green man discussed earlier. He embodies, therefore, a degree of integration between masculine and feminine elements. This figure is more compatible with her "self world," and usually helps lead her away from the values of society toward her own inner depths. This figure represents, then, a change in representation and corresponds to the man's encounter with the positive woman guide noted by Levinson.[72] Just as that female figure no longer entraps and seduces, so the green man image indicates that the masculine now is perceived as a more helpful force, a guide aiding the woman in her transformation.

But before she can claim her inner sense of strength, the woman hero confronts a deeper and often painful examination of herself. This examination occurs first in terms of an inner encounter with her parental figures and the effects these figures had on her development. Once she has worked through this layer of her history, she turns to a fuller realization of her own potential for power. This may be a most difficult and painful process where a woman is likely to encounter her deep sense of shame, self-loathing, and self-hatred as they relate to self-expression. Moreover, since power is an attribute celebrated as masculine but devalued in women, claiming her individuality is often actively discouraged.

One way in which this is done is through the negative stereotype of singlehood in women. Singleness in mythology often connotes a positive state, an inner union in a woman of masculine and feminine traits. However, in novels that state is often considered problematic. In opera, too, a woman's independent pursuit of her individuality often has the most dire consequences, resulting in the fact that most operatic heroines pay for their flirtations with passion and/or independence with death. As Pratt puts it,

Women's rebirth journeys . . . create transformed, androgynous, and powerful human personalities out of socially devalued beings and are therefore more likely to involve denouements punishing the quester for succeeding in her perilous, revolutionary journey.[73]

On a more optimistic note, Gutmann also has argued that the movement from a world of confinement to one of daring openness constitutes a perhaps universal pattern of feminine development. Using Georgia O'Keeffe as an example, Gutmann argues that this painter's early work shows a movement from a micro- to a macroworld. The early work, maintains Gutmann, is characterized by a concern with inner space, with sensuality, with diffuse coloring. This style changes remarkably in later life:

> In old age, O'Keeffe's paintings are of vast spaces, arid desert regions, unpeopled but full of light. . . . Seventy-five percent of the later paintings are of this spacious and hard-edged variety, in which sensuality – to the degree that it is still present – belongs to rounded rock spires and sand dunes rather than to the soft flesh of inner flowers.[74]

Gutmann describes this rebalancing as an "escape from interiority." In a woman's life course, that escape is often depicted as a confrontation with her own authority and a sense of recovering her own "voice." Belenky, Clinchy, Goldberger, and Tarule, in their book *Women's Ways of Knowing*,[75] discuss this issue and suggest that before she discovers this subjective self, a woman is likely to feel herself disempowered and without a voice. I suggest that this process of reclaiming one's voice specifically involves unearthing those aspects of the self that have been censored and deregulated as masculine.

Women's images of the masculine

Young-Eisendrath and Wiedemann argue that this process is reflected in the changing imagery of masculine figures as they are represented in women's dreams. They distinguish different stages of this reflection of male images. Initially, at an early stage, masculine figures appear who are seen as all powerful, but also as distant and nonempathic toward the feminine. An example is a dream reported by Freud in his famous analysis of "Dora":

A house was on fire. My father was standing beside my bed and woke me up. I dressed myself quickly. Mother wanted to stop and save her jewel-case, but Father said: "I refuse to let myself and my two children be burnt for the sake of your jewel-case." We hurried downstairs, and as soon as I was outside I woke up.[76]

Freud interpreted this dream as a seduction wish, but I would propose a more general interpretation. The father here displays all the stereotypical qualities of the masculine: determination, control, decisive judgment. But he is also in conflict with the values of the feminine, here symbolized by the jewel case. Indeed, as Young-Eisendrath and Wiedemann note, Dora's father was a man who devalued the feminine, and Dora had learned to cope with that devaluation, in part, by idealizing the strength of her father. Yet this also left her in a state of fragmentation, a feeling that a "false self" had been erected to cover up a true self experienced as weak, empty, and fearful.

This symbol of a feminine feeling disempowered and overwhelmed by an overvalued masculine element is even more stark in a dream of a 47-year-old woman of our sample:

I had this dream about a year ago, but it still bothers me, especially at night when I go downstairs. The dream is very vivid – I'm down in the basement of my house. I can see the laundry tubs and piles of unwashed clothing. As I bend over to pick something up, a man puts a scarf or nylon around my throat and is strangling me to death and I pass out. I could feel myself dying, not being able to breathe anymore.

For a woman's subsequent development, the task is to withdraw this projection of strength from the masculine and, correspondingly, to realize that this sense of strength is part of herself projected outward. Thus, she can reclaim that sense and utilize it toward the building of inner self-structure. As she does so, her imagery of the masculine often changes from that of a powerful but confining figure into that of a helper. The following dream shows that change in the confrontation between two male figures, one hostile, the other helpful:

There is an old woman locked up in an asylum. The room has been locked for a long time and the woman was kept in a locked closet within. She wanted out, but was being held a prisoner. Her husband came to get her and had gotten into her room without permission. He had some plan to free her, but the male doctor was really shocked that the husband loved her so much, that he was going to save her. This room is in the basement. The old woman had thought the place was a hotel when she came, but then she had not been strong enough to leave. I watched all of this and didn't think the husband knew what was going on, and I was afraid the doctor would lock both of them up. But it was clear at the end that the husband would get the old woman out. I thought to myself, "the husband might be a little crazy too," and concluded, "I don't know because it's hard to tell who's crazy and who's not."[77]

The woman's subsequent task is to integrate fully a sense of authority into a sense of self. Now, dreams occur in which the masculine figure is a full partner to the feminine. In her study of concepts of the masculine, Dougherty[78] also suggests that this encounter with the "green man" constitutes an essential step, typified by a characteristic dream sequence of one woman:

A logos-oriented woman with a developed thinking function has a long series of dreams that feature erotic and intrusive male figures. As the dream ego handles these encounters more competently, the figures exhibit more and more Pan-like qualities (hooves, plays pipes, dances with the woman, dreams take place in the woods, furry body, etc.). As the dream ego becomes less threatened and more receptive and relational, the male figure becomes less unrelated and intrusive. (He feeds her, gives her wool blankets, protects her from danger.)[79]

Here, then, the woman encounters a male principle that balances the principle of logos. The green world guide she meets in her dreams points to the fact that her inner representation of the masculine is moving away from the one-sided spiritualization of the masculine pole to its enrichment with organic elements.

The notion of changes in inner representation of the masculine and the feminine has been worked out in detail in more narrative study, such as that of biography and dreams. But an increasing body of research suggests that the notion of changes in inner representation may form a powerful principle integrating what we know about midlife changes in women. Many authors concur that women's later lives ideally bring a liberation from the confinement of traditional sex roles, and that this liberation is one of the major changes associated with development in the second half of life for women. Thus, from young adulthood to midlife, women have been found to *de*crease their scores on traditional femininity while increasing those on dominance, independence, objectivity, and intellectuality.[80] Overall, these women's scores suggest "an ability to separate thought from feelings, to be detached from affect-laden situations, and to focus attention."[81]

Helson's[82] study of creative, college-educated women offers a good example of such patterns of developmental change. The women in Helson's sample changed considerably between the ages of 27 and 43. They dropped in femininity and increased in social assertiveness, independence, and perceptiveness about self and others. From 43 to 52, there were further changes, with increases in emotional stability, in masculinity, and in cognitive breadth and skill, and decreases in femininity. Thus, these women show a marked increase in assurance, intellectuality, and orientation to values. Helson believes that this increasing confidence and decisiveness in cognitive and moral areas supports the Jungian notion of "integration of the masculine." Moreover, there was higher congruence between actual self and ideal self. All of these changes, Helson argues, were shown to be progressive rather than regressive, since the increase in masculinity brought a gain in confidence and decisiveness, while the decrease in femininity brought a reduction in dependence and vulnerability.

Helson also addresses the question of whether these women had experienced a crisis. Although crisis would be too strong a term, there was evidence that uncertainty and strong affects in the early 40s had given way to stability and calm in the early 50s. These women reported that difficult times had begun in the early 40s, and also that the 40s had been a time of identity questioning and turmoil.

Other studies suggest, too, that while it is often difficult for the young woman to live with her complexity and her creative urges, it may become easier for the older woman to reconcile unconventional strivings. For example, in a study by Livson[83] middle-aged women who were unconventional had displayed a problematic picture of mental health earlier in their adulthood; but later, they were flexible, complex, and well adjusted. Similarly, Maas and Kuypers,[84] in their study of individuals aging from their 30s to their 70s, located a subsample of women who had experienced great discontinuity from early adulthood to late life. These women in their 30s were discontented and poorly adjusted, feeling trapped in their marriages and blaming their husbands for their lack of satisfaction. Some 40 years later, however, these women who had been the most poorly adjusted of the sample had made dramatic readjustments and turned out to be the best-adjusted subsample. These women had developed independent careers and greatly enjoyed the opportunity for identity and growth they afforded.

Gutmann[85] and, before him, Jung[86] believed that such a freeing up of women's lives constitutes a universal aspect of later life development. If so, however, the transformation of later life creativity in women constitutes an ideal rather than a statistical norm, since the literature suggests that perhaps only a few extraordinary women truly are able to break out of the confines of their youthful adaptations. It is perhaps better to state that a woman's reclaiming of her authority to speak her own creative voice constitutes a unique task around which her later life appears to be organized. Thus, her conflicts and her sense of self may be focused around the inner struggle about reclaiming her authority. However, only some women may resolve this struggle, since there have been and continue to be pervasive cultural conditions that discourage women from reaching toward full development of their potentials.

If we reach back far enough historically, evidence of this release of creative energy is extremely rare. As Virginia Woolf[87] noted in *A Room of One's Own*, and as reiterated in Olsen's[88] *Silences* and in Heilbrun's[89] *Writing a Woman's Life*, one is much more overwhelmed with the almost universal degree to which women's efforts at achievement were blunted with terrifying efficacy. As Heilbrun notes, even in relatively recent generations of women writers – for example, Virginia Woolf and Sylvia Plath – one finds that the inner conflicts about achievement and creative expression, though sharply and poignantly articulated, remain a source of pain so deep that it cannot be integrated. Both Woolf and Plath decided to end their suffering and their despair through suicide.

Similarly, in their recent study of gifted women, Tomlinson-Keasey and Blurton[90] note that, paradoxically, a woman's awareness of her superior skills may often diminish rather than enhance her adulthood, weighing her down with a sense of failure and discouragement rather than freeing her energy. Veroff and his co-workers[91] also note in their large survey sample that women who were employed often experience a steep decline in achievement motivation at midlife. Apparently, these women had begun with high career aspirations, but ended up feeling confined by jobs offering little opportunity for advancement. As Huyck[92] suggests, while many women around midlife give voice to their dissatisfaction with the feminine roles they have adopted, this changing discourse about the self in no way guarantees that the resulting conflicts are clearly articulated or even resolved.

To point out the real problems and obstacles women may face in their later life development is not meant to sound an overly discouraging note. Rather, it is to suggest that the course of women's later life development cannot really be discussed without calling attention to the changing social system in which women are embedded. In that regard, Heilbrun points out that it is likely that the achievements of women themselves can work toward transforming social realities. By giving voice to their struggles, earlier generations of women began to reformulate the options available to later generations of women; by building on the work of their predecessors, more recent generations of women can continue the process by which women's lives are rewritten and reinvented. Already, argues Heilbrun, this is evident in successive generations of women poets:

> Only in the last third of the twentieth century have women broken through a realization of the narratives that have been controlling their lives. Women poets of one generation – those born between 1923 and 1932 – can now be seen to have transformed the autobiographies of women's lives, to have expressed, and suffered for expressing, what women had not earlier been allowed to say. . . . These women . . . simultaneously dismantled the past and reimagined the future.[93]

CONCLUSION

This chapter continues the theme of reintegrating the polarities of the mind begun in Chapter 5. In the current chapter, I suggest that a rebalancing or "reenchantment" of the mind requires specifically that we reorganize our imagery of gender that underlies traditional dualist notions of the mind. In this process of rebalancing, the overvalued masculine principle needs to be grounded, while the undervalued feminine principle needs to be elevated. Thus, the process of integration can take on very different experiential qualities, depending on whether it is approached from the masculine or the feminine pole. Approached from the former, the experience is primarily that of disempowerment. But approached from the latter pole, the primary emphasis is on reempowerment.

Evidence of such transformation can be found in contemporary adults who are involved in reorganizing their imagery of gender. That process shows systemic differences, depending on whether it is approached from a masculine or a feminine perspective. From a masculine perspective, the process involves overcoming an attitude of devaluating and belittling the feminine; from a feminine perspective, the main goal is to resist the idealization of the masculine.

This process of transcending culturally bound gender categories is sometimes referred to as the move toward androgyny. I agree, however, with Dougherty who suggests that androgyny is a problematic term, suggesting as it does a blurring of the boundaries between masculinity and femininity. Gender, I suggest, remains extremely critical to an individual's sense of himself or herself. Paradoxically, however, as individuals begin to transcend culturally based gender definitions, they begin to experience themselves as more securely masculine or feminine, indicating a deeper and more integrated sense of self.

Chapter 7

Postlude: The sacred marriage

As Psyche lay in her deathlike sleep, Eros was recovering from his wound. Now healed, he was unable to endure the separation from his bride; and so he slipped through the window of his chamber, and flew to Psyche to rise her from her sleep. He then flew to Zeus and pleaded with the God to have mercy on Psyche, to make her immortal, and to let her come live with him in the heavens. Zeus had pity on Eros, and turning to Aphrodite, he said: "Do not be downcast, for this marriage will be worthy of your son." He then ordered Hermes to bring Psyche to Olympus. When Psyche arrived, he told her: "Psyche, drink of this ambrosia and be immortal. Then Eros shall never leave your arms, and your marriage shall endure forever."

So it happened that Psyche became Eros' bride, and soon a daughter was born to them: she was given the name of Pleasure.

A DIVINE UNION

The myth concludes with Psyche's travails being rewarded when Zeus admits her to Mount Olympus, where she is raised to the status of a goddess and joins her divine husband in a sacred marriage. In ancient times, the sacred or divine marriage (Greek: *hieros gamos*) was a powerful symbol, enacted in story, art, and ritual. It indicated to individuals that the events were based on a proper balance of elements. In Egypt, for example, male royal authority was recognized only if it was properly empowered by a feminine principle in the form of a goddess, as in the marriage of Isis and Osiris. Even in the human realm, that symbolism persisted in the form of a throne that referred to the lap of the goddess; by ascending the throne, the king (and, in religious symbolism, even the pope), now symbolically sitting in the lap of the goddess, indicated his adherence to a broader cosmic order. "The throne," as Frankfort notes, "made manifest a divine power which changed one of several princes into a king fit to rule."[1]

A union of opposites

In ancient mythology[2] the symbol of the sacred marriage thus referred to a relationship of complementarity and wholeness, creating a cooperative union of different polarities of the mind and personified by male and female divinities with their associated symbols of sun and light versus moon and darkness. But, as I have argued throughout this book, mature adulthood in cultural and in individual development has not always been defined as a balance of dualities, a *coincidentia oppositorum*. In cultural development, the evolution of Western consciousness brought a gradual waning of the symbolisms of integration, as the ideals of cosmic order came to be seen as residing in a single pole of mind and human nature. I have referred to this pole as logos – the tendency to view reality primarily from a rational, deterministic, paradigmatic perspective – and contrasted it with mythos – the tendency to perceive the world imaginatively, from the perspective of stories, images, and subjective symbols.

The development of the logos pole of the mind probably was of extreme importance in the evolution of Western thinking about mind and human nature. The new concept of the mind was based on such oppositions as mind versus body, self versus other, self versus society, objective truth versus subjective inclination, and so forth. Thus, as mythos became differentiated from logos, it also became subordinated to it. These two poles were thought to be arranged vertically, with the mental pole the superior, and the organic one, the inferior pole. As a consequence, wisdom and mature reason were assumed to be aimed at a notion of universal objective truth that was, presumably, purged of subjective elements.

I used the story of Psyche and Eros to trace the development of the individual growing to maturity within that vertical structure. Yet the story also suggests that this structure is only a preliminary one (while perhaps a necessary first step). I have referred to that preliminary structure as "primary development," and suggested that within that structure, the individual splits the representations of self and reality along the prevalent cultural paradigm. As a result, primary development does not permit the individual to reach a state of wholeness. Initial adaptation in early adulthood is characterized by a marriage of death in which part of the self is heroically elevated, while part of the self is, to an equal and opposite extent, suppressed.

This verticalization of development is supported by an elaborate imagery of hierarchical control. Good and evil, strong and weak, "up" and "down" – all are dimensions of reality that provide pervasive metaphors that structure our sense of reality in primary development. It has been a core argument of this book that these metaphors are carried over into the domain of gender. Gendered personifications of mental qualities, whether in mythic products such as in religion, art, and literature, or (more indirectly) in logos products such as philosophical and scientific theories, tend to idealize power, strength, and domination as aspects of the masculine. These same elements are considered problematic and evil if encountered in the feminine, which is based on an idealization of surrender, passivity, and suffering.

The development of this vertical mode of adaptation does not permit the achievement of wholeness in either men or women. How such integration becomes the theme in later development is symbolized in the second part of the myth of Psyche and Eros. As Psyche continues on her journey, she dismantles the hierarchical structure she has elaborated and constructs a new, secondary structure. That secondary structure is based on complementarity and the creative tension of a union of opposites. Psyche achieves that secondary structure by engaging in a series of graded tasks that require that logos and mythos, the masculine and the feminine, be integrated and balanced. The divine marriage between Psyche and Eros is the result of these trials. This union of opposites character-izes a new concept of maturity, one that is implied in many recent studies of developmental processes in adulthood.

The union of opposites implied in the divine marriage is not only an ancient symbol, but one that has a surprisingly con-temporary ring. In fact, as Jules and Cashford[3] show, it is a symbol that has never lost its vitality. Though the notion of a balance of the masculine and the feminine was not publicly recognized as a guiding image and was pushed underground, it continued a vigorous life there and persisted in much of Christian symbolism. But in the contemporary era, this sym-bolism has been revived as individuals search for a new sys-tem of metaphors that may guide our wide-ranging search for a new model of wisdom and maturity.

If the process of primary development has been described as one of disenchantment or demythification, that of secondary development sometimes is referred to as one of re-enchantment or remythification.[4] Just as primary develop-ment consists of banning the concrete and organismic, the imaginative and ludic, and the feminine from the arena of "mature functioning," so secondary development requires that these dimensions be restored.

The story of Psyche and Eros is not specific in showing how such a restoration comes to bear on the interaction of the cou-ple. A story that is more specific in that respect is Louisa Molesworth's story "The Brown Bull or Norwa,"[5] a story of the "Beauty and the Beast" type. In Molesworth's rendition, a princess is abducted by a fierce and wild bull to a faraway country. The princess, who was given a set of golden balls at her birth as a sign of her extraordinary potential and who is more skillful at juggling those balls than anyone far and wide, soon finds that the bull is no other than an enchanted prince who sheds his bull skin for three hours a day and joins her ball play. The bull tells the princess that his enchantment will be broken if she is patient for another three years. Of course, the princess' impatience wins out and she must leave the bull-prince. Only after many years and a series of travails are both united: Now, they are able to engage in the back-and-forth tossing of the golden balls without the interruption of their immature features.

Hermes and reason

The story suggests that the restoration of the split in the dissociated polarities is made possible by a playful exchange between two different but equal partners. I have proposed that such a restoration can be achieved through the principle of hermeneutics. The concept of hermeneutics is particularly relevant in this context, as the name derives from the god Hermes.[6] In Greek mythology,[7] Hermes is the messenger god who mediates between the divine and the human realms. Indeed, it is this god who is the final catalyst in facilitating the integration of the divine marriage by escorting Psyche to Olympus.

Hermes is a very different kind of god from Apollo – or his "erotic" counterpart, the Eros of the death marriage. Apollo stands for stable structure, clear boundaries, and logos. He could be called, in fact, the god of primary development. But Hermes is a god who negates Apollonic stability. He personifies agility of movement, shifting across levels and crossing boundaries. Of him, Stassinopoulos says:

> He is the god of the unexpected, of luck, of coincidences, of synchronicity. "Hermes has entered our midst," the ancient Greeks would say when a sudden silence entered the room, descended on conversation, introduced into the gathering another dimension. Whenever things seem fixed, rigid, "stuck," Hermes introduces fluidity, motion, new beginnings – and the confusion that inevitably precedes new beginnings.[8]

Hermes is known for his creative ingenuity and eloquent persuasiveness. On the first day of his life, he invented the lyre when he found a tortoise, killed it, and strung seven strings across the emptied shell. He also is the inventor of the flute, which he created from reeds. Both of those instruments he traded with Apollo who gave him, among others, the gift of augury.[9] Because of his gift of persuasive speech, Zeus made Hermes a messenger who mediated between mortals and immortals. Thus, he is often associated with the ability to move across transitional spaces. As Hermes Psychopompos, he also serves as a guide of souls into the underworld.

Under his Roman name of Mercury, Hermes is the prime god of the alchemists who hoped to transform base matter into refined, spiritual gold. Mercury is "quicksilver," the spirit that existed in matter. Thus, he is a symbol that unites opposites: spirit and matter, life (earth) and soul (underworld), ego and unconscious, logos and mythos. He could be said to personify the principle of hermeneutics as discussed in Chapter 5. As a god who functions as a catalyst, he stands for the transitional and potential spaces Winnicott discussed – those activities that create a bridge between self and other, mind and body, reason and imagination, reality and play.

Like Hermes, many contemporary adults are concerned with a similar restructuring of reality. They do so as they begin to understand that the "Apollonian" perspective on development has provided only a one-sided narrative of life's journey. With its emphasis on ideal, stability, and control, it has split off surrender and suffering. Yet this dark, shadow self continues to live an existence, as powerful as it is unacknowledged. By recovering this neglected narrative and by integrating it with the idealized one, I have suggested, many adults are engaged in creating a fuller and more balanced narrative of their lives. Ideally, that new structure permits the individual to join the two selves in the cooperative union of a lateral structure of life or mind.

In this process of rebalancing, it is particularly critical that we recover the language of mythos that was previously deleted from accounts of mind, self, and human nature. The power of such an integration lies in the fact that mythos consists of and provides, in image and story, a concrete language of the symbols that have served as core metaphors for logos-oriented models of the mind. That concrete representation can also help to change that language by suggesting new guiding images. Ultimately, it is through such a base of imagery that we will be able to evolve new ways of describing human nature.

In Chapter 2, I have discussed how in the course of history, models of mind and self were dissociated along several dimensions. First, the mind evolved as a unit that was differentiated from the physical and the organic. Second, it moved from a communal or transpersonal principle to an individual, intrapsychic one. And finally, it moved the definition of the nature of truth to the rational arena, which was opposed to that of the imaginative and subjectively meaningful.

I suggest that the notion of hermeneutics can restore these dissociations. First, it moves the unit of analysis from the individual to the dyad or group, thus invoking a supra- or transpersonal principle. According to that principle, the search for truth is always embedded in an interpersonal or communicative process. At the same time, this process must follow certain rules that themselves transcend the specific dyad. Those rules are inherent in the process both of objective inquiry and of the mutual respect that is a necessary precondition for such inquiry.

Second, hermeneutics can build a bridge between the mental and conceptual, and the physical and organic dimension of knowledge. It does so because it elaborates the concrete situatedness of knowledge. Yet it also assumes that, once individuals submit to the process of cooperative inquiry, knowledge is changed in a self-regulating way to reveal a more generalized, overarching system. Finally, it rejects the traditional notion of an opposition between objectivity and subjectivity. Instead, it views the two as coordinated, one supporting the other, both defining each other. As in development the realm of objectivity is widened and enlarged, so the realm of subjectivity is explicated and deepened.

Throughout this book, I also suggest that in this process of rebalancing, gender-related imagery has an extremely crucial role. The two types of narratives – the self as hero and the self as sufferer, the self as thinker and controller and the self as a reactor to emotions – have been widely associated with masculinity and femininity. Those two narratives, I suggest, also have quite different (though complementary) relationships with masculine and feminine core identity. As we have seen historically, however, it has been the masculine pole that has been especially well elaborated and idealized, while the feminine pole has been less well elaborated, and seen primarily in a pejorative sense.

It is this asymmetry that creates the particular dynamics of the myth and its meaning as a metaphor for the individual's journey through the course of life. The story of Psyche, as Neumann suggests, indicates that in that process of restoration, the feminine takes on a leading role. Much as primary development has been defined by the ascendancy of the masculine principle, so secondary development happens as the locus of activity moves to the feminine one. Even Eros' transformation is achieved through Psyche's actions, through her taking on a leading role and claiming her own heroism. And, claiming her own heroic attitude, Psyche is able to achieve the status of a goddess herself and to join the god Eros in a transformed union of balanced opposites.

Neumann[10] suggests a further feature that indicates how important it is to attend to the feminine element and the process of creating a union of wholeness. The story ends with the birth of a daughter to Psyche and Eros. The birth of a divine child is an important event in mythology and in the inner life of individuals. It indicates a sense of renewal of a self aspect that has not yet found appropriate expression. Conventional religion, of course, has placed primary emphasis of the birth of a masculine divine spirit, as in the birth of Jesus. Indeed, Eros earlier in the myth has predicted the birth of a son. However, the myth significantly breaks with that tradition, suggesting that a particularly redemptive aspect of the restoration of wholeness will be an attention to the feminine dimension of mind and spirit.

Postlude

SOME QUESTIONS FOR THE FUTURE

In this book, I have suggested a fairly wide-ranging view of development throughout the life course using the Psyche and Eros myth as an illustration. While details of this view remain to be worked out, I have attempted to show how it will integrate a wide body of research and thinking about development from early to late life. Nevertheless, in discussing the notions I have presented here with a wide range of colleagues and friends over the years, several questions have been raised consistently and with insistence. In ending this discussion, I would like to reply to several of those.

A place for idealism?

The questions often raised usually seem to converge on a few core issues. The first core issue is whether it is still a timely endeavor to evoke a "grand scheme" of development of the nature of rationality. As contemporary thinkers have abandoned the lavish hopes and claims of philosophies past, grand narratives about the nature of the mind and self are often considered hopelessly outdated. In an age of postmodernism and poststructuralism, is it necessary that we forgo such grand themes, searching instead for a pattern in local conditions?

I agree with the postmodern stance that our past narratives of development have been based on an extremely narrow form of idealism – what we might call an "Apollonian" idealism. To offer a critique and a deconstruction of that idealism by criticizing its static emphasis, its obsession with control and domination, and ultimately its egocentrism, has been an extremely valuable result of recent intellectual efforts. By dismantling the transcendentalism of logos-oriented theories of the mind, these theories have been shown to be divisive and dualistic. In an effort to avoid those errors of the past, a new intellectual fashion has taken hold: to celebrate relativism rather than holism, fragmentation rather than integration, local validity rather than universal applicability.

However, by providing primarily a negation of past Apollonian idealism, many postmodern and poststructuralist voices have provided mainly a negation rather than a new integration. In the process of negation, they still have remained embedded in the assumptions of logos-oriented models, which say that we have to opt for one or the other of a set of polarities. By negating the Apollonian pole, however, these critiques have not provided a constructive and overarching language within which that dualism can be analyzed and transcended. Instead, they have tended to erect a new form of dogmatism, according to which integration, holism, and universality are "out" and to be avoided at all cost.

The way of thinking I am advocating in this book does not rest with either of these polar opposites. Rather than thinking of the two as related in an either–or fashion, I suggest that they are related in a both–and relationship. Thus, part and whole or particular and overarching principles are related in a mutually codependent, codefining, and cooperative fashion. The next task facing those who study the mind, then, is to define a new language that can encompass both polarities.

Instead of casting my vote for a commitment to relativism, I am suggesting that the next step in theory construction must consist of developing a new language of mind and self. Such a language will not only reveal the problematic nature of Apollonian idealism but also locate that attitude within a more general framework. One such framework, I have suggested, would discuss Apollonian idealism in terms of the language of mythos on which it is based. By restoring such a complementarity between mythos and logos, we both expose a more general language on which the language of logos is based, and point the way to changing that language into one that is more wholesome and complete.

It is not necessary to throw away ideals in restoring this complementarity. Criticizing the rigidity of logos-based theories does not mean that more flexible forms of idealism are not possible. In keeping with the theme of this book, we might think of such a flexible form of idealism by invoking Hermes rather than Apollo. Thus, the emphasis on stability and one-

sided control would be replaced by an emphasis on transformation and on dialogue. Indeed, I suggest that such a concept
of "hermeneutic" idealism is particularly apt to summarize the
view of mind and self I have proposed in this book.

Hermeneutic idealism is a form of idealism quite different
from that associated with Apollo. It is a form of idealism that
accepts the differentiation between the polarities of mind and
self, yet also maintains that this differentiation must be held
together by a unifying principle. This unifying principle is not
held with the heavy hand of Apollo; it is held more tentatively,
more playfully. Louisa Molesworth's image of the princess
and prince tossing back and forth their golden balls is an apt
symbol of that principle of unification. It accepts the fact that
uncertainty is part and parcel of the search for truth. Yet, it
holds that understanding of uncertainty with a paradoxical
attitude, one that nevertheless maintains a vision or hope of
transcendental ideals.[11]

In fact, I further surmise that to speak about models of mind
and human nature presupposes ideals. Take, for example, the
field of medicine and physical health – fields in which these
notions are much less controversial than when talking about
theories of the mind and self. Any statement about the health
of an individual presupposes an ideal of health from which
such a statement derives. It would be quite impossible to make
such statements without an underlying model of ideals. Yet to
work with such ideals does not mean that we consider them
fixed or unchangeable. The mature individual may be quite
aware that these ideals are historically situated and subject to
revision. Yet, this knowledge may not need to create a relativistic paralysis in which a lack of certain standards justifies
nonaction.

The example of health also elucidates another problem often
associated with idealism. According to that critique, the fact
that only few if any individuals may embody standards of
wholeness is "proof" that such standards are useless. Again, I
disagree with that view. To hold an ideal standard does not
require that it is embodied in any quantity of individuals. In
fact, not a single individual may embody it. What matters,

instead, is that the standard serves as a useful tool to diagnose *deviations*. Thus, we can talk about such factors as exposure to a virus, air pollution, diet, and so forth, that will create inevitable deviations from some ideal. I suggest that, in a similar fashion, theories of mind and self in the future must resist the tendency to reify ideal standards.

In fact, the discussion of gender throughout this book is based on just such a conceptualization. It begins from the assumption that men and women are constituted with an equal set of potentialities. However, realized development is viewed as constituting deviation from that idealized model. At the same time, these deviations are related within a dialectical and systems perspective. Thus, both masculine and feminine patterns of development form different, though interrelated and complementary, deviations from an idealized pathway.

In a related fashion, the reader might also object that I have tended to evoke a broad historical-evolutionary scheme. In a way, I agree that one easily moves into slippery waters by doing so. As I have argued elsewhere, the tendency to use such schemes as pejorative standards of evaluation for some cultural and subcultural groups is a most unfortunate one.[12] Yet, such misuse of standards derives exactly from the kind of Apollonian idealism I am rejecting. It is quite alien to hermeneutical idealism. The latter is committed to a deep understanding of the ways in which ideals constellate their negatives, and out of that attitude of interpenetrating subjectivities comes a commitment to the process of communication rather than domination. In that process of cooperative communication, the game is not "who is better," but "how do we each see the world."

To engage in that game does not preempt the concept of evolution; it may, however, change our notion of it. Models of development still profoundly reflect the tenets of individualism. However, these tenets can be transformed within a more systemic and ecological perspective. In such a perspective, evolution reflects not just individual fates, but also an overarching balance and integration among the individual elements of the system.

Within such a whole systems perspective, the idealism of the Apollonian attitude can be reframed. Thus, a discussion of evolutionary movements is no longer a presumption that "our way is best." Neither is it necessary to rule out that certain regular and developmental movements are possible and even likely. For example, Donald[13] has recently reiterated and documented the suggestion quoted in Chapter 2 that changes in concepts of mind and self are a necessary consequence of increases in community size. Such changes necessarily bring new modes of thinking and of regulating behavior, along with a reorganization of the nature of self and its development across the life span. Whether these changes are "better" in any absolute sense is not really the issue here. What is at issue is that certain worldwide changes have created a new type of community, a global community in which communication requires a fairly universal type of language.

Gender as dialectical balance

Throughout this book, I have argued that one of the polarities particularly crucial in theories of mind and human nature is that of gender. This has easily been the assertion that has created the most vigorous and even passionate reactions. It is perhaps in keeping with the theme of this book that this should be so. However, many of the questions raised have paralleled those I discussed in the previous section, and can be briefly restated here.

One set of questions relates to the origin and generality of the polarizations of masculine and feminine. Do these classifications refer to a general and universal set of attributes? Jung suggests so, claiming that logos is masculine while relatedness is feminine.[14] The argument I present is somewhat different. It suggests that we must deal with a complex process of social and symbolic construction, lasting over many centuries and even millennia. In this process, masculine and feminine attributes came to refer not only to biological categories, but also to how these categories were symbolically experienced and elaborated. In that process of symbolic construction, a prime

265

factor was one correlated with sex though not logically identical with it: that of social power.[15] And, since the major world cultures developed societies with patriarchal structures, the so-called masculine and feminine attributes represent a way in which issues of power are delegated.

The argument has been raised, of course, that the near universality of masculine power speaks to a kind of necessity of such arrangements. If not rooted in biological dictate, they nevertheless can spring from the symbolic construction of gender. Perhaps, as Blos, Chodorow, and Stoller[16] suggest, the evolution of a solid sense of masculinity requires a turning against the feminine, of construing it as an inferior category. However, to that argument I would counter that even though the male control of power is nearly universal, it is not completely so, and considerable deviation exists across cultures in the completeness and severity of the devaluation of femininity. In fact, such devaluation may be most severe in cultures in which men are raised for extreme violence, such as the Sambia described by Herdt.[17] Interestingly, too, Gutmann[18] has argued that gender polarization is motivated by the duality of nurturance versus fighting of wars. If that argument is correct, a changing world environment certainly would suggest that the value of such polarizations, with their associated gender dualism, must be reassessed.

The interpretation I favor stresses two components. First, it assumes that the regulation of gender attributes is embedded in the structure of a particular population. Second, it stresses a historical dimension in which populations have grown in size and complexity. Accordingly, I suggest that the ascendancy of the masculine principle over the feminine one is a temporary and transitional one. Quite possibly, it has been instrumental in the rapid expanse of major cultures, permitting both growth of populations and expansion of territories.

However, the contemporary world hardly requires such a model any longer. In particular, one by-product of the expanse of major cultures may have turned rather problematic: namely, that they have tended to erect systems of laws and regulations that, even though they may have served local adaptive functions, claimed universal validity, and did so vehemently. Thus, even though there is wide-ranging concern with preserving the local integrity of different cultures, it is also necessary to search for a model that is more unifying. In that model, the ideal individual no longer can be the one raised to preserve the integrity of local systems. Rather, a new model needs to aim at the participant of a worldwide community that, even though it respects diversity, also perceives those qualities that hold all of humanity together.

Again, my interpretation raises the issue of universality. How can we, from the perspective of Western culture, make judgments over the practices of other cultures? Do we not, I find myself admonished,[19] need to take at face value the young Indian woman who walks to her immolation joyously singing, convinced that her death reunites her with her dead husband-god? Should we not resist passing judgment on the millions of women who believe that painful genital mutilation of girls makes them proper women?[20]

I suggest a more general stance is possible than such relativism. Feelings, we know, can be altered by social practices and social discourses, and those related to gender socialization are ones that can involve extreme violence and horror. Thus, we cannot take the resulting structure of feelings and convictions at face value. Instead, we can look to see if those feelings and convictions allow the individual to speak a language of wholeness. If not, do they persist only in the presence of social strictures? If so, the individual's affirmation of a public language may go hand in hand with a private one that contradicts that very affirmation.

Bateson[21] has talked about gender-related rituals in those terms, suggesting that the very rigidity of polarization is so alien to the maintenance of internal equilibrium that some societies create outlets in which traditional gender roles are ritualistically reversed. Thus, as a means of restoring equilibrium, some cultures may enact a public ritual in which men and women dress up in the costumes of members of the other sex and act out their characteristic behavior, right down to sexual behavior. Bettelheim also has suggested that the sexual rites related to initiation are a (unconscious) way in which one gender may appropriate qualities and characteristics of the other. Finally, in her recent study of the *zar* cult of Sudanese women, Boddy[22] suggests that, in this cult, women are able to express – if only in veiled form – feelings not permitted in the more general ideology that legally and materially privileges men. Thus, this cult forms a kind of "antilanguage" that runs parallel to and serves to neutralize a public one.

The evolution to such antilanguages assumes, of course, that there exists some kind of self that is not completely contained by culture. This issue raises another aspect of dialectical tension, and one that is particularly relevant when we discuss how individuals are able to transform cultural languages rather than merely recite them. One criticism I have often encountered, for example, originates out of the postmodern stance that there really is no self or development without culture. Again, I maintain that cultural relativism is a principle that can enrich our past views of human nature. At the same time, *taken by itself*, it is no less absurd than the assumption it aims at rejecting. For if there is no self without culture, neither is there culture without selves. According to that view, while the self is formed in interaction with others and with culture, it cannot be reduced to those. Rather, it forms a principle that is partially autonomous.

Thus, even though the self is a cultural construction, it is also more than that, more than instantiated culture or language. I envision self as a dialectic: In that view, the self is constituted by incorporating the tensions between two dialectically related poles. On one hand, the self reproduces culture; yet on the other, individuals assert themselves against culture. Such dialectical opposition between self and culture creates a degree of slippage in which the self not only reproduces culture, but also can transform it creatively. In fact, by making room for the validity of such opposition, we can create new visions of change. As Freud's work shows, models that are based on a cultural eclipse of the self tend to deal with change in revolutionary and violent images of overthrow and destruction of the old. Instead, I suggest, a dialectical model can embrace change as a more orderly and benign process.

Toward lateral models of thinking

A final set of criticisms I sometimes encounter is the fear that, by liberating mythos or the feminine, one runs a danger of assuming a hostile attitude toward the pole rejected. Indeed, I have argued throughout this work that my aim is to strive for a dialectical balance. True, in working toward such a balance, individuals often negate a stand that has appeared "natural" at first. Thus, "logos bashing" or bashing of the masculine sometimes results from the attempt at evolving a new, more critical language.

I wish to emphatically assert, however, that I reject any attempt that looks for resolution in a simple negation. Instead, I am envisioning a new model in which the polarities of mind and self engage in a cooperative and constructive dialogue. In such a model, a genuine balance is achieved in which the past categories are integrated and become irrelevant. Such balances are revealed, for example, in the observations of outstanding artists on their process of creation.

One artist who has written extensively on the nature of artistic action is the painter Henri Matisse. Matisse felt that it was important that the artist "draw without thinking" and "saw that the mind which is composing should keep a sort of virginity for certain chosen elements, and reject what is offered by reasoning."[23] At first blush, this may suggest an association of the artistic attitude with a lack of the discipline of logos. But in actuality, it required a new form of "discipline," since Matisse's artistic training had been in "the dead part of tradition, in which all that derived from feeling or memory was scorned and condemned as bogus."[24] However, it was important that the artist, after so many studies performed in cool deliberation, be able to empty his mind of preconceptions – "of all influences which prevented me from seeing nature from my own personal view"[25] – and approach the final work with a kind of naiveté, as an almost unconscious transcription process. Thus

> Having cleaned and emptied my mind of all preconceived ideas, I traced this preliminary outline with a hand completely given over to my unconscious sensations which sprang from the model. I was careful not to introduce into this representation any conscious observation, or any correction of physical error.[26]

Nevertheless, once the spontaneous creative process has taken its course, rational judgment and conscious deliberation were called for. This rational process "takes charge, holding things in check, and makes it possible to have new ideas using the initial drawing as a springboard."[27] The same process is also evident in music, where the artist, after much discipline, must move to a new level of expression and artistic height by surrendering to a more indefinite, personal, and emotive process. This is well indicated in a statement by violinist Isaac Stern:

> People very rarely realize that the real happening in the arts comes out of the most enormous discipline, because when you've disciplined yourself thoroughly, you know what is possible. That's when you let your imagination move, because you know that by discipline and study and thought you've created the limits. . . .
> When you're really disciplined, and you know what the possibilities are beyond which you don't dare to go because of taste and knowledge, that's when something really begins to happen, when you throw away all the rigidities and simply make music.[28]

Thus, Stern suggests that human performance, at its best, marries discipline to deeply felt experience. In that view, creativity – doing creative science, performing creative art, or living a creative life – is more than an outpouring of feeling; it is also more than mere technical expertise. It is the blending of both in one act that gives structure to feeling and human depth to discipline.

Appendix: List of goddesses, gods, other mythological figures, and sacred sites

Achilles: A major figure of the *Iliad* and a major warrior of the Trojan War.

Agamemnon: One of the principal warriors of the Trojan War, and a figure of *The Oresteia*. As king of Argos, he led the Achean fleet to Troy; but when the fleet had been assembled at Argos, there was no favorable wind and Agamemnon, who had offended Artemis by bragging he was a better hunter than the goddess, learned that he was to sacrifice his daughter Iphigenia so as to secure a favorable wind. Agamemnon tricked his wife, Clytemnestra, into letting her daughter go to her death. When Agamemnon returned from the Trojan War, Clytemnestra avenged Iphigenia's death by murdering her husband. Her son Orestes, in turn, killed both his mother and her lover. The Odyssey and later Greek drama raised the issue of which crime was worse, Clytemnestra's murder of her husband or her son's matricide of Clytemnestra, and concluded that the former was a more hateful crime.

Amor: Roman version of the Greek god of love, Eros. Although in Greek mythology Eros was one of the most powerful original divinities, he later appeared in the disempowered version of the boy-god Cupid.

Aphrodite: The Greek goddess of beauty, love, and fertility, Aphrodite is a later development of more ancient goddesses who unite in themselves such diverse powers as knowledge, authority, wisdom, love, and fertility. Examples are the goddesses Astarte, Inanna, or Isis. In Greek mythology, these powers have become split and appear as different goddesses. Some, like Athena, are associated with wisdom and war, or like Artemis, with hunt and

271

wild, untamed strength. Others came to represent more stereotypically feminine qualities. For example, Persephone was associated with suffering and victimization and with deep emotional
knowledge, while Aphrodite came to represent beauty and sexual love.

Apollo: Son of Zeus and one of the most powerful of the Greek gods,
Apollo represents the values most appreciated by the Greek
philosophers. He is associated with rational control, music, and
medicine. His symbols are light and gold, lyre and flute. Greek
myth and theater also make him a god victorious over the feminine principle, as when he gains ascendancy by slaying the primordial she-dragon. His ascendancy over the feminine is widely
celebrated in the Greek tragedy sequences such as *The Oresteia*.

Artemis: Twin sister of Apollo, Artemis was the Greek goddess of the
hunt and lady of the beasts and wild things. Hesiod's *Theogeny*
acknowledges her association with childbirth by telling how,
after she was born, she helped her mother Leto birth her brother
Apollo.

Astarte: An ancient goddess mentioned in the Bible (Asthoreth in
Hebrew) whose cult was widespread in Canaan and into Egypt.
Like the Sumerian Inanna, she is often depicted as standing on
lions.

Asthoreth: The Hebrew name for Astarte.

Athena: Greek goddess associated with wisdom and crafts and also
with war. Athena was the favorite daughter of Zeus. Her mother
was Metis, a wisdom goddess. When Zeus learned that Metis
was to give birth to an extremely powerful divinity, Zeus
changed her into a fly and swallowed her. Athena continued to
gestate in Zeus' head and was delivered by Hephaestus, the god
of the forge and creativity. Although Athena's roots are much
more ancient and point to an old association of femininity with
power and creativity, in Greece she became a figure friendly to
the men and the masculine, and upholding the masculine right
to creation. Nevertheless, many of her symbols and activities
(owl, snakes, and weaving) indicate the gradual repression of
her own femininity. As a sign of that repressed femininity, she
wore on her breastplate the mask of Medusa, a terrifying female

figure whose head is surrounded by snakes and who caused those who looked at her to turn to stone.

Clytemnestra: Wife of Agamemnon. She killed her husband to avenge his slaughter of their daughter Iphigenia. Her subsequent killing by their son Orestes is the main theme of Greek tragedy sequences such as *The Oresteia*.

Cronus: One of the Titans, the children of Gaia and Uranus, the earth goddess and the god of heaven. Cronus and his sister Rhea were to become the parents of Zeus, his brothers Hades and Poseidon, and his sisters Demeter and Hera.

Delphi: Sacred site in Greece that was the home of the Delphic Oracle. Originally, the site was called Pytho and dedicated to Gaia, but eventually Apollo appropriated the oracle when he slew the serpent that inhabited the grounds.

Delphyne: A primordial female monster who was slain by Apollo when he was a little boy. Delphyne was the sister of Typhon. Both monsters were born by Gaia because she resented the growing power of Zeus who had defeated the Titans, giants and the original children of Gaia and Uranus.

Demeter: Sister of Zeus who took on the role of the fruitful earth mother and grain goddess. She is closely associated with her daughter Persephone, who was abducted by Hades and had to live in the underworld. Demeter grieved and caused the earth to be barren until a deal was struck by which Persephone stayed in the underworld every winter, but could return to the earth in the spring to bring new growth and vegetation. Demeter and Persephone came to symbolize the mysteries of death and resurrection. These mysteries were celebrated twice yearly at Eleusis, and initiates into the mysteries were sworn to secrecy.

Dionysus: Son of Zeus and brother of Apollo and in many ways his brother's opposite. Dionysus is associated with the cultivation of grapes and with wine making, and became the god of emotional excess and of ecstatic frenzy. He was a god to whom women were attracted, and everywhere bands of frenzied women followed him. He was not honored as a god in his youth, but in his later life he was admitted to Delphi where he joined Apollo's shrine. Much of the imagery surrounding Dionysus was later appropriated in the Christian imagery of Satan.

Enlil: An original father god of Sumer, and one of the divine figures of various cultures who coalesced into the Hebrew father-god Yahweh-Elohim.

Eros: One of the two main protagonists of the myth recounted in this book and a powerful Greek god, perhaps as old as Gaia. Eros represented the power of love that can overwhelm and even destroy people. Over the course of time, his awesome power was degraded and eventually emerged as the chubby and insipid Roman Amor or Cupid, who shoots his victims with his arrows.

Erynome: According to Graves' rendition of the Pelasgian creation myth, the original goddess of all things who danced the universe into being.

Gaia: In Greece, Gaia is the original feminine divinity, mother of the earth and all the universe, including her later husband Uranus, the father of the skies.

Green man. The green man is a masculine divine figure of pagan origin, a figure occurring widely in northeastern Europe and the Mediterranean basin. Unlike the transcendent god of logos and disembodied spirit, it is an earth and fertility figure. It derives its name from the form in which it most often occurs: a male head formed out of a leaf mask or surrounded by leaves or other vegetation. This composite of leaves and a man's head symbolizes the union of the organismic plant and the human world, especially its mental and spiritual aspects. It is a symbol of renewal and rebirth. He was considered a remnant of pagan religions but has remained extremely pervasive, widely occurring in the folk habits of Europe as well as its architecture, especially churches and cathedrals. Though a specifically European figure with its concentration on the head, similar masculine deities representing the union of the plant and the human world were pervasive in other cultures. Examples are the Aztec corn god or the Egyptian Osiris, both of whom are often depicted as bodies from whom new growth arises in the form of shoots of grain.

Hades: Brother of Zeus and Poseidon. When the three brothers divided heaven, the seas, and the underworld between them,

Hades became the king of the underworld, also called Hades. He abducted the youthful Persephone from the earth and made her his bride.

Hephaestus: God of creativity and the forge. In Rome, he took on the name of Vulcan.

Hera: Sister of Demeter, Zeus, Poseidon, and Hades who married Zeus. She was a goddess of marriage, family life, and children, all qualities pointing to her preeminence in pre-Hellenic times. In Greek mythology, she was disempowered and became the archetype of an unhappy, jealous, and quarrelsome wife.

Hermes: A Greek god associated with the crossing of boundaries between heaven and earth, divine and human. He functioned as Zeus' ambassador and, as *psychopomp,* he guided the souls of the deceased to Hades.

Hestia: Greek goddess of the hearth and of life-giving fire. She kept away from the disputes of Olympus and was considered the preserver of its peace. She has no elaborate mythology but she seems to have commanded almost universal reverence as the sacred center of the domestic hearth, representing security, happiness, and hospitality.

Inanna: Goddess of Sumer and central figure of earliest epic poems ever recorded in writing. Inanna was the goddess of heaven and earth, and her powers spanned those of love and fertility and those of culture, war, and royal authority. Her epic records both her reign as a queen and her travels to the underworld, where she died and was resurrected. Aspects of her myth anticipate later death-and-resurrection myths such as those of Osiris and Jesus.

Iphigenia: Agamemnon's and Clytemnestra's daughter who was sacrificed by her father in return for a favorable wind to sail his ships to the Trojan War.

Ishtar: The Semitic counterpart of Inanna in Babylonia.

Isis: An important Egyptian goddess, Isis is closely associated with her twin brother and husband Osiris. Twin children of Nut, the goddess of heaven, they were engaged in loving embrace already in their mother's womb. As adults, they worked together in harmony and brought writing, agriculture, and other gifts of culture to their people. Like other early goddesses, she thus represents not only fertility, but also power and authority. Her association both with fertility and authority is indicated by the dual meaning of her name. Isis means "black soil," referring to the rich, fertile soil of the Nile Delta; but her hieroglyph, a part of her headdress on many of her statues, also is the form of a throne, indicating her royal authority.

Medusa: An early goddess who once was beautiful but was changed by Athena into a terrifying creature, a monster with serpent hair and glaring eye that would turn men who looked at her into stone. Since the crime for which Medusa was punished was that of making love with Poseidon in one of Athena's temples, she is widely thought to represent masculine fear of and repression of feminine power and sexuality. The father-identified Athena wore Medusa's image on her breastplate. After Medusa was beheaded by Perseus, her children fathered by Poseidon arose from her body: One of them was the winged horse Pegasus.

Mercury: Roman version of the Greek god Hermes, Mercury played a particular role among the medieval alchemists who hoped to transform mercury to gold.

Metis: According to Hesiod, one of the earliest consorts of Zeus. Her name means counsel, and she was the wisest of all the gods and mortals. When Metis was pregnant, Zeus was warned by Gaia and Uranus that her child, combining both Zeus' power and Metis' wisdom, would overthrow Zeus. Therefore, Zeus changed Metis into a fly and swallowed her. Now pregnant, Zeus eventually gave birth to his daughter Athena who, motherless, sprang from his head in full golden armor; but Metis stayed confined inside Zeus and continued to counsel him.

Mount Olympus: The highest peak in Greece, it was thought to be the home of the Greek gods.

Muses: Nine daughters of Zeus who represented the arts.

Nestor: A Greek king who went off to the Trojan War, and a major figure in Homer's *Iliad* and *Odyssey*.

Nut: Egyptian goddess of heaven and the mother of Isis and Osiris.

Oedipus: The son of Laius and Jocasta, king and queen of Thebes. Warned at his birth that he would one day kill his father, his parents told a servant to abandon him after his birth, but the servant saved the infant who was raised by a neighboring king.

Appendix

As a young man, following another oracle, Oedipus traveled to Thebes and on the way got into a fight with a stranger, Laius, who challenged him and whom Oedipus killed. He then went to Thebes and married his mother. The legend was borrowed by Freud to refer to young boys' sexual fantasies about their mothers.

Ophion: Original serpent who mated with Erynome, goddess of the Pelasgian creation myth.

Orestes: Son of Agamemnon and Clytemnestra, and sister of Iphigenia and central figure of a series of Greek tragedies focusing on the victory of the masculine principle over the feminine one.

Osiris: The Egyptian Osiris was the twin brother and husband of Isis. According to Egyptian legend, Osiris brought the arts of civilization and agriculture to Egypt. He taught his people to cultivate wheat and barley, to pick fruit from the trees and train vines on poles, and to make wine and beer. Through trickery Osiris eventually was killed by his jealous brother Set who tore his body into pieces, which he dispersed over the land of Egypt. The murdered Osiris was resurrected by his sister-wife Isis. Osiris' cycle of death and rebirth came to be associated with the cycle of changing seasons. Each spring, his body was thought to be reborn like the planted earth and to sprout forth new life.

Pan: A Greek god who typically is pictured as part goat, part man. A nature god, he was also noted for his playing of reed pipes, the pan flutes.

Pandora: According to Hesiod, the first mortal woman who was crafted by the god of the forge, Haephestus. Like the biblical Eve, she was thought to be the origin of much evil and misfortune for humankind. Like Eve, too, this was due to her unbridled curiosity. The misfortune she created was said to have resulted when she opened a jar that Prometheus, the creator of man, had warned should never be opened. The jar contained such scourges as old age, sickness, insanity, vice, and passion. According to Spretnak (1971), this myth represents a downgrading of an earlier goddess associated with grain and abundance.

Persephone: Daughter of the grain goddess Demeter who was abducted by Hades into the underworld and made Hades' bride.

Persephone is often felt to stand for the vulnerability of a young woman who sacrifices her sense of selfhood. However, her myth also is a variant of the death-and-resurrection theme that states that going underground and suffering may be a necessary stage of growth, followed by a new flowering and wisdom. Thus Persephone would have been able to return to earth, had she not accepted and eaten some pomegranate seeds Hades gave her. As a result, she was to stay in Hades for part of the year, while the earth grieved and grew barren. But she was allowed to return to earth every spring, causing the earth to break out in bloom.

Phaeton: The son of Phoebus, the sun god who wanted to drive his father's fiery chariot. The boy could not control the fierce winged horses and the chariot fell to the earth and scorched it. The earth could only be saved by having Zeus kill the boy and return the control of the chariot to his father.

Phanes: In Orphic creation myths, an alternate name for Eros.

Phoebus: Latin name for Helios, the Greek sun god. His mythology is not extensive and sometimes blurred with that of Apollo, the god of light and reason.

Poseidon: Brother of Zeus and Hades. The three brothers divided among themselves the world: Zeus received the heavens, Hades the underworld, and Poseidon the sea.

Psyche: One of the two main protagonists of the myth retold in this book. Psyche was the human bride of Eros who had warned her never to look at him. Overcome by curiosity, one night she lit a lamp and saw that she was married to the god of love. But her curiosity was punished when Eros left and cursed her. Only after a series of difficult trials was Psyche reunited with Eros when Zeus agreed that she could join him on Mount Olympus as a divinity.

Rhea: Daughter of Gaia and Uranus and brother-wife of Cronos. Her children were the first generation of the Olympian gods and goddesses: Hestia, Demeter, Hera, Hades, Poseidon, and Zeus.

Set: Brother of Isis and Osiris who represented a dark and negative principle and who caused Osiris' death and dismemberment.

Appendix

Styx: The main river of the underworld. For the Greeks, an oath by the river Styx was held to be extremely sacred and never to be violated.

Titans: The children of Gaia and Uranus, and a generation that preceded the Olympians.

Uranus: The original Greek god of sky and heaven who was born by the primordial earth goddess Gaia and subsequently became her husband. Together they parented the Titans. Uranus grew fearful of the power of his children and tried to confine them in Gaia's womb, but eventually Gaia asked her son Cronos to overthrow his father. Cronos took the sickle his mother gave him and castrated his father. When Uranus' genitals fell into the ocean, a foam arose and gave birth to Aphrodite.

Zephyr: Personification of the west wind in Greek mythology.

Zeus: Son of Rhea and Cronos, Zeus came to be the all powerful god of the universe when he overthrew his father with Rhea's help. He shared with his son Apollo the symbolism of gold and light. But being of an earlier generation, he was a less refined god, known for his lust and vengefulness.

Notes

1. *Logos* throughout this book is used in a sense wider than the term logic, and refers to a particular mode of relating to and processing experience. This mode will be defined more technically in Chapter 2.

2. To be sure, what is referred to here as "Greek thought" in actuality is not a homogeneous theory, but itself constitutes a wide diversity of approaches. To quote Betrand Russell's *A History of Western Philosophy* (1945, pp. 41–42): "There were, in fact, two tendencies in Greece, one passionate, religious, mystical, otherworldly, the other cheerful, empirical, rationalistic, and interested in acquiring knowledge of a diversity of facts. . . . It seems probably that educated Athenians, even in the best period, however rationalistic they may have been in their explicitly conscious mental processes, retained from tradition and from childhood a more primitive way of thinking and feeling, which was liable to be victorious in times of stress. Therefore no simple analysis of the Greek outlook is likely to be adequate." Nevertheless, despite the diversity of approaches that Russell points out, what seems to have been a pervasive aspect of Greek philosophy is that it attempted to talk about and define a tension between two ways of being and of knowing. This issue is discussed in detail in Chapter 2.

3. See Labouvie-Vief (1980, 1982, 1985); Labouvie-Vief & Hakim-Larson (1989).

4. This work has been extensively reviewed elsewhere. See Labouvie-Vief (1985, 1990, 1992a); Labouvie-Vief & Hakim-Larson (1989).

5. Rubinstein (1968), p. 409.

6. I am using the term logic here, as did Wittgenstein (1972), in a rather loose and colloquial sense. To be more precise, I am referring to classical bivalent logic. In reality, the technical field of logic comprises a variety of more complex "logics," such as dialectical, trivalent, fuzzy, modal, and so forth. For fuller discussion, the reader is referred to Chinen (1984); E. Harris (1987); Reich (1992).

7. Piaget (1967); see also Labouvie-Vief (1980).

8. See Labouvie-Vief (1980, 1982, 1985); Labouvie-Vief & Hakim-Larson (1989).

9. See Case (1991c) Fischer (1980); Gardner (1983); P. Miller (1983).

10. Langer (1942), pp. 292–293.

11. Freud (1911/1957), pp. 43–44.

12. Freud (1911/1957), p. 43.

13. I am using the term *romantic* here not necessarily to refer to a precise historical period but, in Russell's (1945) sense, to a movement or sensibility that emphasizes the significance of nonrational forms of experience that are held to be direct and quite uninformed by thought.

14. Mann (1978).

15. Jung (1933, 1964).

16. For excellent overviews of Jung's theory, see Fordham (1966); Jacobi (1962); Whitmont (1969).

17. Campbell (1986, 1988).

18. Plato (1961e), pp. 543–544 (*Symposium*, 190e–191e).

19. See Gilligan (1982); also Belenky et al. (1986); Brown & Gilligan (1992); Miller (1986).

20. See Faludi (1991); Tavris (1992).

21. For a recent review, see Unger & Crawford (1992).

22. See Unger & Crawford (1992); AAUW (1992).

23. See especially Bettelheim (1962); Brown & Gilligan (1992); Lloyd (1984); Miller (1986); Ortner (1974); and Schott (1988).

24. Neumann (1956); see also Downing (1988); Johnson (1989); Young-Eisendrath & Wiedemann (1987).

25. Franz (1992); see also Downing (1988); Houston (1987); Lewis (1980).

CHAPTER 2. THE RANGE OF APHRODITE:
THE VERTICAL MIND

1. Neumann (1956), p. 3. This and all further summaries of the myth of Psyche and Eros are based on Neumann (1956).

2. Ibid., pp. 4–5.

3. Ibid., (1956), p. 3.
4. Freud (1900/1965); Jung (1964).
5. Bruner (1990); McAdams (1990); Sarbin (1986); Spence (1982).
6. Campbell (1988); Pratt (1993); Whitmont (1969).
7. See Labouvie-Vief (1990).
8. Neumann (1954, 1955, 1956, 1973).
9. Some readers may consider such a sweeping proposition a bit outlandish. It is not offered here, however, as a dogmatic point to be followed. It is offered more from the perspective of playfulness, inviting the reader to suspend disbelief and to enter the story with such an attitude. As I suggest in this book, the "truthfulness" of stories is to a great extent only apparent if one is willing to surrender to them, watching what they tend to unfold as they involve the reader.
10. This point has been made in a scholarly version by Gould's *Ontogeny and Phylogeny* (1977) and by Piaget and Garcia (1989). Specific parallels between stages of historical evolution of consciousness and individual development have been suggested by Donald (1991), Whyte (1948), and Wilber (1981). However, the notion of certain parallels between individual and historical development is no longer accepted in the simple version originally proposed by Herbert Spencer around the turn of the century. Rather, more modern versions of the hypothesis are more complex in assuming that historical development feeds back on the process of individual development, as will be suggested throughout this book.
11. Neumann (1956). Amor is the Latin name for Eros.
12. Hesiod (1983).
13. See Kerenyi (1951); Stone (1978).
14. According to a map of principal Mesopotamian cities of 2500–1000 B.C.E. (Baring & Cashford [1992], p. 179), Akkadia was an ancient country in what now roughly is referred to as Iraq. Spread along the river Tigris, its western border was Babylonia which spread along the river Euphrates in the east. In the south it was bordered by Sumer, a coastal region of the Persian Gulf.
15. Bly (1990).
16. Emphasis on one or the other component inevitably raised questions of undue dualism. Throughout this book, however, my position is that gender concepts are neither solely fixed culturally nor biologically, but rather reflect an interaction of the two. Accordingly, culture transforms biological givens, but, vice versa, biology also constrains the power of culture to transform.

17. Kerenyi (1951).
18. Graves (1960), p. 30.
19. See Gilligan (1982); Bakan (1966).
20. Whitmont (1982).
21. Quoted in B. Walker (1983), p. 766.
22. See Scribner & Cole (1981).
23. Havelock (1963, 1978); Goody & Watt (1963); McLuhan (1962, 1964); Olson (1977); Postman (1982); Donald (1991).
24. Scribner & Cole (1981).
25. Plato, (1961d), p. 831 (*Republic*, 605d).
26. Buber (1958).
27. Cassirer (1946), pp. 32–33.
28. See Whitmont (1982); Lorenz (1967).
29. See Labouvie-Vief, Hakim-Larson, DeVoe, & Schoeberlein (1989).
30. Havelock (1978).
31. Ibid., pp. 42–43.
32. Klein (1967); Liddell & Scott (1958); Partridge (1966).
33. Watzlawick (1978).
34. See Koestler (1964); Shlain (1991).
35. For discussions, see Campbell (1982); Schon (1983).
36. See Abrams (1958).
37. See Rorty (1979).
38. To be sure, Christian religion also incorporated an important mystical trend. Indeed, I am indebted to K. Helmut Reich (personal communication, November 1992) for pointing out that in its religious usage, logos never was completely divorced from a mystic basis; logos referred to a divine principle that became flesh in Jesus.
39. Freud (1923/1957), pp. 210–235.
40. Piaget (1962).
41. Bruner (1986).
42. Goldberg & Costa (1981); Pribram & McGuiness (1975); Tucker & Williamson (1984).
43. Hofstadter (1980).
44. Russell (1945), p. 43.
45. Whyte (1948), p. 196.
46. In fact, it is interesting to note that for Heraclitus this transformative tension that results from a dialectic of complementary processes itself still is called logos, whereas later the term logos took on the more narrow meaning of a mode of knowledge that referred to a

single pole of a dialectical tension (J. Jarred, personal communication, December 2, 1992).

47. Quoted from Fromm (1956), p. 63.
48. Fromm (1956), p. 63.
49. Russell (1945), p. 49.
50. Erikson (1958).
51. See Collingwood (1945); Keller (1985); Russell (1945).
52. See Logan (1986); Scribner & Cole (1981).
53. Jaynes (1976); Vernant (1982); Whyte (1948).
54. Elias (1978, 1982).
55. See Jaynes (1976); Onians (1954); Simon (1978).
56. Collingwood (1945); Frankfort & Frankfort (1949).
57. Berman (1984); Habermas (1981).
58. Onians (1954).
59. Simon (1978), p. 72.
60. Ibid., p. 58.
61. Ibid., p. 62.
62. Plato (1961f), pp. 895–896 (*Thaetetus*, 189e–190a).
63. See Berman (1981); Habermas (1970).
64. Cassirer (1944, 1946).
65. Frankfort & Frankfort (1946).
66. Cassirer (1944), p. 45.
67. Quotation from DeLong (1970).
68. Plato (1961a), p. 290 (*Gorgias*, 508a).
69. Frankfort & Frankfort (1946).
70. Ibid., p. 253.
71. DeLong (1970); Vernant (1982).
72. See Macmurray (1978).
73. DeLong (1970).
74. Plato (1961c), p. 314 (*Protagoras*, 315a).
75. Ibid., p. 313 (313 c–d).
76. Plato (1961b), p. 48 (*Phaedo*, 65c).
77. Ibid., p. 48 (65d).
78. Ibid., p. 49 (66b–d).
79. Plato (1961d), p. 798 (*Republic*, 571c–d).
80. Ibid., p. 820 (595b).
81. Ibid., pp. 825–826 (601a–c).
82. Simon (1978).
83. Aeschylus (1953), p. 112 (*The Libation Bearers*).
84. See Gergen (1992).

CHAPTER 3. THE MARRIAGE OF DEATH:
ASCENT AND LOSS IN DEVELOPMENT

1. See Whitmont (1969).
2. Neumann (1973), pp. 400–401.
3. Bettelheim (1983).
4. Neumann (1973).
5. Whitmont (1982).
6. Ibid.
7. Hesiod.
8. Stapleton (1986).
9. Whitmont (1982), p. 50.
10. Neumann (1973).
11. Ibid.; see also Kurtz (1993).
12. Kerenyi (1951).
13. Stapleton (1986).
14. Neumann (1956).
15. Ibid.
16. Neumann (1973), p. 318.
17. See among others Bruner (1986, 1990); Case (1991b); Fischer (1980); Gardner (1983); Gilligan (1982); Labouvie-Vief (1980, 1982, 1992a); Noam (1988); Riegel (1973, 1976).
18. Piaget (1981).
19. Ibid., p. 14.
20. Piaget (1965); see also Labouvie-Vief & Lawrence (1985); Youniss (1980).
21. Piaget (1965), p. 280.
22. Ibid., p. 393.
23. Ibid.; see also Labouvie-Vief & Lawrence (1985); Youniss (1980).
24. For summaries, see Flavell (1963); Gruber & Voneche (1977).
25. A comment is in order here as to why I should choose Piaget's theory, because that choice is not entirely without problems. One obvious reason for doing so is that no theory has had as profound an effect on restructuring our views of the process of development as has Piaget's broad view of the nature of cognitive stages from infancy to adolescence. However, as noted in the section to follow, this rather sweeping view of the process of development, with the claim that it has achieved a mapping of cognitive capacities universally, has become widely criticized, and a number of extensions, amendments, and modifications have recently been proposed. In the process of formulating necessary modifications, it has been useful to

discuss aspects of this influential theory that are problematic and that should be modified, and to differentiate them from those that are important and should be maintained. Thus, to facilitate the analysis to follow, I begin with a brief account of Piaget's stages of cognitive development. My specific rendition of these stages is somewhat modified from Piaget's own, following the labeling proposed by Fischer (1980).

26. Piaget (1930), p. 274.
27. Piaget (1965).
28. Longstreth (1968), p. 521.
29. Piaget (1980), p. 5.
30. Ibid., p. 15.
31. Ibid., p. 18.
32. Gruber & Voneche (1977), p. 438.
33. Ibid., pp. 442–443.
34. See Case (1991b); Gardner (1983); P. Miller (1983).
35. See Labouvie-Vief (1980, 1992a).
36. See Case (1991b); Fischer (1980).
37. Kohlberg (1969, 1984).
38. Selman (1980); Selman & Schultz (1991); Damon (1988); Damon & Hart (1982).
39. Case, Hayward, Lewis, & Hurst (1988); Fischer, Shaver, & Cornochan (1990); Labouvie-Vief, DeVoe, & Bulka (1989).
40. E.g., Werner (1955); Werner & Kaplan (1963).
41. Freud (1911/1957), p. 43.
42. Ibid., p. 43.
43. Ibid., p. 40.
44. Piaget (1962).
45. Gruber & Voneche (1977), p. 492.
46. Piaget (1955).
47. Ibid., p. 43.
48. Ibid.
49. Ibid., p. 45.
50. Ibid., p. 44.
51. Bettelheim (1977), pp. 119–120.
52. Turner (1973).
53. See Stern (1985); Trevarthen (1989).
54. For a review, see Mitchell (1988).
55. Piaget (1965), p. 393.
56. See Benjamin (1988); Greenberg & Mitchell (1983).
57. Winnicott (1971); see also Davis & Wallbridge (1981).

58. Davis & Wallbridge (1981), p. 65.
59. Ibid., p. 64.
60. For somewhat similar accounts, see also Bretherton (1990); Case (1991a,b,c); Fischer & Pipp (1985); Noam (1988).
61. Erikson (1984).
62. Werner & Kaplan (1963).
63. For a review, see Bretherton (1990).
64. Stern (1985).
65. See Greenberg & Mitchell (1983).
66. Kohut (1977).
67. For a review, see Bretherton (1990); Main (1991); Main, Kaplan, & Cassidy (1985).
68. Sroufe (1983); Sroufe & Fleeson (1986).
69. Case (1990).
70. Stern (1985), p. 182.
71. Labouvie-Vief (1981); Labouvie-Vief & Schell (1982).
72. Nelson & Gruendel (1981); cited in Bretherton (1990).
73. Harter & Buddin (1977); Fischer (1991); Fischer et al. (1990); Selman (1980).
74. Bowlby (1969, 1980); see also Bretherton (1990).
75. Bretherton (1990).
76. Kohlberg (1969): Children who are raised in sex-role tolerant settings often begin to display clear preferences to behave in a fashion typical of "boys" or "girls."
77. Elias (1978, 1982).
78. Werner & Kaplan (1963).
79. Main (1983); Main, Kaplan, & Cassidy (1985); Solomon & George (1991).
80. See Higgins (1991); Labouvie-Vief, Orwoll, & Manion (1994).
81. Kohlberg (1969).
82. Foulkes (1979).
83. See Bettelheim (1977); Fromm (1951).
84. Fein (1979); Gardner (1983).
85. See Gardner (1980); Winner (1982).
86. E.g., Kohlberg (1984); Selman (1980).
87. See Blanchard-Fields (1986); Kitchener & King (1981); Labouvie-Vief & Hakim-Larson (1989).
88. Benner (1984).
89. Coles (1977).
90. Tedlock (1987), p. 8.
91. Ashmore & Ogilvie (1992).

92. Ogilvie & Clark (1992).
93. For a review, see Janoff-Bulman (1992).
94. Dabrowski (1970); Piechowski (1975).

CHAPTER 4. NIGHT AND DAY: REASON AND GENDER

1. Neumann (1956), p. 13.
2. Ibid., p. 18.
3. Mayer (1978).
4. Barlow (1988).
5. See also Chinen (1992); May (1980).
6. May (1980); see also Bakan (1966); Chinen (1992).
7. Evelyn-Whyte (1920).
8. Ibid., (1920), p. 289.
9. E.g., Baring & Cashford (1991).
10. Klein & Riviere (1964); Segal (1974).
11. See Goldstein (1991); Zinner (1989).
12. In Goldstein (1991), p. 159.
13. Euripides (1929).
14. Ibid., p. 94.
15. Ibid., p. 94.
16. See Neumann (1954, 1955).
17. E.g., Bachofen (1967); Gimbutas (1982).
18. Aeschylus (1953).
19. Ibid., pp. 140, 141.
20. Ibid., p. 158.
21. Ibib., p. 158.
22. Deutsch (1969), p. 79.
23. Aeschylus (1953).
24. von Franz (1980).
25. Foucault (1986).
26. Hesiod (1983), (*Theogeny*, 590–601).
27. Spretnak (1971), p. 97.
28. Graves (1960).
29. Graves cites evidence to indicate that her origin may be even more ancient and be located in Libya where she was born near or by Lake Triton.
30. Lerner (1986).
31. See Lloyd (1984); Schott (1989).

32. Spretnak (1971), p. 53.
33. Hesiod (1983).
34. Deuteronomy, 4.19–4.23.
35. Ibid., 13.7 - 13.10.
36. Freud (1925/1963), p. 187.
37. Ibid.
38. Ibid., p. 188.
39. Ibid., pp. 188–189.
40. Ibid., p. 193.
41. Zilboorg (1944), p. 294.
42. Bettelheim (1962).
43. Ibid., p. 10.
44. Herdt (1987); Herdt & Stoller (1990).
45. Stoller (1985); Herdt & Stoller (1990).
46. Stoller (1985), p. 18.
47. Bettelheim (1962) argues that the envy is heightened in social settings that attempt to minimize the overlap between sex/gender. This point will be discussed in more detail in Chapter 7.
48. Bettelheim (1962), p. 11.
49. Lacqueur (1990).
50. Hillman (1972), p. 221.
51. Aristotle (1912), 729a, 28–34.
52. Ibid., 737a, 26–31.
53. Aristotle (1932), 1254b, 4–6, 12–16.
54. Ibid., 1254b 24–26; 1255a, 2–5.
55. Daly (1978).
56. Richter (1979).
57. Ibid., p. 103.
58. Ibid., p. 110.
59. Ibid., p. 112.
60. Ibid., p. 113.
61. LeBon; quoted in Gould (1981), p. 104–105.
62. Thorndike (1910) p. 10.
63. Hollingsworth (1926), p. 11.
64. Noble (1992), p. 282.
65. Ashmore (1990); Lipps (1988); Maccoby & Jacklin (1974).
66. Kerr (1987); Maccoby & Jacklin (1974).
67. AAUW report.
68. Kaufman & Richardson (1982).
69. Bardwick (1971), p. 149. For a more recent version of this notion,

see Gilligan (1982). Gillligan's argument is more complex, however, and maintains that women's interpersonal orientation gives rise to a different form of reasoning.

70. Maccoby & Jacklin (1974).
71. Ibid., p. 132.
72. Dweck & Elliot (1983); Kaufman & Richardson (1982).
73. Block (1983); Heilbrun (1988); Horner (1989); Lipps (1988).
74. Peplau (1976), pp. 249–258; Weisfeld (1986), pp. 278–299.
75. Bundtzen (1983).
76. Plath (1971), p. 26.
77. Ibid., p. 69.
78. Ibid.
79. Ibid., p. 58.
80. Ibid., p. 68.
81. Ibid., pp. 61–62.
82. Rich (1951).
83. Rich (1969).
84. Rich, quoted in Pope (1984), p. 144.
85. Heilbrun (1988), p. 23.
86. Ibid., p. 24.
87. Olsen (1978).
88. In Olsen (1978); quoted from Anaïs Nin's diaries, vol. 3, 1939–1944.
89. Terman & Oden (1925).
90. Kerr (1987), p. 99.
91. Ibid., p. 23.
92. Terman & Oden (1947, 1959).
93. Kerr (1987), p. 24.
94. Ibid., p. 21.
95. Ibid.
96. Peterson (1987).
97. See AAUW (1992); McGrath, Keita, Strickland, & Russo (1990).
98. See AAUW (1992); Byrne, Shavelson, & March (1992); Dweck & Bush (1976); Martin & Nivens (1987); Roberts & Nolen-Hoeksema (1989); Yee & Eccles (1988).
99. Gilligan (1982, 1990); Gilligan, Lyons, & Hanmer (1990).
100. Gilligan (1990), p. 26.
101. Cramer (1979).
102. Cramer (1990).
103. Labouvie-Vief, Hakim-Larson, & Hobart (1987).

104. For a review, see Labouvie-Vief, Orwoll, & Manion (1994).
105. Block (1984).
106. Ibid., p. 137.

CHAPTER 5. KNIFE AND LAMP: MYTHOS
REDISCOVERED

1. Neumann (1956), p. 70.
2. Jung (1933); see also Chinen (1989).
3. Neumann (1956), p. 15.
4. Ibid., pp. 16–17.
5. Ibid., p. 22.
6. Ibid., p. 74.
7. Ibid.
8. Ibid., p. 5.
9. Ulanov & Ulanov (1983).
10. Horner (1989); Klein & Riviere (1964); Segal (1974).
11. Ulanov & Ulanov (1983), p. 49.
12. Neumann (1956), p. 18.
13. Ibid., p. 19.
14. Ibid., p. 26.
15. Dabrowski (1970); Piechowski (1975).
16. Barker (1969).
17. Frege (1953), p. 20e.
18. Lakatos (1970), pp. 8–9.
19. DeLong (1970); Hofstadter (1980).
20. DeLong (1970), pp. 225–226. More recently, Sheldrake (1988) has suggested that as a result of similar movements, it is necessary to think of "laws of nature" as habits, of coming-into-being of forms that are subject to constant evolution.
21. Whitehead (1938), p. 189.
22. Wittgenstein (1953), no. 12.
23. Blumenberg (1987), p. 454; Horkheimer & Adorno (1972). Also see Flax (1990).
24. Plato, (1961d).
25. Boole (1958), p. 409.
26. Nozick (1981), p. 4.
27. Lakoff & Johnson (1980).
28. Reddy (1979).

29. Gadamer (1976); Flax (1990); Lyotard (1987); Welsch (1988).
30. Geertz (1983).
31. Habermas (1984); Popper (1963).
32. Blumenberg (1987).
33. Popper (1963); Ricoeur (1970).
34. Lakoff (1987).
35. Baynes, Bohman, & McCarthy (1987).
36. See Bernstein (1991); Putnam (1987).
37. Dabrowski (1970).
38. Lakoff & Johnson (1980), pp. 4–5.
39. See Warnke (1987).
40. Gadamer (1975).
41. Gadamer (1976), p. 66.
42. Gadamer (1979), quoted in Bernstein (1991), p. 137.
43. Habermas (1970, 1984).
44. Apel (1980).
45. Labouvie-Vief & Lawrence (1985).
46. See Reich (1990, 1992).
47. See Berman (1981).
48. Perry (1968).
49. Ibid., pp. 135–136.
50. Kitchener & King (1981); see also King, Kitchener, Wood, & Davison (1989); Kitchener & Brenner (1990); Kitchener, King, Wood, & Davison (1989).
51. Kitchener & King (1981), p. 90.
52. Ibid., p. 96.
53. Ibid., p. 90.
54. See Basseches (1984); Labouvie-Vief (1992a).
55. See Broughton (1980); Reich (1992).
56. Reich (1992), p. 33.
57. Adams, Labouvie-Vief, Hakim-Larson, DeVoe, & Hayden (1988).
58. see Baltes (1987); Baltes & Smith (1990); Basseches (1984); Belenky, Clinchy, Goldberger, & Tarule (1986); Blanchard-Fields (1986, 1989); Clinchy & Zimmerman (1982); Commons, Richards, & Armon (1984); Fischer, Hand, & Russell (1984); Kramer (1989); Kramer & Woodruff (1986); Kuhn (1991); Kuhn, Pennington, & Leadbeater (1983); Reich (1990; 1992). For review, see Labouvie-Vief (1990, 1992a).
59. Broughton (1980).

60. Colby, Kohlberg, Gibbs, & Lieberman (1983); Kohlberg (1969, 1984).
61. Riegel (1973).
62. See Labouvie-Vief (1993); Loevinger (1993).
63. Erikson (1984).
64. Armon (1984).
65. Orwoll, Chiodo, & Goguen (1991); Orwoll, Chiodo, Goguen, Labouvie-Vief, & Murphey (1993).
66. Fowler (1981).
67. Armon (1984, 1989); Colby et al. (1983); Cook-Greuter (1989); Hauser (1976); Redmore & Loevinger (1979).
68. For a review, see Labouvie-Vief (1992a).
69. Labouvie-Vief & Hakim-Larson (1989).
70. E.g., Neugarten (1968).
71. Adams (1986, 1991); Adams, Labouvie-Vief, Hobart, & Dorosz (1990); Jepson & Labouvie-Vief (1992).
72. Labouvie-Vief, Schell, & Weaverdyck (1982), pp. 12–13.
73. Adams (1991), p. 333.
74. Ibid., p. 333.
75. Adams et al. (1991); Jepson & Labouvie-Vief (1992).
76. Monod (1971).
77. See Koestler (1964).
78. See Fordham (1966); Whitmont (1969).
79. Mann (1978).
80. Fowler (1981).
81. Ibid., p. 197.
82. Ricoeur (1970).
83. Chinen (1989).
84. Piaget (1981).
85. See Case et al. (1988); Fischer & Pipp (1984); Fischer et al. (1990); Harter (1983); Kegan (1982); Saarni & Harris (1989); Selman (1980).
86. Donaldson & Westerman (1986); P. Harris (1983); Harter (1983); Saarni & Harris (1989); Selman (1980); see also Labouvie-Vief & DeVoe (1991).
87. E.g., Damon (1988); Damon & Hart (1982); Kegan (1982); Kohlberg (1969).
88. Gutmann (1987); see also Neugarten (1968).
89. Labouvie-Vief, DeVoe, & Bulka (1989); Labouvie-Vief, Hakim-Larson, DeVoe, & Schoeberlein (1989).
90. Belenky et al. (1986).

CHAPTER 6. PSYCHE'S TRIAL: THE
TRANSFORMATION OF DESIRE

1. Neumann (1956), p. 32.
2. Ibid., p. 40.
3. Neumann (1954).
4. Freud (1918/1952).
5. Jung (1933).
6. Neumann (1956), pp. 41–42.
7. See Bakan (1966).
8. Houston (1987).
9. See Chinen (1992).
10. Jellouschek (1989).
11. Plato, *Symposium*, 209b; quoted in Keller (1985), p. 24.
12. Keller (1985), p. 39.
13. Richter (1979), p. 103.
14. Ibid., p. 108.
15. Battersby (1989).
16. Kant (1764/1960), p. 78; quoted in Battersby (1989), p. 77.
17. Bachofen (1967); see Georgoudi (1992).
18. Plutarch (1969).
19. Baring & Cashford (1991).
20. See Eisler (1987); Gimbutas (1982); Stone (1978).
21. See Badinter (1989); Georgoudi (1991); Ortner (1974).
22. Bamberger (1974).
23. Georgoudi (1992).
24. Ibid., p. 463.
25. Ibid.
26. Ibid., p. 456.
27. Kramer (1989), p. 71.
28. See Wolkstein & Kramer (1983).
29. Engelsman (1979).
30. Cady, Ronan, & Taussig (1986).
31. Pagels (1979).
32. Quoted from Baring & Cashford (1991), p. 631.
33. See Baring & Cashford (1991); Bolen (1984).
34. See Heine (1989).
35. See Anderson & Hicks (1990).
36. Ibid.
37. Bly (1990).

38. Jung (1954).
39. See also Neugarten (1968).
40. Jung, quoted in Pratt (1981), p. 136.
41. See Dougherty (1992).
42. Stevens-Long & Commons (1992); see also Chiriboga (1989); Rosenberg & Farrell (1976); Tamir (1982); Vaillant & McArthur (1972).
43. Vaillant & McArthur (1972), quoted in Stevens-Long & Commons (1992), pp. 306–307.
44. Levinson, Darrow, Klein, Levinson, & McKee (1978), p. 107.
45. Ibid., p 237.
46. Jaques (1965).
47. Noam (1988).
48. Jaques (1965), p. 511.
49. Gutmann (1987).
50. Ibid., pp. 73–74.
51. Ibid., p. 74.
52. Ibid., p. 78.
53. Jung (1954).
54. Dougherty (1992).
55. Labouvie-Vief (1992a).
56. Dougherty (1992).
57. Turner (1982); in Stevens-Long & Commons (1992).
58. Troll & Bengtson (1982); in Stevens-Long & Commons (1992), p. 432.
59. See Costa & McRae (1988).
60. Rosenberg & Farrell (1976).
61. Livson (1981a,b); see also Stevens-Long & Commons (1992), p. 325.
62. Jellouschek (1989).
63. See also Chinen (1992).
64. See Fox (1985); Hart & Bishop (1990).
65. Fox (1985), p. 27.
66. Ibid., p. 27.
67. Ibid.
68. Jung (1954).
69. Fox (1985).
70. Pratt (1981); see also Pratt (1993).
71. Fordham (1966); Jacobi (1962); Whitmont (1969, 1982).
72. Levinson et al. (1978).
73. Pratt (1981), p. 142.

74. Gutmann (1987), p. 152.
75. Belenky et al., (1986).
76. Freud (1905/1953), p. 64, quoted in Young-Eisendrath & Wiedemann (1987), p. 95.
77. Young-Eisendrath & Wiedemann (1987), p. 126.
78. Dougherty (1992).
79. Ibid., p. 36.
80. Helson & Moane (1987); see also Cooper & Gutmann (1987); Haan (1981, 1985).
81. Helson & Moane (1987), p. 179.
82. Helson & Wink (1992).
83. Livson (1981a,b).
84. Maas & Kuypers (1974).
85. Gutmann (1987).
86. Jung (1954).
87. Woolf (1929).
88. Olsen (1978).
89. Heilbrun (1988).
90. Tomlinson-Keasey & Blurton (1991).
91. Veroff, Reumann, & Feld (1984).
92. Huyck (1994).
93. Heilbrun (1988), p. 60.

CHAPTER 7. POSTLUDE: THE SACRED MARRIAGE

1. Frankfort (1961), pp. 6–7.
2. Baring & Cashford (1991).
3. Ibid.
4. Berman (1981); Chinen (1989).
5. Molesworth (1879).
6. See Palmer (1969); Valle, King, & Halling (1989). See also *Random House Dictionary of the English Language,* 2nd ed. (1987), s.v. "hermeneutics."
7. See Bolen (1989).
8. Stassinopoulos (1983), quoted in Bolen (1989), p. 162.
9. Bolen (1989); Graves (1960); Kerenyi (1951).
10. Neumann (1956).
11. See Labouvie-Vief & Lawrence (1985).
12. Labouvie-Vief (1980).

13. Donald (1991).
14. Stevens (1982).
15. J. Miller (1986); see also Brown & Gilligan (1992) and Gilligan (1982).
16. Blos (1962); Chodorow (1978); Stoller (1985).
17. Herdt (1987); Herdt & Stoller (1990).
18. Gutmann (1987).
19. See Shweder (1984).
20. Boddy (1989); A. Walker (1992).
21. Bateson (1972).
22. Boddy (1989).
23. Quotation is from Elderfield (1984), p. 27.
24. Ibid.
25. Ibid., p. 29.
26. Ibid., p. 27.
27. Ibid.
28. Sweeney (1980), p. 132.

References

Abrams, M. H. (1953). *The mirror and the lamp: Romantic theory and the critical tradition.* New York: Oxford University Press.

[American Association of University Women]. (1992). *The AAUW Report: How schools short change girls.* Washington, DC: AAUW Educational Foundation.

Adams, C. (1986). *Qualitative changes in text memory from adolescence to mature adulthood.* Unpublished doctoral dissertation, Wayne State University, Detroit, MI.

Adams, C. (1991). Qualitative age differences in memory for text: A life-span developmental perspective. *Psychology and Aging, 6,* 323–336.

Adams, C., Labouvie-Vief, G., Hakim-Larson, J., DeVoe, M., & Hayden, M. (1988). *Modes of thinking and problem solving: Developmental transitions from preadolescence to middle adulthood.* Unpublished manuscript, University of Michigan, Ann Arbor.

Adams, C., Labouvie-Vief, G., Hobart, C. J., & Dorosz, M. (1990). Adult age group differences in story recall style. *Journal of Gerontology, 25,* 17–27.

Aeschylus (1953). *Oresteia* (Trans. R. Lattimore). Chicago: University of Chicago Press.

Anderson, W., & Hicks, C. (1990). *The green man: The archetype of our oneness with the earth.* San Francisco: Harper Collins.

Apel, K. O. (1980). Scientistics, hermeneutics, and the critique of ideology: Outline of a theory of science from a cognitive-anthropological standpoint. In G. Adey & D. Fisby (Eds.), *Towards a transformation of philosophy* (pp. 46–76). Boston: Routledge & Kegan Paul.

Aristotle (1912). *De generatione animalium* (Trans. A. Platt). In J. A. Smith & W. D. Ross (Ed.), *The works of Aristotle* Oxford: Clarendon Press.

References

Aristotle (1932). *Politics* (Trans. H. Rackham). Cambridge, MA: Harvard University Press.

Armon, C. (1984). Ideals of the good life and moral judgment: Ethical reasoning across the lifespan. In M. L. Commons, F. A. Richards, & C. Armon (Eds.), *Beyond formal operations: Late adolescent and adult cognitive development* (pp. 357–380). New York: Praeger.

Armon, C. (1989). Individuality and autonomy in adult ethical reasoning. In M. L. Commons, J. D. Sinnott, F. A. Richards, & C. Armon (Eds.), *Adult development. Vol. 1: Comparisons and applications of developmental models* (pp. 179–196). New York: Praeger.

Ashmore, R. D. (1990). Sex, gender, and the individual. In L. Pervin (Ed.), *Handbook of personality: Theory and research* (pp. 486–526). New York: Guilford Press.

Ashmore, R. D., & Ogilvie (1992). He's such a nice boy . . . when he's with grandma: Gender and evaluation in self-with-other representations. In T. M. Brinthaupt & R. P. Lipka (Eds.). *The self: Definitional and methodological issues* (pp. 236–290). Albany, NY: State University of New York Press.

Bachofen, J. J. (1967). *Myth, religion, and mother right: Selected writings of J. J. Bachofen.* Princeton, NJ: Princeton University Press.

Badinter, E. (1989). *Man/woman: The one is the other* (Trans. B. Wright). London: Collins Harvill.

Bakan, D. (1966). *The duality of human existence.* Chicago: Rand McNally.

Baltes, P. B. (1987). Theoretical propositions of life-span developmental psychology: On the dynamics between growth and decline. *Developmental Psychology, 23,* 611–626.

Baltes, P. B., & Smith, J. (1990). Toward a psychology of wisdom and its ontogenesis. In R. J. Sternberg, *Wisdom: Its nature, origins, and development* (pp. 87–120). Cambridge: Cambridge University Press.

Bamberger, J. (1974). The myth of matriarchy: Why men rule in primitive society. In M. Z. Rosaldo & L. Lamphere (Eds.), *Women, culture, and society* (pp. 263–280). Stanford, CA: Stanford University Press.

Bardwick, J. (1971). *Psychology of women: A study of biocultural conflicts.* New York: Harper & Row.

Baring, A., & Cashford, J. (1991). *The myth of the goddess.* New York: Penguin Group.

Barker, S. F. (1969). *Philosophy of mathematics.* Englewood Cliffs, NJ: Prentice-Hall.

References

Barlow, G. (1988). *East of the sun and west of the moon.* New York: Philomel Books.

Basseches, M.A. (1984). Dialectical thinking as a metasystematic form of cognitive organization. In M. L. Commons, F. A. Richards, & C. Armon (Eds.), *Beyond formal operations: Late adolescent and adult cognitive development* (pp. 216–238). New York: Praeger.

Bateson, G. (1972). *Steps to an ecology of mind.* New York: Ballantine.

Battersby, C. (1989). *Gender and genuis: Towards a feminist aesthetics.* Indianapolis: Indiana University Press.

Baynes, K., Bohman, J., & McCarthy, T. (1987) *Philosophy: End or transformation.* Cambridge, MA: MIT Press.

Belenky, M. F., Clinchy, B. M., Goldberger, N. R., & Tarule, J. M. (1986). *Women's ways of knowing.* New York: Basic Books.

Benjamin, J. (1988). *Bonds of love: Psychoanalysis, feminism, and the problem of domination.* New York: Pantheon Books.

Benner, P. (1984). *From novice to expert: Excellence and practice in clinical nursing.* Reading, MA: Addison-Wesley.

Berman, M. (1981). *The re-enchantment of the world.* Ithaca, NY: Cornell University Press.

Bernstein, R. J. (1991). *Beyond objectivism and relativism: Science, hermeneutics, and practice.* Philadelphia: University of Pennsylvania Press.

Bettelheim, B. (1962). *Symbolic wounds: Puberty rites and the envious male* (rev. ed.). New York: Collier Books.

Bettelheim, B. (1977). *The uses of enchantment: The meaning and importance of fairy tales.* New York: Knopf.

Bettelheim, B. (1983). *Freud and man's soul.* New York: Knopf.

Blanchard-Fields, F. (1986). Reasoning on social dilemmas varying in emotional saliency: An adult developmental perspective. *Psychology and Aging, 1,* 325–333.

Blanchard-Fields, F. (1989). Postformal reasoning in a socioemotional context. In M. L. Commons, J. D. Sinnott, F. A. Richards, & C. Armon (Eds.), *Adult development. Vol. 1: Comparisons and applications of developmental models* (pp. 73–93). New York: Praeger.

Block, J. H. (1983). Differential premises arising from differential socialization of the sexes: Some conjectures. *Child Development, 54,* 1335–1354.

Blos, P. (1962). *On adolescence: A psychoanalytic interpretation.* New York: Free Press.

Blumenberg, H. (1987). An anthropological approach to the contemporary significance of rhetoric. In K. Baynes, J. Bohman, & T.

References

McCarthy (Eds.), *After philosophy: End or transformation?* (pp. 429–458). Cambridge, MA: MIT Press.

Bly, R. (1990). *Iron John.* Reading, MA: Addison-Wesley.

Boddy, J. (1989) *Wombs and alien spirits: Women, men, and the Zar cult in northern Sudan.* Madison: University of Wisconsin Press.

Bolen, J. S. (1989). *Gods in everyman: A new psychology of men's lives and loves.* San Francisco: Harper & Row.

Boole, G. (1958). *The laws of thought.* New York: Dover (Original work published 1854).

Bowlby, J. (1969). *Attachment and loss: Attachment* (Vol. I). New York: Basic Books.

Bowlby, J. (1973). *Attachment and loss: Separation* (Vol. II). New York: Basic Books.

Bowlby, J. (1980). *Attachment and loss: Depression* (Vol III). London: Hogarth Press.

Bretherton, I. (1990). Open communication and internal working models: Their role in the development of attachment relationships. In R. A. Thompson (Ed.), *Nebraska symposium on motivation* (Vol. 36, pp. 57–113). Lincoln: University of Nebraska Press.

Broughten, J. M. (1980). Genetic metaphysics: The developmental psychology of mind-body concepts. In R. W. Rieber (Ed.), *Body and mind* (pp. 177–221). New York: Academic Press.

Brown, L. M., & Gilligan, C. (1992). *Meeting at the crossroads: Women's psychology and girls' development.* Cambridge, MA: Harvard University Press.

Bruner, J. (1986). *Actual minds, possible worlds.* Cambridge, MA: Harvard University Press.

Bruner, J. (1990). *Acts of meaning.* Cambridge, MA: Harvard University Press.

Buber, M. (1958). *I and Thou.* New York: C. Scribner.

Bundtzen, L. (1983). *Plath's incarnations: Woman and the creative process.* Ann Arbor: University of Michigan Press.

Byrne, B. M., Shavelson, R. J., & March, H. W. (1992). Multigroup comparisons in self concept research: Reexamining the assumptions of equivalent structure and measurement. In T. M. Brinhaupt & R. P. Lipka (Eds.), *The self: Definitional and methodological issues.* Albany: State University of New York Press.

Cady, S., Ronan, M., & Taussig, H. (1986). *Sophia: The future of feminist spirituality.* New York: Harper & Row.

Campbell, J. (1982). *Grammatical man: Information, entropy, language, and life.* New York: Simon & Schuster.

References

Campbell, J. (1986). *The inner reaches of outer space: Metaphor as myth and as religion.* New York: Van Der Mark.

Campbell, J. (1988). *The power of myth.* New York: Doubleday.

Case, R. (1991). Stages in the development of the young child's first sense of self. *Developmental Review, 11,* 210–230.

Case, R. (1991b). *The mind's staircase.* Hillsdale, NJ: Erlbaum.

Case, R. (1991c, April). *The role of primitive defenses in the representation and regulation of early attachment relations.* Paper presented at the Society for Research in Child Development, Seattle, WA.

Case, R., Hayward, S., Lewis, M., & Hurst, P. (1988). Toward a neo-Piagetian theory of cognitive and emotional development. *Developmental Review, 8,* 1–51.

Cassirer, E. (1944). *An essay on man.* New Haven, CT: Yale University Press.

Cassirer, E. (1946). *Language and myth.* New York: Harper and Brothers. Reprint. New York: Dover Publications, 1953.

Cassirer, E. (1953–1957). *Philosophy of symbolic form* (Vols. 1–4). New Haven, CT: Yale University Press.

Chinen, A. B. (1984). Modal logic: A new paradigm of development and late-life potential. *Human Development, 27,* 42–56.

Chinen, A. B. (1989). *In the ever after: Fairy tales and the second half of life.* Wilmette, IL: Chiron.

Chinen, A. B. (1992). *Once upon a mid life: Classic stories & mythic tales for the middle years.* New York: J.P. Tarcher.

Chiriboga, D. (1989). Mental health at the midpoint: Crisis, challenge or relief? In S. Hunter & M. Sundel (Eds.), *Midlife myths* (pp. 116–144). Newbury Park, CA: Sage.

Chodorow, N. (1978). *The reproduction of mothering.* Los Angeles: University of California Press.

Clinchy, B., & Zimmerman, C. (1981). Epistemology and agency in the development of undergraduate women. In P. Perun (Ed.), *The undergraduate woman: Issues in educational equity* (pp. 161–181). Boston: D. C. Heath.

Colby, A., Kohlberg, L., Gibbs, J., & Lieberman, M. (1983). A longitudinal study of moral development. *Monographs of the Society for Research in Child Development, 49* (2, Serial No. 206).

Coles, R. (1977). *The children of crisis. Vol. 5: Privileged ones.* Boston: Little, Brown, & Co.

Collingwood, R. G. (1945). *The idea of nature.* Oxford: Clarendon Press.

References

Commons. M. L., Richards, F. A., & Armon, C. (1984). *Beyond formal operations: Late adolescent and adult cognitive development.* New York: Praeger.

Cook-Greuter, S. (1990). Maps for living: Ego development theory from symbiosis to conscious universal embeddedness. In M. L. Commons, J. D. Sinnott, F. A. Richards, & C. Armon (Eds.), *Adult development. Vol. 2: The development of adult thinking and perception* (pp. 79–104). New York: Praeger.

Cooper, K. L., & Gutmann, D. L. (1987). Gender identity and ego mastery style in middle-aged and post-empty nest women. *Gerontologist, 27,* 347–352.

Costa, B. J., & McCrae, R. R. (1988). Personality in adulthood: A six-year longitudinal study of self-reports and spouse ratings on NEO Personality Inventory. *Journal of Personality and Social Psychology, 54,* 853–863.

Cramer, P. (1979). Defense mechanisms in adolescence. *Developmental Psychology, 15,* 476–477.

Cramer, P. (1990). *The development of defense mechanisms: Theory, research, and assessment.* New York: Springer-Verlag.

Dabrowski, K. (1970). *Mental growth through positive disintegration.* London: Gryf Publications.

Daly, M. (1978). *Gyn-ecology.* Boston: Beacon Press.

Damon, W. (1988). *Self-understanding in childhood and adolescence.* Cambridge: Cambridge University Press.

Damon, W. & Hart, D. (1982). The development of self-understanding from infancy through adolescence. *Child Development, 53,* 841–864.

Davis, M., & Wallbridge, D. (1981). *Boundary and space: An introduction to the work of D. W. Winnicott.* New York: Brunner Mazel.

DeLong, H. (1970). *A profile of mathematical logic.* Reading, MA: Addison-Wesley.

Deutsch, H. (1969). *A psychoanalytic study of the myth of Dionysus and Apollo.* New York: International Universities Press.

Donald, M. (1991). *Origins of the modern mind: Three stages in the evolution of culture and cognition.* Cambridge, MA: Harvard University Press.

Donaldson, S. K., & Westerman, M. A. (1986). Development of children's understanding of ambivalence and causal theories of emotion. *Developmental Psychology, 22,* 655–662.

Dougherty, N. (1992). *Unfolding Neumann's map: Imagining masculine archetypal wholeness*. Thesis presented to the Chicago Jung Institute, Evanston, IL.

Downing, C. (1988). *Psyche's sisters: Re-imagining the meaning of sisterhood*. San Francisco: Harper & Row.

Dweck, C. S., & Bush, E. (1976). Sex differences in learned helplessness: II. The contingencies of evaluation feedback in the classroom and III. An experimental analysis. *Developmental Psychology, 14,* 268–276.

Dweck, C. S., & Elliot, E. S. (1983). Achievement motivation. In P. H. Mussen (Ed.), *Handbook of child psychology* (4th ed., Vol. 4, pp. 643–692). New York: Wiley.

Eisler, R. (1987). *The chalice and the blade*. San Francisco: Harper & Row.

Elias, N. (1978). *The civilizing process. Vol. 1: The history of manners*. New York: Pantheon Books.

Elias, N. (1982). *The civilizing process. Vol. 2: Power and civility*. New York: Pantheon Books.

Elderfield, J. (1984). *The drawings of Henri Matisse*. London: Thames & Hudson.

Engelsman, J. C. (1979). *Feminine dimensions of the divine*. Philadelphia, Westminster Press.

Erikson, E. H. (1958). *Young man Luther: A study in psychoanalysis and history*. New York: Norton.

Erikson, E. (1984). *The life cycle completed*. New York: Norton.

Euripides. (1972). *Iphigenia in Aulis* (Trans. F. M. Stawell). New York: Oxford University Press.

Evelyn-White, H. G. (1920). *Hesiod, the Homeric Hymns, and Homerica*. Loeb Classical Library. Cambridge, MA: Harvard University Press.

Faludi, S. (1991). *Backlash*. New York: Crown Publishers.

Fein, G. G. (1979). Play and the acquisition of symbols. In L. Katz (Eds.), *Current topics in early childhood education* (pp. 195–225). Norwood NJ: Ablex.

Fischer, K. W. (1980). A theory of cognitive development: The control and construction of hierarchies of skills. *Psychological Review, 87,* 477–531.

Fischer, K. W. (1991). Emotional splitting as an organizer of functional and dysfunctional development. In *Newsletter of the International Society for the Study of Behavioral Development, 19,* 4.

Fischer, K. W., Hand, H. H., & Russell, S. (1984). The development of abstractions in adolescence and adulthood. In M. L. Commons,

References

F. A. Richards, & C. Armon (Eds.), *Beyond formal operations: Late adolescent and adult cognitive development* (pp. 43–72). New York: Praeger.

Fischer, K. W., & Pipp, S. L. (1984). Development of the structures of unconscious thought. In K. Bowers & D. Meichenbaum (Eds.), *The unconscious reconsidered* (pp. 88–148). New York: Wiley.

Fischer, K. W., Shaver, P. R., & Carnochan, P. (1990). How emotions develop and how they organize development. *Cognition and Emotion, 4,* 81–127.

Flavell, J.H. (1963). *The developmental psychology of Jean Piaget.* New York: Van Nostrand.

Flax, J. (1990). *Thinking fragments: Psychoanalysis, feminism, and post-modernisms in the contemporary West.* Berkeley: University of California Press.

Fordham, F. (1966). *An introduction to Jung's psychology.* New York: Pelikan.

Foucault, M. (1986). *The care of the self.* New York: Pantheon Books.

Foulkes, D. (1979). Children's dreams. In B. B. Wolman (Ed.), *Handbook of dreams: Research, theories, and applications* (pp. 131–167). New York: Van Nostrand Reinhold.

Fowler, J. W. (1981). *Stages of faith: The psychology of human development and the quest for meaning.* San Francisco: Harper & Row.

Fox, M. (1985). *Illuminations of Hildegard of Bingen.* Santa Fe, NM: Bear.

Frankfort, H. (1961). *Ancient Egyptian religion: An interpretation.* New York: Harper.

Frankfort, H., & Frankfort, H. A. (1946). *Before philosophy: The intellectual adventure of ancient man.* Baltimore: Penguin Books.

Franz, M. L. V. (1992). *The golden ass of Apuleius: The liberation of the feminine in man.* Boston: Shambala Publications.

Frege, G. (1953). *The foundations of arithmetic: A logico-mathematical enquiry into the concept of number* (2nd rev. ed.). Oxford: Blackwell.

Freud, S. (1900/1965). *The interpretation of dreams* (Transl. J. Strachey). New York: Avon Books.

Freud, S. (1905/1953). Fragment of an analysis of a case of hysteria. In J. Strachey (Ed. and Trans.), *The standard edition of the complete psychological works of Sigmund Freud* (Vol. 7, pp. 7–122). London: Hogarth Press.

Freud, S. (1911/1957). Formulations regarding the two principles in mental functioning. In J. Rickman (Ed.), *A general selection from the works of Sigmund Freud* (pp. 43–44). Garden City, NY: Doubleday.

Freud, S. (1918/1952). *Totem and Tabu* (Trans. J. Strachey). New York: Norton.

Freud, S. (1923/1957). The id and the ego. In J. Rickman (Ed.), *A general selection from the works of Sigmund Freud* (210–235). Garden City, NY: Doubleday.

Freud, S. (1925/1963). Some psychological consequences of the anatomical differences between the sexes. In P. Rieff (Ed.), *Sexuality and the psychology of love* (pp. 183–193). New York: Macmillan.

Fromm, E. (1951). *The forgotten language.* New York: Grove Press.

Fromm, E. (1956). *The art of loving.* New York: Harper & Row.

Gadamer, H. G. (1976). *Philosophical hermeneutics* (Trans. D. E. Linge). Berkeley: University of California Press.

Gadamer, H. G. (1979). The problem of historical consciousness. In P. Rabinow & W. M. Sullivan (Eds.), *Interpretive social science: A reader.* Berkeley: University of California Press.

Gardner, H. (1980). *Artful scribbles: The significance of children's drawings.* New York: Basic Books.

Gardner, H. (1983). *Frames of mind: The theory of multiple intelligences.* New York: Basic Books.

Geertz, C. (1983). *Local knowledge.* New York: Basic Books.

Georgoudi, S. (1992). Creating a myth of patriarchy. In P. S. Pantel (Ed.), *A history of women: From ancient goddesses to Christian Saints* (pp. 449–477). Cambridge, MA: Harvard University Press.

Gergen, K. J. (1992). *Psychology in the postmodern era.* Invited address to the American Psychological Association, Washington, DC.

Gilligan, C. (1982). *In a different voice.* Cambridge, MA: Harvard University Press.

Gilligan, C. (1990). Teaching Shakespeare's sister: Notes from the underground of female adolescence. In C. Gilligan, N. P. Lyons, & T. J. Hanmer (Eds.), *Making connections* (pp. 6–29). Cambridge, MA: Harvard University Press.

Gilligan, C., Lyons, N. P., & Hanmer, T. J. (Eds.). (1990). *Making connections.* Cambridge, MA: Harvard University Press.

Gilligan, C., & Murphy, J. M. (1979). Development from adolescence to adulthood: The philosopher and the dilemma of fact. In D. Kuhn (Ed.), *Intellectual development beyond childhood* (pp. 85–99). New York: Jossey-Bass.

Gimbutas, M. (1982). *The goddesses and gods of old Europe: Myths and cult images.* Berkeley: University of California Press.

References

Goldberg, E., & Costa, L. (1981). Hemisphere differences in the acquisition and use of descriptive systems. *Brains and Language, 14,* 144–173.

Goldstein, W. N. (1991). Clarification of projective identification. *American Journal of Psychiatry, 148,* 153–161.

Goody, J., & Watt, I. (1963). The consequences of literacy. *Comparative Studies in Society and History, 5,* 304–345.

Gould, S. J. (1977). *Ontogeny and phylogeny.* Cambridge, MA: Belknap Press of Harvard University Press.

Gould, S. J. (1981). *The mismeasure of man.* New York: Norton.

Graves, R. (1960). *The Greek myths* (Vols. 1 and 2). New York: Penguin Books.

Greenberg, J. R., & Mitchell, S. A. (1983). *Object relations in psychoanalytic theory.* Cambridge, MA: Harvard University Press.

Gruber, H. E. & Voneche, J. J. (1977). *The essential Piaget: An interpretive reference and guide.* New York: Basic Books.

Gutmann, D. (1987). *Reclaimed powers: Toward a new psychology of men and women in later life.* New York: Basic Books.

Haan, N. (1981). Common dimensions of personality development: Early adolescence to middle life. In D. Eichorn, N. Haan, J. Calusen, M. Honzik, & P. Mussen (Eds.), *Present and past in middle life* (pp. 117–151). New York: Academic Press.

Haan, N. (1985). Common personality dimensions or common organizations across the life-span? In J. M. A. Munnichs, P. Mussens, E. Olbrich, & P. G. Coleman (Eds.), *Life-span and change in a gerontological perspective* (pp. 17–44). New York: Academic Press.

Habermas, J. (1970). *Zur Logik der Sozialwissenschaften.* Frankfurt: Suhrkamp.

Habermas, J. (1984). *The theory of communicative action. Vol. 1: Reason and the rationalization of society.* Boston: Beacon Press.

Harris, E. E. (1987). *Formal, transcendental, and dialectical thinking: Logic and reality.* Albany, NY: State University of New York Press.

Harris, P. L. (1983). Children's understanding of the link between situation and emotion. *Journal of Experimental Psychology, 36,* 490–509.

Hart, C., & Bishop, J. (1990). *Hildegard of Bingen: Scivias.* New York: Paulist Press.

Harter, S. (1983). Developmental perspectives on the self system. In P. Mussen (Series Ed.), & E. M. Hetherington (Vol. Ed.), *Handbook of child psychology* (Vol. 4, pp. 275–385). New York: Wiley.

Harter, S. & Buddin, B. J. (1987). Children's understanding of the simultaneity of two emotions: A five-stage developmental acquisition sequence. *Developmental Psychology, 23,* 388–399.

Hauser, S. T. (1976). Loevinger's model and measure of ego development: A critical review. *Psychological Bulletin, 83,* 928–955.

Havelock, E. A. (1963). *Preface to Plato.* Cambridge, MA: Belknap Press of Harvard University Press.

Havelock, E. A. (1978). *The Greek concept of justice.* Cambridge, MA: Harvard University Press.

Heilbrun, C. (1988). *Writing a woman's life.* New York: Ballantine Books.

Heine. S. (1989). *Matriarchs, goddesses, and images of god.* Minneapolis: Augsburg.

Helson, R., & Moane, G. (1987). Personality change in women from college to midlife. *Journal of Personality and Social Psychology, 53,* 176–186.

Helson, R., & Wink, P. (1992). Personality change in women from the early 40's to the early 50's. *Psychology and Aging, 7(1),* 46–55.

Herdt, G. H. (1987). *Guardians of the flutes: Idioms of masculinity.* New York: Columbia University Press.

Herdt, G. H., & Stoller, R. J. (1990). *Intimate communications: Erotics and the study of culture.* New York: Columbia University Press.

Hesiod. (1983). Theogeny. In A. N. Athanassakis (Ed.), *Hesiod: Theogeny, work and days, shield* (pp. 590–601). Baltimore: Johns Hopkins University Press.

Higgins, E. T. (1991). Development of self-regulatory and self-evaluative processes: Costs, benefits, and tradeoffs. In M. R. Gunnar & L. A. Sroufe (Eds.), Self processes in development. *Minnesota Symposia on Child Development, 23,* 125–165.

Hillman, J. (1972). *The myth of analysis.* Evanston, IL: Northwestern University Press.

Hofstadter, D. R. (1980). *Gödel, Esher, Bach: An eternal golden braid.* New York: Vintage Books.

Hollingsworth, L. (1926). *Gifted children: Their nature and nurture.* New York: Macmillan.

Horkheimer, M., & Adorno, T. (1972). *Dialectic of enlightenment.* New York: Herder & Herder.

Horner, A. (1989). *The wish for power and the fear of having it.* Northvale, NJ: Jason Aronson.

Houston, J. (1987). *The search for the beloved.* Los Angeles: J. Tarcher.

Huyck, M. H. (1994). The relevance of psychodynamic theories for understanding gender among older women. In B. F. Turner & L.

E. Troll (Eds.), *Growing older female: Theoretical directions in the psychology of aging*. Newbury Park, CA: Sage.

Jacobi, J. (1962). *The psychology of C. G. Jung*. New Haven, CT: Yale University Press.

Janoff-Bulman, R. (1992). *Shattered assumptions: Towards a new psychology of trauma*. New York: Free Press.

Jaques, E. (1965). Death and the mid-life crisis. *International Journal of Psychoanalysis, 46*, 502–514.

Jaynes, J. (1976). *The origin and history of consciousness in the breakdown of the bicameral mind*. Boston: Houghton Mifflin.

Jellouschek, H. (1989). *The frog princess*. Zurich: Kreuz Verlag.

Jepson, K. & Labouvie-Vief, G. (1992). Symbolic processing in the elderly. In J. Sinnott & R. West (Eds.), *Everyday memory and aging: Current research and methodology* (pp. 124–137). New York: Springer-Verlag.

Johnson, R. A. (1989). *She: Understanding feminine psychology* (rev. ed.). San Francisco: Harper Collins.

Jung, C. G. (1933). *Modern man in search of a soul* (Trans. W. S. Dell & C. F. Baynes). New York: Harcourt, Brace & World.

Jung, C. G. (1954). *The psychology of transference* (Trans. R. F. C. Hull). Princeton, NJ: Princeton University Press.

Jung, C. G., von Franz, M. L., Henderson, J. L., Jacobi, J., & Jaffe, A. (1964). *Man and his symbols*. Garden City, NY: Doubleday.

Kant, I. (1764/1960). *Observations on the feeling of the beautiful & sublime* (Trans. J. T. Goldthwait). Berkeley: University of California Press.

Kaufman, D. R., & Richardson, B. L. (1982). *Achievement and women: Challenging the assumptions*. New York: Free Press.

Kegan, J. (1982). *The evolving self*. Cambridge MA: Harvard University Press.

Keller, E. F. (1985). *Reflections on gender & science*. New Haven: Yale University Press.

Kerenyi, C. (1951). *The gods of the Greeks*. London: Thames & Hudson.

Kerr, B. A. (1987). *Smart girls, gifted women*. Columbus: Ohio Publishing.

King, P. M., Kitchener, K. S., Wood, P. K., & Davison, M. L. (1989). Relationships across developmental domains: A longitudinal study of intellectual, moral, and ego development. In M. L. Commons, J. D. Sinnott, F. A. Richards, & C. Armon (Eds.), *Adult development. Vol. 1: Comparisons and applications of developmental models* (pp. 57–72). New York: Praeger.

References

Kitchener, K. S., & Brenner, H. G. (1990). Wisdom and reflective judgment: Knowing in the face of uncertainty. In R. Sternberg (Ed.), *Wisdom: Its nature, origin, and development* (pp. 212–229). Cambridge: Cambridge University Press.

Kitchener, K. S., & King, P. M. (1981). Reflective judgment: Concepts of justification and their relationship to age and education. *Journal of Applied Developmental Psychology, 2,* 89–116.

Kitchener, K. S., King, P. M., Wood, P. K., & Davison, M. L. (1989). Consistency and sequentiality in the development of reflective judgment: a six year longitudinal study. *Journal of Applied Developmental Psychology, 10,* 73–95.

Klein, E. (1967). *A comprehensive etymological dictionary of the English language.* Amsterdam: Elsevier Publishing.

Klein, M., & Riviere, J. (1964). *Love, hate, and reparation.* New York: Norton.

Koestler, A. (1964). *The act of creation.* New York: Macmillan.

Kohlberg, L. (1969). Stage and sequence: The cognitive-developmental approach to socialization. In D. A. Goslin (Ed.), *Handbook of socialization theory and research* (pp. 347–380). Chicago: University of Chicago Press.

Kohlberg, L. (1984). *Essays on moral development. Vol. 2: The psychology of moral development.* San Francisco: Harper & Row.

Kohut, H. (1977). *The restoration of the self.* New York: International Universities Press.

Kramer, D. A. (1989). Development of an awareness of contradiction across the life span and the question of post-formal operations. In M. L. Commons, J. D. Sinnott, F. A. Richards, & C. Armon (Eds.), *Adult development. Vol. 1: Comparisons and applications of developmental models* (pp. 133–160). New York: Praeger.

Kramer, D. A., & Woodruff, D. (1986). Relativistic and dialectical thought in three adult age-groups. *Human Development, 29,* 280–290.

Kuhn, D. (1991). *The skills of argument.* New York: Cambridge University Press.

Kuhn, D., Pennington, N., & Leadbeater, B. (1983). Adult thinking in developmental perspective. In P. B. Baltes & O. G. Brim, Jr. (Eds.), *Life-span development and behavior* (Vol. 5, pp. 158–195). New York: Academic Press.

Kurtz, S. R. (1993). *All the mothers are one: Hindu India & the cultural reshaping of psychoanalysis.* New York: Columbia University Press.

References

Labouvie-Vief, G. (1980). Beyond formal operations: Uses and limits of pure logic in life span development. *Human Development, 23,* 141–161.

Labouvie-Vief, G. (1981). Re-active and pro-active aspects of constructivism: Growth and aging in life span perspective. In R. M. Lerner & N. A. Busch-Rossnagel (Eds.), *Individuals as producers of their development: A life-span perspective.* (pp. 197–320). New York: Academic Press.

Labouvie-Vief, G. (1982). Dynamic development and mature autonomy. *Human Development, 25,* 161–191.

Labouvie-Vief, G. (1985). Intelligence and cognition. In J. E. Birren & K. W. Schaie (Eds.), *Handbook of the psychology of aging* (2nd ed., pp. 500–530). New York: Academic Press.

Labouvie-Vief, G. (1990). Wisdom as integrated thought: Historical and developmental perspectives. In R. J. Sternberg (Ed.), *Wisdom: Its nature, origins, and development* (pp. 52–83). Cambridge: Cambridge University Press.

Labouvie-Vief, G. (1992a). A neo-Piagetian on adult cognitive development. In R. L. Sternberg & C. A. Berg (Eds.), *Intellectual development* (pp. 197–228). Cambridge: Cambridge University Press.

Labouvie-Vief, G. (1992b). Modes of knowledge and the organization of development. In M. L. Commons, C. Armon, L. Kohlberg, F. A. Richards, T. A. Grotzer, & J. D. Sinnott (Eds.), *Adult development. Vol 2: Models and methods in the study of adolescent and adult thought* (pp. 43–62). New York: Praeger.

Labouvie-Vief, G. (1993). Ego processes in adulthood: A comment on Jane Loevinger. *Psychological Inquiry, 4,* 34–47.

Labouvie-Vief, G., & CeVoe, M. R. (1991). Emotions in adulthood and later life: A cognitive-developmental perspective. In K. W. Schaie (Ed.), *Handbook of geriatrics* (pp. 172–194). New York: Springer.

Labouvie-Vief, G., Devoe, M., & Bulka, D. (1989). Speaking about feelings: Conceptions of emotion across the life span. *Psychology and Aging, 4,* 425–437.

Labouvie-Vief, G., & Hakim-Larson, J. (1989). Developmental shifts in adult thought. In S. Hunter & M. Sundel (Eds.), *Midlife myths: Issues, findings, and practice implications* (pp. 69–96). Newbury Park, CA: Sage.

Labouvie-Vief, G., Hakim-Larson, J., Devoe, M., & Schoeberlein, S. (1989). Emotions and self-regulation: A life span view. *Human Development, 32,* 279–299.

References

Labouvie-Vief, G., Hakim-Larson, J., & Hobart, C. (1987). Age, ego level, and life-span development of coping and defense processes. *Psychology and Aging, 2,* 286–293.

Labouvie-Vief, G., & Lawrence, R. (1985). Object knowledge, personal knowledge, and processes of equilibration in adult cognition. *Human Development, 28,* 25–39.

Labouvie-Vief, G., Orwoll, L., & Manion, M. (1994). *Narratives of mind, gender, and the life course.* Unpublished manuscript, Wayne State University, Detroit, MI.

Labouvie-Vief, G., & Schell, D. (1982). Learning and memory in later life: A developmental perspective. In B. Wolman & G. Stricker (Eds.), *Handbook of developmental psychology* (pp. 829–846). Englewood Cliffs, NJ: Prentice-Hall.

Labouvie-Vief, G., Schell, D. A., & Weaverdyck, S. E. (1982). *Recall deficit in the aged: A fable recalled.* Unpublished manuscript.

Lacqueur, T. (1990). *Making sex: Body and gender from the Greeks to Freud.* Cambridge, MA: Harvard University Press.

Lakatos, I. (1970). *Criticism and the growth of knowledge.* International Colloquium in the Philosophy of Science, 1965. Cambridge, MA: Cambridge University Press.

Lakoff, G. (1987). *Women, fire & dangerous things.* Chicago: University of Chicago Press.

Lakoff, G. (1980). *Metaphors we live by.* Chicago: Chicago University Press.

Langer, S. (1942). *Philosophy in a new key: A study in the symbolism of reason, rite, and art.* Cambridge MA: Harvard University Press.

Lerner, G. (1986). *The creation of patriarchy.* New York: Oxford University Press.

Levinson, D. J., Darrow, C. N., Klein, E. B., Levinson, M. H., & McKee, B. (1978). *The seasons of a man's life.* New York: Ballantine.

Lewis, C. S. (1980). *Till we have faces: A myth retold.* Ft. Worth, TX: Harcourt, Brace & Jovanovich.

Liddell, H. G., & Scott R. (1958). *A Greek–English lexicon.* Oxford: Clarendon.

Lipps, H. M. (1988). *Sex & gender.* Mountain View, CA: Mayfield.

Livson, F. B. (1981a). Paths to psychological health in the middle years: Sex differences. In D. H. Eichorn, N. Haan, J. Clausen, M. Honzik, & P. Mussen (Eds.), *Present and past in middle life* (pp. 195–221). New York: Academic Press.

Livson, F. B. (1981b). Patterns of personality development in middle-aged women: A longitudinal study. In J. Hendricks (Ed.), *Being and becoming old* (pp. 133–140). Farmingdale, NY: Baywood.

Lloyd, G. (1984). *The man of reason: "male" and "female" in Western philosophy*. Minneapolis: University of Minnesota Press.

Logan, R. K. (1986). *The alphabet effect: The impact of the phonetic alphabet on the development of Western civilization*. New York: William Morrow.

Longstreth, L. (1968). *Psychological development of the child*. New York: Ronald Press.

Loevinger, J. (1993). Measurement of personality: True or false. *Psychological Inquiry, 4*, 1–16.

Lorenz, K. (1967). *On aggression*. London: Methuen.

Lyotard, J. F. (1987). The postmodern condition. In K. Baynes, J. Bohman, & T. McCarthy (Eds.), *Philosophy: End or transformation* (pp. 73–94). Cambridge, MA: MIT Press.

Maas, H. S., & Kuypers, J. A. (1974). *From thirty to seventy*. San Francisco: Jossey-Bass.

McAdams, D. P. (1990). *The person: An introduction to personality psychology*. New York: Harcourt, Brace & Jovanovich.

Maccoby, E. E., & Jacklin, C. N. (1974). *The psychology of sex differences*. Stanford, CA: Stanford University Press.

McGrath, E., Keita, G. P., Strickland, B. R., & Russo, N. F. (1990). *Women and depression: Risk factors and treatment issues*. Washington, DC: American Psychological Association.

McLuhan, H. M. (1962). *The Gutenberg galaxy: The making of typographic man*. Toronto: University of Toronto Press.

McLuhan, H. M. (1964). *Understanding media: The extensions of man*. New York: McGraw-Hill.

Macmurray, J. (1978). *The self as agent*. Atlantic Highlands, NJ: Humanities Press.

Main, M. (1991). Metacognitive knowledge, metacognitive monitoring, and singular (coherent) vs. multiple (incoherent) model of attachment: Findings and directions for future research. In C. M. Parkes, J. Stevenson-Hinde, & P. Marris (Eds.), *Attachment across the life cycle* (pp. 127–159). London: Tavistock/Routledge.

Main, M., Kaplan, N., & Cassidy, J. (1985). Security in infancy, childhood, and adulthood: A move to the level of representation. *Monographs of the Society for Research in child Development, 50*, 66–104.

Mann, T. (1978). Freud und die Zukunft. In T. Kurzke (Ed.), *Thomas Mann: Essays* (Vol. 3, pp. 173–192). Frankfurt: Fischer.

References

Martin, V., & Nivens, M. K. (1987). The attributional response of males and females to noncontingent feedback. *Sex Roles, 16,* 453–462.

May, R. (1980). *Sex and fantasy: Patterns of male and female development.* New York: Norton.

Mayer, M. (1978). *Beauty and the beast.* New York: Four Winds Press.

Miller, J. B. (1986). *Towards a new psychology of women.* Boston: Beacon Press.

Miller, P. H. (1983). *Theories of developmental psychology.* San Francisco: Freeman.

Mitchell, S. A. (1988). Relational concepts in psychoanalysis: An integration. Cambridge, MA: Harvard University Press.

Molesworth, L. (1879). *The tapestry room: A child's romance.* New York: Random House.

Monod, J. (1971). *Chance and necessity: An essay on the natural philosophy of modern biology.* New York: Knopf.

Nelson, K., & Gruendel, J. (1981). Generalized event representations: Basic building blocks of cognitive development. In M. E. Lamb & A. L. Brown (Eds.), *Advances in developmental psychology* (Vol. 1, pp. 131–158). Hillsdale, NJ: Erlbaum.

Neugarten, B. L. (1968). The awareness of middle age. In B. L. Neugarten (Ed.), *Middle age and aging* (pp. 93–98). Chicago: University of Chicago Press.

Neumann, E. (1954). *The origins and history of consciousness.* Princeton, NJ: Princeton University Press.

Neumann, E. (1955). *The great mother.* Princeton, NJ: Princeton University Press.

Neumann, E. (1956). *Amor and Psyche: The psychic development of the feminine.* Princeton, NJ: Princeton University Press.

Neumann, E. (1973). *The origins and history of human consciousness.* Princeton, NJ: Princeton University Press.

Noam, G. G. (1988). The self, adult development, and the theory of biography and transformation. In D. K. Lapsley & F. L. Power (Eds.), *Self, ego, and identity: Integrative approaches.* (pp. 3–29). New York: Springer.

Noble, D. F. (1992). *A world without women.* New York: Knopf.

Nozick, R. (1981). *Philosophical explanations.* Cambridge, MA: Harvard University Press.

Ogilvie, D. M., & Clark, M. D. (1992). The best and worst of it: Age and sex differences in self-discrepancy research. In R. P. Lipka & T. M. Brinthaupt (Eds.), *Self-perspectives across the life span* (pp. 1–282). Albany: State University of New York Press.

References

Olsen, T. (1978). *Silences.* New York: Delacorte Press/Seymour Lawrence.

Olson, D. R. (1977). From utterance to text: The bias of language in speech and writing. *Harvard Educational Review, 47,* 257–281.

Onians, R. B. (1954). *The origins of European thought: About the body, the mind, the soul, world, time, and fate.* Cambridge: Cambridge University Press.

Ortner, S. (1974). Is female to male as nature is to culture? In M. Z. Rosaldo & L. Lamphere (Eds.), *Woman, culture, and society* (pp. 67–88). Stanford, CA: Stanford University Press.

Orwoll, L., Chiodo, L. M., Goguen, L. A., Labouvie-Vief, G., & Murphy, D. (1993, August). *Representations of the self across the life span.* Poster presented at the annual meeting of the American Psychological Association, Toronto.

Pagels, E. H. (1979). *Gnostic Gospels.* New York: Random House.

Palmer, R. E. (1969). *Hermeneutics: Interpretion theory in Scheiermacher, Dilthey, Heidegger, and Gadamer.* Evanston, IL: Northwestern University Press.

Partridge, E. (1966). *Origins: A short etymological dictionary of modern English.* London: Routledge & Kegan Paul.

Peplau, L. A. (1976). Fear of success in dating couples. *Sex Roles, 2,* 249–258.

Perry, W. G. (1968). *Forms of intellectual and ethical development in the college years.* New York: Holt, Rinehart, & Winston.

Peterson, A. C. (1987). Those gangly years. *Psychology Today, 21,* 28–34.

Piaget, J. (1930). *The child's conception of physical causality* (Trans. M. Gabain). New York: Harcourt Brace.

Piaget, J. (1955). *The language and thought of the child* (Trans. M. Gabain). New York: New American Library.

Piaget, J. (1962). *Play, dreams, and imitation in childhood* (Trans. C. Gattegno & F. M. Hodgeson). New York: Norton.

Piaget, J. (1965). *The moral judgment of the child* (Trans. M. Gabain). New York: Free Press.

Piaget, J. (1967). *Six psychological studies* (Trans. A. Tenzer). New York: Random House.

Piaget, J. (1980). *Experiments in contradiction* (Trans. D. Coleman). Chicago: University of Chicago Press.

Piaget, J. (1981). *Intelligence and affectivity: Their relationship during child development* (Trans. T. A. Brown & C. E. Kaegi). Palo Alto, CA: Annual Reviews.

References

Piaget J., & Garcia, R. (1989). *Psychogenesis and the history of science* (Trans. H. Feider). New York: Columbia University Press. (Original work published 1896)

Piechowski, M. M. (1975). A theoretical & empirical approach to the study of development. *Genetic Psychological Monograph, 92,* 231–297.

Plath, S. (1971). *The bell jar.* New York: Harper & Row.

Plato (1961a). *Gorgias* (Trans. W. D. Woodhead). In E. Hamilton & H. Cairns (Eds.), *Plato: Collected dialogues* (pp. 229–307). Princeton, NJ: Princeton University Press.

Plato (1961b). *Phaedo* (Trans. H. Tredennick). In E. Hamilton & H. Cairns (Eds.), *Plato: Collected dialogues* (pp. 40–98). Princeton, NJ: Princeton University Press.

Plato (196lc). *Protagoras* (Trans. W. K. C. Guthrie). In E. Hamilton & H. Cairns (Eds.), *Plato: Collected dialogues* (pp. 308–352). Princeton, NJ: Princeton University Press.

Plato (1961d). *The Republic* (Trans. P. Shorey). In E. Hamilton & H. Cairns (Eds.), *Plato: Collected dialogues* (pp. 575–844). Princeton, NJ: Princeton University Press.

Plato (1961e). *Symposium* (Trans. M. Joyce). In E. Hamilton & H. Cairns (Eds.), *Plato: Collected dialogues* (pp. 526–574). Princeton, NJ: Princeton University Press.

Plato (1961f). *Thaetetus* (Trans. F. M. Cornford). In E. Hamilton & H. Cairns (Eds.), *Plato: Collected dialogues* (pp. 845–919). Princeton, NJ: Princeton University Press.

Plutarch (1969). Isis and Osiris. In *Moralia,* Book 5 (Trans. F. C. Babbitt). Loeb Classical Library. London: William Heinemann.

Pope, D. (1984). *A separate vision: Isolation in contemporary women's poetry in America.* Baton Rouge, LA: Louisiana State University Press.

Popper, K. R. (1963). *Conjecture and refutations: The growth of scientific knowledge.* New York: Harper & Row.

Postman, N. (1982). *The disappearance of childhood.* New York: Delacorte Press.

Pratt, A. (1981). *Archetypal patterns in women's fiction.* Brighton, Sussex: Harvester Press.

Pratt, A. (1993). *Archetypal empowerment in poetry: Medusa, Aphrodite, Artemis, Bears: Gender comparisons.* Bloomington: Indiana University Press.

Pribram, K. H., & McGuiness, D. (1975). Arousal, activation, and effort in the control of attention. *Psychological Review, 82,* 116–149.

References

Putnam, H. (1987). Why reason can't be naturalized. In K. Baynes, J. Bohman, & T. McCarthy (Eds.), *After philosophy: End or transformation?* (pp. 217–244). Cambridge, MA: MIT Press.

Reddy, M. J. (1979). The conduit metaphor. In A. Ortony (Ed.), *Metaphor and thought* (pp. 284–324). Cambridge: Cambridge University Press.

Redmore, C. D., & Loevinger, J. (1979). Ego development in adolescence: Longitudinal studies. *Journal of Youth and Adolescence, 8,* 129–134.

Reich, K. H. (1990). *Commonalities and differences of Piagetian operations and complementary reasoning: A conceptual model and its support by empirical data.* Paper presented at the meeting of the Jean Piaget Society, Philadelphia.

Reich, K. H. (1992). Definitionen der Komplementaritaet. In E. P. Fischer, H. S. Herzka, & K. H. Reich (Eds.), *Widerspruechliche Wirklichkeit* (pp. 18–28). Munich: Piper.

Rich, A. C. (1951). *A change of world.* New Haven, CT: Yale University Press.

Rich, A. C. (1969). *Leaflets.* New York: Norton.

Richter, H. E. (1979). *Der Gotteskomplex: Die Geburt und Krise des Glaubens and die Allmacht des Menschen* Reinbeck: Rowohlt.

Ricoeur, P. (1970). *Freud and philosophy: An essay on interpretation.* New Haven, CT: Yale University Press.

Riegel, K. F. (1973). Dialectical operations: The final period of cognitive development. *Human Development, 16,* 346–370.

Riegel, K. F. (1976). The dialectics of human development. *American Psychologist, 31,* 679–700.

Rorty, R. (1979). *Philosophy and the mirror of nature.* Princeton, NJ: Princeton University Press.

Rosenberg, S. D., & Farrell, M. P. (1976). Identity and crisis in middle-aged men. *International Journal of Aging and Human Development, 7,* 153–170.

Rubinstein, S. L. (1968). *Grundlagen der allgemeinen Psychologie.* Berlin: Volkseigener Verlag Berlin.

Russell, B. (1945). *A history of Western philosophy.* New York: Simon & Schuster.

Saarni, C., & Harris, P. L. (1989). *Children's understanding of emotion.* Cambridge: Cambridge University Press.

Sarbin, T. R. (1986). *Narrative psychology: The storied nature of human conduct.* New York: Praeger.

Schon, D. A. (1983). *The reflective practitioner.* New York: Basic Books.

References

Schott, R. M. (1988). *Cognition and eros*. Boston: Beacon Press.

Scribner, S., & Cole, M. (1981). *The psychology of literacy*. Cambridge, MA: Harvard University Press.

Segal, H. (1974). *Introduction to the work of Melanie Klein*. New York: Basic Books.

Selman, R. L. (1980). *The growth of interpersonal understanding: Developmental and clinical analyses*. New York: Academic Press.

Selman, R., & Schultz, L. (1991). *Making a friend in youth: Developmental theory and pair therapy*. Chicago: University of Chicago Press.

Sheldrake, R. (1988). The laws of nature as habits: A post-modern basis for science. In D. R. Griffin (Ed.), *The re-enchantment of science: Post-modern proposals* (pp. 79–86). Albany: State University of New York Press.

Shlain, L. (1991). *Art & physics: Parallel visions in space, time, and light*. New York: William Morrow.

Shweder, R. (1984). *Culture theory: Essays on mind, self, and emotion*. Cambridge: Cambridge University Press.

Simon, B. (1978). *Mind and madness in ancient Greece*. Ithaca, NY: Cornell University Press.

Solomon, J., & George, C. (1991, April). *Working models of attachment of children classified as controlling at age six: Disorganization at the level of representation*. Paper presented at the biennial meeting of the Society for Research in Child Development, Seattle, WA.

Spence, D. P. (1982). *Narrative truth and historical truth*. New York: Norton.

Spretnak, C. (1971) *Lost goddesses of early Greece*. Boston: Beacon Press.

Sroufe, L. A. (1983). Infant-caregiver attachment and patterns of adaptation in preschool: The roots of maladaptation and competence. In M. Perlmutter (Ed.), *Minnesota symposium on child psychology* (Vol. 16, pp. 41–83). Hillsdale, NJ: Erlbaum.

Sroufe, L. A., & Fleeson, J. (1986). Attachment & the construction of relationships. In W. Hartup & Z. Rubin (Eds.), *Relationships & development* (pp. 51–71). Hillsdale, NJ: Erlbaum.

Stapleton, M. (1986). *The illustrated dictionary of Greek and Roman mythology*. New York: Peter Bedrick Books.

Stassinopoulos, A. (1983). *The gods of Greece*. New York: Abrams.

Stern, D. L. (1985). *The interpersonal world of the infant*. New York: Basic Books.

Stevens, A. (1982). *Archetypes*. New York: William Morrow.

Stevens-Long, J., & Commons, M. L. (1992). *Adult life* (4th ed.). Mountain View, CA: Mayfield Publishing.

References

Stoller, R. J. (1985). *Presentations of gender*. New Haven: Yale University Press.

Stone, M. (1978). *When god was a woman*. New York: Harcourt, Brace & Jovanovich.

Sweeney, L. (1980, September 30). Isaac Stern, concertmaster of the world. *Christian Science Monitor*, September 30, p. 132.

Tamir, L. (1982). *Men in their forties*. New York: Springer.

Tavris, C. (1992). *The mismeasure of woman*. New York: Simon & Schuster.

Tedlock, B. (1987). Dreaming and dream research. In B. Tedlock (Ed.), *Dreaming: Anthropological and psychological interpretations* (pp. 1–30). Cambridge: Cambridge University Press.

Terman, L. M., & Oden, M. (1925). *Genetic studies of genius. Vol. 1: Mental and physical traits of a thousand gifted children*. Stanford, CA: Stanford University Press.

Terman, L. M., & Oden, M. (1947). *Genetic Studies of Genius. Vol 4: The gifted child grows up*. Stanford, CA: University of California Press.

Terman, L. M., & Oden, M. (1959). *Genetic Studies of Genius. Vol 5: The gifted group at mid-life*. Stanford, CA: University of California Press.

Thorndike, E. (1910). *Educational psychology* (2nd. ed.). New York: Teachers College, Columbia University.

Tomlinson-Keasey, C., & Blurton, E. (1991). Gifted women's lives: Aspirations, achievements, and personal adjustment. In J. Carlson (Ed.), *Cognition and educational practice: An international perspective* (pp. 151–176). Greenwich: JAI Press.

Trevarthen, C. (1989, August). Origins and directions for the concept of infant intersubjectivity. *SRCD Newsletter*.

Troll, L. E., & Bengston, V. (1982). Intergenerational relations throughout the life-span. In B. B. Wolman (Ed.), *Handbook of developmental psychology* (pp. 890–908). Englewood Cliffs, NJ: Prentice-Hall.

Tucker, D. M., & Williamson, P. A. (1984). Asymmetric neural control system in human self-regulation. *Psychological Review, 91,* 185–215.

Turner, B. F. (1982). Sex related differences in aging. In B. B. Wolman (Ed.), Handbook of developmental psychology (pp. 201–253). New York: Van Nostrand.

Turner, T. (1973). Piaget's structuralism. *American Anthropologist, 75,* 351–373.

Ulanov, A., & Ulanov, B. (1983). *Cinderella and her sisters: The envied and the envying*. Philadelphia: Westminster Press.

References

Unger, R., & Crawford, M. (Eds.) (1992). *Women and gender: A feminist psychology.* New York: McGraw-Hill.

Vaillant, G. E., & McArthur, C. C. (1972). Natural history of male psychological health: The adult life cycle from eighteen to fifty. *Seminars in Psychiatry, 4,* 415–427.

Valle, R. S., King, M., & Halling, S. (1989). Introduction to existential-phenomenological perspectives in psychology (pp. 3–16). New York: Plenum.

Vernant, J. P. (1982). *The origins of Greek thought.* Ithaca, NY: Cornell University Press.

Veroff, J., Reuman, D., & Feld, S. (1984). Motives in American men and women across the adult life span. *Developmental Psychology, 20,* 1142–1158.

von Franz, M. L. (1980). *An interpretation of Apuleius' Golden Ass.* Irving, TX: Spring Publications.

Walker, A. (1992). *Possessing the secret of joy.* New York: Harcourt, Brace & Jovanovich.

Walker, B. (1983). *Women's encyclopedia of myths and secrets.* New York: Harper & Row.

Warnke, G. (1987). *Gadamer: Hermeneutics, tradition, and reason.* Stanford, CA: Stanford University Press.

Watzlawick, P. (1978). *The language of change.* New York: Basic Books.

Weisfeld, C. (1986). Female behavior in mixed-sex competition: A review of the literature. *Developmental Review, 6,* 278–299.

Welsch, W. (1988). *Unsere postmoderne Moderne.* Weinheim: VCH.

Werner, H. (1955). *On expressive language.* Worcester MA: Clark University Press.

Werner, H., & Kaplan, B. (1963). *Symbol formation.* New York: Wiley.

Whitehead, A. N. (1938). *Modes of thought.* New York: Macmillan.

Whitmont, E. C. (1969). *The symbolic quest: Basic concepts of analytical psychology.* Princeton, NJ: Princeton University Press.

Whitmont, E. C. (1982). *Return of the goddess.* New York: Crossroad Publishing.

Whyte, L. L. (1948). *The next development in man.* New York: Holt.

Wilber, K. (1981). *Up from Eden: A transpersonal view of human evolution.* Garden City, NY: Anchor Press/Doubleday.

Winner, E. (1982). *Invented worlds: The psychology of the arts.* Cambridge, MA: Harvard University Press.

Winnicott, D. W. (1971). *Playing and reality.* London: Tavistock Publications.

Wittgenstein, L. (1953). *Philosophical investigations.* Oxford: Blackwell.

References

Wittgenstein, L. (1972). *Tractatus logico-philosophicus*. New York: Humanities Press.

Wolkstein, D., & Kramer, S. N. (1983). *Inanna: Queen of heaven and earth – Her stories and hymns from Sumer*. New York: Harper & Row.

Woolf, V. (1929). *A room of one's own*. London: Harcourt, Brace & Jovanovich.

Yee, D. K., & Eccles, J. S. (1988). Parent perceptions and attributions for children's math achievement. *Sex Roles, 19*, 317–333.

Young-Eisendrath, P., & Wiedemann, F. (1987). *Female authority*. New York: Guilford Press.

Youniss, J.(1980). *Parents and peers in social development*. Chicago: University of Chicago Press.

Zilboorg, G. (1944). Masculine and feminine. *Psychiatry, 7*, 294.

Zinner, J. (1989). The implications of projective identification for marital interaction. In J. Scharff (Ed.), *Object relations family therapy* (pp. 155–173). Dumone, PA: Aronson.

Author index

Author index

Bruner, J., 283n5 (25), 284n41 (43), 286n17 (74)
Buber, M., 35, 284n26 (35)
Bundtzen, L., 291n75 (149)
Byrne, B. M., 291n98 (156)

Cady, S., 295n30 (224)
Campbell, J., 282n17 (10), 283n6 (25), 284n35 (41)
Case, R., 103, 282n9 (6), 286n17 (74), 287n34 (85), n36 (86), n39 (86), 288n60 (99), n69 (103), 294n85 (204)
Cassirer, E., 35, 54, 284n27 (35), 285n64 (54), n66 (55)
Chinen, A. B., 282n6 (4), 289n5 (118), n6 (120), 292n2 (162), 294n83 (203), 295n9 (216), 296n63 (239), 297n4 (256)
Chiriboga, D., 296n42 (228)
Chodorow, N., 138, 266, 298n16 (266)
Clinchy, B. M., 244, 293n58 (192)
Colby, A., 294n60 (193), n67 (198)
Coles, R., 288n89 (110)
Collingwood, R. G., 285n51 (48), n56 (50)
Commons, M. L., 293n58 (192)
Cook-Greuter, S., 294n67 (198)
Cooper, K. L., 297n80 (247)
Costa, B. J., 296n59 (238)
Cramer, P., 156, 291n101 (156), n102 (156)

Dabrowski, K., 113, 169, 177, 289n94 (113), 292n15 (169), 293n37 (177)
Daly, M., 141, 290n55 (141)
Damon, W., 287n38 (86), 294n87 (204)
Davis, M., 287n57 (97), 288n58 (98), n59 (98)
DeLong, H., 58, 172, 285n67 (56), n71 (57), n73 (58), 292n19 (172), n20 (173)
Deutsch, H., 127, 289n22 (127)
Donald, M., 283n10 (26), 284n23 (33), 298n13 (265)
Donaldson, S. K., 294n86 (204)
Dougherty, N., 235, 246, 296n41 (228), n54 (235), n56 (236), 297n78 (246), n79 (246)
Downing, C., 282n24 (15), n25 (15)
Dweck, C. S., 291n72 (148), n98 (156)

Eisler, R., 295n20 (221)
Elderfield, J., 298n23 (269), n24 (269), n25 (269), n26 (270), n27 (270)
Elias, N., 49, 106, 285n54 (49), 288n77 (106)
Engelsman, J. C., 223, 295n29 (223)

Erikson, E. H., 285n50 (46), 288n61 (99), 294n63 (195)
Euripides, 289n13 (125), n14 (125), n15 (125)
Evelyn-Whyte, H. G., 289n7 (120), n8 (121)

Faludi, S., 282n20 (12)
Fein, G. G., 288n84 (108)
Fischer, K. W., 282n9 (6), 286n17 (74), 287n25 (79), n36 (86), n39 (86), 288n60 (99), n73 (105), 293n58 (192), 294n85 (204)
Flavell, J. H., 286n24 (78)
Flax, J., 292n23 (174), 293n29 (176)
Fordham, F., 282n16 (9), 294n78 (202), 296n71 (242)
Foucault, M., 289n25 (128)
Foulkes, D., 288n82 (107)
Fowler, J. W., 197, 294n66 (197), n80 (203), n81 (203)
Fox, M., 296n64 (240), n65 (240), n66 (240), n67 (241), n69 (241)
Frankfort, H. A., 56, 285n56 (50), n65 (54), n69 (56), n70 (56), 297n1 (254)
Franz, M. von, 15, 128, 282n25 (15), 289n24 (128)
Frege, G., 171, 292n17 (171)
Freud, S., 282n11 (8), n12 (8), 283n4 (24), 284n39 (43), 287n41 (89), n42 (90), n43 (90), 290n36 (134), n37 (134), n38 (135), n39 (135), n40 (135), 295n4 (211), 297n76 (245)
Fromm, E., 285n47 (45), n48 (45), 288n83 (108)

Gadamer, H. G., 179–181, 293n29 (176), n40 (179), n41 (179), n42 (180)
Gardner, H., 282n9 (6), 286n17 (74), 287n34 (85), 288n84 (108), n85 (108)
Geertz, C., 293n30 (177)
Georgoudi, S., 222, 295n17 (221), n21 (221), n23 (222), n24 (222), n25 (222), n26 (223)
Gergen, K. J., 285n84 (62)
Gilligan, C., 156, 282n19 (12), 284n19 (31), 286n17 (74), 291n69 (147), n99 (156), n100 (156), 298n15 (266)
Gimbutas, M., 289n17 (126), 295n20 (221)
Goldberg, E., 284n42 (43)
Goldberger, N. R., 244
Goldstein, W. N., 123, 289n11 (122), n12 (123)
Goody, J., 284n23 (33)

324

Author index

Gould, S. J., 143, 283n10 (26), 290n61 (143)
Graves, R., 129, 284n18 (30), 289n28 (129), n29 (130), 297n9 (258)
Greenberg, J. R., 287n56 (97), 288n65 (101)
Gruber, H. E., 286n24 (78), 287n32 (84), n33 (85), n45 (91)
Gutmann, D., 204, 233–235, 244, 248, 266, 294n88 (204), 296n49 (233), n50 (234), n51 (235), n52 (235), 297n74 (244), n85 (248), 298n18 (266)

Haan, N., 297n80 (247)
Habermas, J., 180, 285n57 (50), n63 (54), 293n31 (177), n43 (180)
Harris, E. E., 282n6 (4)
Harris, P. L., 294n86 (204)
Hart, C., 296n64 (240)
Harter, S., 288n73 (105), 294n85 (204), n86 (204)
Hauser, S. T., 294n67 (198)
Havelock, E. A., 37, 38, 284n23 (33), n30 (37), n31 (38)
Heilbrun, C., 152–153, 249, 250, 291n73 (148), n85 (153), n86 (153), 297n89 (249), n93 (250)
Heine, S., 295n34 (225)
Helson, R., 247, 297n80 (247), n81 (247), n82 (247)
Herdt, G. H., 266, 290n44 (137), 298n17 (266)
Hesiod, 283n12 (26), 286n7 (68), 289n26 (128), 290n33 (132)
Hicks, C., 226
Higgins, E. T., 288n80 (107)
Hillman, J., 139, 290n50 (139)
Hofstadter, D. R., 284n43 (44), 292n19 (172)
Hollingsworth, L., 144–145, 290n63 (145)
Horkheimer, M., 292n23 (174)
Horner, A., 291n73 (148), 292n10 (166)
Houston, J., 282n25 (15), 295n8 (214)
Huyck, M. H., 249, 297n92 (249)

Jacklin, C. N., 147
Jacobi, J., 282n16 (9), 296n71 (242)
Janoff-Bulman, R., 289n93 (112)
Jaques, E., 231–233, 296n46 (231), n48 (233)
Jaynes, J., 285n53 (49), n55 (50)
Jellouschek, H., 295n10 (216), 296n62 (239)
Jepson, K., 294n71 (200), n75 (202)

Johnson, R. A., 282n24 (15)
Jung, C. G., 282n15 (9), 283n4 (24), 292n2 (162), 295n5 (211), 296n38 (227), n40 (228), n53 (235), n68 (241), 297n86 (248)

Kaufman, D. R., 290n68 (146), 291n72 (148)
Kant, I., 171, 220, 295n16 (220)
Kegan, R., 294n85 (204), n87 (204)
Keller, E. F., 217–218, 285n51 (48), 295n11 (218), n12 (219)
Kerenyi, C., 283n13 (27), 284n17 (30), 286n12 (71), 297n9 (258)
Kerr, B. A., 154, 155, 290n66 (146), 291n90 (154), n91 (154), n93 (155), n94 (155), n95 (155)
King, P. M., 185–189, 293n50 (185)
Kitchener, K. S., 185–189, 288n87 (109), 293n50 (185), n51 (186), n52 (187), n53 (187)
Klein, M., 122, 166, 284n32 (39), 289n10 (122), 292n10 (166)
Koestler, A., 284n34 (40), 294n77 (202)
Kohlberg, L., 108, 193–194, 195, 196, 199, 287n37 (86), 288n76 (105), n81 (107), n86 (108), 294n60 (193), n87 (204)
Kohut, H., 101, 288n66 (101)
Kramer, D. A., 293n58 (192), 295n27 (223)
Kuhn, D., 293n58 (192)
Kurtz, S. R., 286n11 (70)
Kuypers, J. A., 248

Labouvie-Vief, G., 281n3 (2), n4 (2), 282n7 (5), n8 (5), 283n7 (25), 284n29 (36), 286n17 (74), n20 (76), n23 (77), 287n35 (86), n39 (86), 288n71 (104), n80 (107), n87 (109), 291n103 (156), 292n104 (157), 293n45 (181), n54 (188), n58 (192), 294n62 (194), n68 (198), n69 (199), n71 (200), n72 (200), n86 (204), n89 (204), 296n55 (236), 297n11 (263), n12 (264)
Lacqueur, T., 290n49 (139)
Lakatos, I., 171, 292n18 (172)
Lakoff, G., 176, 292n27 (176), 293n34 (177), n38 (178)
Langer, S., 282n10 (8)
Lerner, G., 130–131, 289n30 (130)
Levinson, D. J., 229–231, 243, 296n44 (229), n45 (231), n72 (243)
Lewis, C. S., 282n25 (15)
Liddell, H. G., 284n32 (39)

Author index

Lipps, H. M., 290n65 (146), 291n73 (148)
Livson, F. B., 238, 248, 296n61 (238), 297n83 (248)
Lloyd, G., 282n23 (13), 289n31 (131)
Loevinger, J., 294n62 (194)
Logan, R. K., 285n52 (49)
Longstreth, L., 287n28 (82)
Lorenz, K., 284n28 (36)
Lyotard, J. F., 293n29 (176)

Maas, H. S., 248, 297n84 (248)
McAdams, D. P., 283n5 (25)
McArthur, C. C., 228
Maccoby, E. E., 147, 290n65 (146), n66 (146), 291n70 (147), n71 (147)
McGrath, E., 291n97 (155)
McLuhan, H. M., 284n23 (33)
Macmurray, J., 285n72 (57)
Main, M., 288n67 (102), n79 (107)
Mann, T., 8, 94, 202, 282n14 (8), 294n79 (202)
Martin, V., 291n98 (156)
May, R., 120, 289n5 (118), n6 (120)
Mayer, M., 289n3 (117)
Mead, G. H., 108
Miller, J. B., 282n19 (12), n23 (13), 298n15 (266)
Miller, P. H., 282n9 (6), 287n34 (85)
Mitchell, S. A., 287n54 (95)
Molesworth, L., 256, 263, 297n5 (256)
Monod, J., 202, 294n76 (202)

Nelson, K., 288n72 (104)
Neugarten, B. L., 199, 294n70 (199), n88 (204), 296n39 (227)
Neumann, E., 15, 25, 26, 66, 67, 68, 70, 72, 164, 210, 212, 260, 282n24 (15), n1 (23), n2 (23), 283n3 (24), n8 (25), n11 (26), 286n2 (66), n4 (68), n10 (70), n11 (70), n14 (71), n15 (72), n16 (73), 289n1 (115), n2 (116), n16 (126), 292n1 (162), 292n3 (163), n4 (164), n5 (164), n6 (164), n7 (164), n8 (165), n12 (168), n13 (169), n14 (169), 295n1 (209), n2 (209), n3 (210), n6 (212), 297n10 (260)
Noam, G. G., 286n17 (74), 288n60 (99), 296n47 (232)
Noble, D. F., 145, 290n64 (145)
Nozick, R., 175, 292n26 (176)

Ogilvie, D. M., 289n92 (111)
Olsen, T., 153, 249, 291n87 (153), n88 (153), 297n88 (249)
Olson, D. R., 284n23 (33)

Onians, R. B., 285n55 (50), n58 (51)
Ortner, S., 282n23 (13), 295n21 (221)
Orwoll, L., 294n65 (196)

Pagels, E. H., 295n31 (224)
Palmer, R. E., 297n6 (257)
Partridge, E., 284n32 (39)
Peplau, L. A., 291n74 (149)
Perry, W. G., 183, 188, 293n48 (183), n49 (185)
Peterson, A. C., 291n96 (155)
Piaget, J., 282n7 (5), 283n10 (26), 284n40 (43), 286n18 (76), n19 (76), n20 (76), n21 (77), n22 (77), n23 (77), n25 (79), 287n26 (80), n27 (81), n29 (82), n30 (83), n31 (84), n44 (90), n46 (91), n47 (92), n48 (92), n49 (92), n50 (93), n55 (96), 294n84 (203)
Piechowski, M. M., 289n94 (113), 292n15 (169)
Plath, S., 149, 249, 291n76 (149), 291n77 (150), n78 (150), n79 (150), n80 (150), n81 (151)
Plato, 10–11, 33–34, 37–38, 48–53, 174, 218, 282n18 (11), 284n25 (34), 285n62 (53), n68 (56), n74 (58), n75 (58), n76 (59), n77 (59), n78 (59), n79 (60), n80 (60), n81 (61), 292n24 (174), 295n11 (218)
Plutarch, 221, 295n18 (221)
Pope, D., 291n84 (152)
Popper, K. R., 293n31 (177), n33 (177)
Postman, N., 284n23 (33)
Pratt, A., 241, 243, 283n6 (25), 296n40 (228), n70 (241), n73 (243)
Pribram, K. H., 284n42 (43)
Putnam, H., 293n36 (177)

Reddy, M. J., 292n28 (176)
Redmore, C. D., 294n67 (198)
Reich, K. H., 188, 282n6 (4), 284n38 (42), 293n46 (182), n55 (188), n56 (189), n58 (192)
Rich, A. C., 151–152, 291n82 (151), n83 (151), n84 (152)
Richter, H. E., 290n56 (141), n57 (141), n58 (142), n59 (142), n60 (142), 295n13 (219), n14 (220)
Ricoeur, P., 293n33 (177), 294n82 (203)
Riegel, K. F., 193, 286n17 (74), 294n61 (193)
Rorty, R., 284n37 (42)
Rosenberg, S. D., 296n42 (228), n60 (238)

326

Author index

Rubinstein, S. L., 281n5 (3)
Russell, B., 173, 281n2 (1), 282n13 (8), 284n44 (44), 285n49 (46), n51 (48)

Saarni, C., 294n85 (204), n86 (204)
Sarbin, T. R., 283n5 (25)
Schon, D. A., 284n35 (41)
Schott, R. M., 282n23 (13), 289n31 (131)
Scribner, S., 284n22 (33), n24 (34), 285n52 (49)
Segal, H., 289n10 (122), 292n10 (166)
Selman, R. L., 108, 287n38 (86), 288n73 (105), n86 (108), 294n85 (204), n86 (204)
Sheldrake, R., 292n20 (173)
Shlain, L., 284n34 (40)
Shweder, R., 298n19 (267)
Simon, B., 285n55 (50), n59 (51), n60 (51), n61 (52), n82 (61)
Solomon, J., 288n79 (107)
Spence, D. P., 283n5 (25)
Spretnak, C., 129, 289n27 (129), 290n32 (131)
Sroufe, L. A., 288n68 (102)
Stapleton, M., 286n8 (70), n13 (71)
Stassinopoulos, A., 297n8 (257)
Stern, D. L., 100, 101, 104, 287n53 (95), 288n64 (101), n70 (104)
Stevens, A., 298n14 (265)
Stevens-Long, J., 296n42 (228), n43 (229), n57 (238), n58 (238), n61 (238)
Stoller, R. J., 137–138, 266, 290n45 (137), n46 (138), 298n16 (266)
Stone, M., 283n13 (27), 295n20 (221)
Sweeney, L., 298n28 (270)

Tamir, L., 296n42 (228)
Tarule, J. M., 244
Tavris, C., 282n20 (12)
Tedlock, B., 110, 288n90 (111)
Terman, L. M., 153, 154, 291n89 (153), n92 (154)
Thorndike, E., 144, 290n62 (144)
Tomlinson-Keasey, C., 249, 297n90 (249)
Trevarthen, C., 95, 97, 100, 287n53 (95)
Troll, L. E., 296n58 (238)

Tucker, D. M., 284n42 (43)
Turner, T., 94, 287n52 (94)
Turner, B. F., 296n57 (228)

Ulanov, A., 166, 167, 292n9 (166), n11 (167)
Ulanov, B., 166, 167, 292n9 (166), n11 (167)
Unger, R., 282n21 (13), n22 (13)

Vaillant, G. E., 228, 296n42 (228), n43 (229)
Valle, R. S., 297n6 (257)
Vernant, J. P., 285n71 (57)
Veroff, J., 249, 297n91 (249)

Walker, A., 298n20 (267)
Walker, B., 284n21 (32)
Warnke, G., 293n39 (178)
Watzlawick, P., 284n33 (40)
Weisfeld, C., 291n74 (149)
Welsch, W., 293n29 (176)
Werner, H., 106, 287n40 (88), 288n62 (100), n78 (106)
Whitehead, A. N., 173, 292n21 (173)
Whitmont, E. C., 31, 68, 282n16 (9), 283n6 (25), 284n20 (31), n28 (36), 286n1 (65), n5 (68), n6 (68), n9 (70), 294n78 (202), 296n71 (242)
Whyte, L. L., 283n10 (26), 284n45 (44)
Wiedemann, F., 244, 245
Wilber, K., 283n10 (26)
Winner, E., 288n85 (108)
Winnicott, D. W., 97–98, 101, 287n57 (97)
Wittgenstein, L., 173–174, 282n6 (4), 292n22 (174)
Wolkstein, D., 295n28 (223)
Woolf, V., 152, 249, 297n87 (249)

Yee, D. K., 291n98 (156)
Young-Eisendrath, P., 244, 245, 282n24 (15), 297n76 (245), n77 (246)
Youniss, J., 286n20 (76), n23 (77)

Zilboorg, G., 136, 290n41 (136)
Zinner, J., 289n11 (122)

Subject index

abstract period, 109–112
  disconnections in, 109–112
  Piagetian, 82–85
  problem solving in, 109
accommodation, Piagetian, 87–88
achievement and men, 154, 155, 157
achievement and women, 143–147
  achievement gap, 146–149
  conflicts about achievement, 147–157
  emotional problems related to, 155–157
  in midlife, 249
  and socialization, 148–149
  study of female intelligence, 143–145
Achilles, 51–52, 271
adolescence
  abstract period, 82–85, 108–112
  concrete orientation of, 108–109, 189–191, 201
  gender and emotional problems, 156–157
  self in, 111–112
adulthood
  conventional thought in, 196–197
  dialectical thinking in, 188–189
  emotional development, 203–206
  expansion of self in, 195–196
  generativity in, 194–195, 211, 235
  hermeneutical thinking of, 189–192, 193
  midlife reevaluation, 162–163, 227–239
  and position of relativism, 183–187
  postconventional thought in, 193–195, 196, 198, 203
  sex-role changes and aging, 238
  symbolic thinking in, 199–203
Agamemnon, 124–125
aging

concept of descent in, 2–3
  and wisdom, 3–5
animism, Piagetian, 80–81
Aphrodite, in Psyche and Eros myth, 23–29, 47–48, 165, 208, 210, 212, 214
Apollo, 69–70, 71, 73, 126–127, 257, 272
Apuleius, 25, 28, 30
art, Platonic view, 60–61
Artemis, 272
assimilation, Piagetian, 43, 87–88
Astarte, 272
Asthoreth, 272
Athena, 73, 128–129, 272
attachment
  secure/insecure attachment, 102–103, 107
  and splits in self, 105
autonomy, 77, 96

Bacon, Francis, 218–219
"Beauty and the Beast," 117
"Brown Bull of Norwa, The," 256–257

Carus, Carl Gustav, 219–220
cathexis, 31
Clytemnestra, 61, 125, 127, 273
concrete operational stage, 81–82
creation myths, 129–131
  and differentiation of self, 68–74
  male versus female imagery in, 129–133
creativity
  conflicts of creative women, 149–153, 249
  and development, 66, 240–241
  and feminine, 128–133
  and feminine development, 244, 247–250

329

Subject index

representational period, 79–82
sensorimotor period, 79
of social development, 96
play
  Piaget's theory, 90–91
  requirements of, 179–180
  Winnicott's view, 97–98
pleasure principle, 8, 67, 89
Politics, 140
Poseidon, 69, 278
postconventional thought, 193–195, 196, 198, 203, 210
preoperational stage, 80–81
primary process, 7, 42–43, 89
projective identification, 122–123
Protagoras, 58
Psyche, 278
Psyche and Eros
  background of myth, 25–28
  Eros, significance of role in, 29–33
  and marriage of death, 116, 118
  as myth of development, 72, 118, 123, 162, 163–166, 167–170, 255–256
  recounting of story, 23–24, 64–65, 115–116, 161–162, 208–209, 212–216, 253–254
themes in, 29, 65, 116, 162, 209

rationalism, 46–47
  bias toward, 7–8
  new standards of, 177–182, 184–185
  as relic of past, 174–177
reality principle, 8, 66, 89
reason
  and demythification of mind, 53–54, 57–61
  Platonic view, 37, 38, 48–53
reflective thinking, 84
relativism, 183–188
  and adult development, 183–187
religion
  Freudian view, 90
  levels of religious thinking, 197
representational period
  distorted development in, 104–108
  Piagetian, 79–82
Republic, 34, 60
Rhea, 278
Romantic Age, 172, 219, 220
Rousseau, Jean-Jacques, 46, 219
rules, child's conception of, 81–82

Sambia initiation rites, 137, 266
Schopenhauer, 142, 172
secondary process, 7, 43
self

in adolescence, 111–112
differentiation of self and myth, 68–74
distortions in development of, 101–103
ego, formation of, 67–71
relationships to others, development of, 96–98
in sensorimotor period, 96, 97, 100
sensorimotor period
  distorted development in, 100–103
  Piagetian, 79
  sense of self in, 96, 97, 100
Set, 278
shadow, Jungian, 112
social development, 96–98
Socrates, 56, 58, 59
Sophia, 223–224
Sophists, 58
space, conceptions of, 54–55
splitting, of self, 105–106, 112, 228
Steig, William, 234
Stern, Isaac, 270
strange situation paradigm, attachment patterns in, 102–103
Styx, 279
subjectivity
  in adult thinking, 190–192
  in symbolic thinking, 199–202
symbolic thinking, 199–203
Symposium, 10, 218

Thaetetus, 52
Theogeny, 26, 30
thinking
  effects of writing/literacy on, 33–38
  mimetic mode, 34–36
  paradoxical mode, 43–45
time, conceptions of, 54
Titans, 279

Uranus, 68, 69, 70, 279

vitalism, 202

Weber, Max, 54
Werner, Heinz, theory of development, 88–89, 100
wisdom, and aging, 3–5
written communication, 36–37, 38

Young-Eisendrath, P., 244, 245

Zeno, 43–44
Zephyr, 279
Zeus, 69, 279